MISS
SCANDALOUS

Praise for

Miss Scandalous

"Miss Scandalous" is a fast paced read that will keep you turning the pages till the end only to find the reader wanting the next sequel

~Arlena Dean

I was so angry I couldn't just vegetate in my bed and just read. My life could not stop so that I could get lost in this book, but oh man did I want to

~Urban Christian Author, Krystal Milton

"I find myself on an emotional roller-coaster along with the characters...so many of the issues are real life which speaks of the incredible talent of this author."

~Just Judy's Jumbles

Miss Nobody

"Everybody has secrets and they are revealed just when you think you have it all figured out..."

~OSSA Book Club

"Their life experiences took my emotions to the ringer... Definitely a series I'll look forward to, Kleenex in hand."

~Just Judy's Jumbles

"Authentic characters... Miss Nobody was a page-turner of suspense and drama. The twists and turns are shocking."

• ~APOOO Book Club

"Engaging... The suspense builds... Dunlap carries the reader through a saga where you are constantly wondering..."

~Patricia Garcia Schaack

MISS
SCANDALOUS

BOOK TWO
A SHAW FAMILY SAGA

BY
NICOLE DUNLAP

*Hi Arlena,
Thanks for taking this writing trip with me. Here's to your collection!*

Nicole Dunlap

ALSO BY NICOLE DUNLAP

The Shaw Family Saga
MISS NOBODY

MISS SCANDALOUS

MISS PERFECT (Fall 2013)

Copyright © 2013 by Nicole Dunlap. All rights reserved
Cover image: © Robert Dunlap/ IeMobiTech

All rights reserved. No portion of this book may be reproduced, stored in a retrieval system, or transmitted in any form or by any means—electronic, mechanical, photocopy, recording, or any other—except for brief quotations in printed reviews, without the prior written permission of the publisher.

This novel is a work of fiction. Any references to real events, businesses, organizations, and locales are intended only to give the fiction a sense of reality and authenticity. Any resemblance to actual persons, living or dead is entirely coincidental.

Library of Congress Cataloging-in-Publication Data
Dunlap, Nicole.
Miss Scandalous/ Nicole Dunlap.
    p. cm. – (A Shaw Family Saga. bk, 2
ISBN -10: 1483903230
ISBN-13: 978-1483903231 (pbk.)
1. African American Fiction–Fiction. 2. Family Saga–Fiction.

Printed in the United States of America

To my sister,
Natasha

CHAPTER 1

His deep, smooth voice created a mesmerizing melody as he caressed the piano keys. It traveled from the stage of Manna Church of Dallas and across an empty stadium-like sanctuary. Raven Shaw walked out of Bible Study in one of the smaller classes when the notes wrapped around her, pulling her to the main auditorium. *I'll just sit in the nose bleed section and wait for choir rehearsal to begin*, she decided, padding through the double doors.

Instead of listening to reason, she found herself continuing down the center aisle, past hundreds of plush-purple seats. Surroundings darkened and faded away as she zeroed in on Stephen, the Piano Man. Her handsome friend, with a good Christian heart—the type of man that any woman would want, but it wasn't *him* that had her mesmerized. His soulful voice and the words that he sang to the Lord drew her in.

I should just go back. Soul shaking, her heart waged war against rationale as her brain warned her to sit—to *wait*. She passed between potted stargazers lining the stairs to the stage as her heart melted to the song. When she stood on the platform in his line of view, dimples appeared on Stephen's cheeks. He scooted over on the bench and tapped the leather cushion. To her brains dismay, she sat.

Raven hadn't *really* sung, not since conducting the children's choir back in Bellwood, North Carolina almost four years ago. At Manna, she usually stood in the back, halfheartedly singing hell, sometimes she even "lipped it." With no desire to sing, she joined because being a part of a choir helped vent her frustration from a week of school and work.

I'm just going to listen, she vowed as he started over, a catchy tune. With a sneaky grin, Stephen kept repeating the notes. Sighing, her heart took control and she harmonized with him.

"Beautiful," Stephen said when they finished the piece.

"Well, you really know how to write good music." She stood, noticing choir members trickling in from the corner of her blue eyes.

"No, I meant *you*," he replied as she made her way to the soprano section on the large stage.

Thank you, Jesus. Raven was glad she didn't have to respond as most of the members greeted them with a hug. Choir practice commenced, yet there was one person that was always late–Tiwanda, the lead singer. Maybe in another lifetime the self proclaimed diva had a record with a leading gospel label.

"Okay. Y'all on fire," Stephen said after they completed two songs they hadn't sung in a while. "I have new music to share."

Everyone excitedly started talking at once. Stephen's composition was awesome. Besides, his unique pieces helped them win nationals. He put his hands up, dimples playful as he said, "And Raven's gonna sing this one."

At that exact moment, Tiwanda straggled in. Head high, she stopped right before the steps and gave Raven the evil eye, to which Raven cringed.

"Re-Re, you'd be perfect." Stephen smiled, probably waiting for some type of "yippy" response.

"Thanks," Raven replied, wishing she hadn't opened her mouth. *Maybe God's angry that I haven't been using the voice He's gifted me with?* She tried tearing her eyes away from Tiwanda's satanic face. *But, who's going to tell her that I hadn't kicked off the take-Tiwanda's-shine-initiative?*

Arms crossed, Tiwanda sucked on her teeth. Nobody else noticed her, because they were all chattering at Raven and waiting to hear her vocals.

"Stephen, you were just excited about the new song. I think Tiwanda does a great job…." Raven attempted to smooth things over. Still, no one saw the self-proclaimed diva, so she threw those black-eyed daggers like a circus pro as Raven did the Christian thing and smiled back. *Aw, shit she might assume my smile is mocking her?*

"You *think*," Tiwanda said under her breath.

Yup, she thinks I'm playing games with her.

Still they laughed and chided Raven to sing as she watched Tiwanda mouth a word that rhymed with "witch." Raven looked up, wondering when God would strike her down.

"C'mon, Re-Re. Do it the way we practiced." Stephen used those dimples as motivation. The tall man leaned down and played the notes before she could start another round of protesting.

Not giving it her all, Raven sang the chorus. Hardly hitting the high notes as high as she could, knowing she could hit them higher *than* Tiwanda. The finish was flat, but that was a personal critique. To her horror, they all love it–well, except for Tiwanda.

"Yeah, Raven, you got that down!"

"I *love* it!"

"This is a great surprise, from hearing the same person all the time. No offense, Tiwanda," said Melody. Her fat arm went around Tiwanda for a quick hug as the woman finally made her way into the Soprano section, right behind Raven.

We're at church, so she won't hurt me; right? Besides, a depiction of Jesus on the cross was in the color-stained, arched window right behind Tiwanda. Despite some of the things she'd done… wrong, she knew God had her back.

At the end of choir rehearsal, Stephen pulled her waist to him as they walked toward the exit and as usual asked, "Raven, where'd you park?"

"In the parking structure," she mentioned the furthest lot as she ran her hand through long black hair.

"Okay. Wait for me. I'll only be five minutes," Stephen said before disappearing down the hall.

She would've walked out with the group; except, they were all flocked around Tiwanda. Being the first to arrive when the inner lots were full during Bible study, she had to park far. A few minutes later, Raven checked her cell phone and saw a missed call from home. Already antsy, she decided to leave. Passing through the sliding-glass doors, her only light was from the moon except for a few streetlamps at the end of the rows. Pressing the message button, she listened to her voicemail.

Royael said, "Mommy, Mommy?" as if waiting for an answer, then seconds later in that three-year-old chipmunk voice of hers, she added,

"Hurry up, Mommy! Come tuck me in."

Smiling, Raven strolled through the first lot of Manna Church. It was now dotted with cars, from people who stayed to chat after Bible study. Rubbing the chill that seeped through the shoulders of her sweater, she grumbled about having to walk almost a mile.

The sound of heels made Raven turn around to see a shadowy figure, about twenty yards away. Squinting, she tried to determine if that was someone she knew, but the person was doing a great job at stealthily walking around the street lights. When the figure walked around the glow of the streetlamp at the end of a row, she perceived a trench coat and a cap. *Are you serious? It's not that cold.* About to turn around, she saw a flicker of something…silver in the person's hand.

Thinking of the fight or flight process she learned from Intro to Psychology, her instincts were yelling. She'd done her fair share of fighting as a kid, trying to take up for a mother who abandoned her. As a mother now, she chose a different route. Instead, she froze–the theory was blown away.

Eyes closed, an image of Elise Dubois sprawled on her stream room floor appeared. Even though she willed herself not to think about her ex-boyfriend's mother, Raven was plunged deeper into the past. Raven's breaths came in short increments. She placed her hands over Elise's pale mouth, taking the life from her tormentor's body. Royael had been in her womb at the time, Elise's grandbaby, was kicking and spurting her to leave, and to not get caught…

Bringing her fingertips to her face, she felt wetness. *Oh, my God, why are there tears on my face?* Opening her eyes, she saw wisps of blond hair escape from underneath the cap. It was a lady in the trench coat, and she was only a few yards away.

Finally, Raven ran.

Crossing the remainder of the outer lot as fast as she could go in three inch boots–instantly hating her five-foot-two frame as rapid footsteps echoed dangerously close.

Thank God the parking structure was well lit at night. Thank God her car was on the first floor, yet at the other end. Rummaging through her purse, she felt like a bimbo in a stab flick. She'd always been the type to cuss out fake-booby chicks for doing stupid stuff like dropping their keys or tripping over their tramp heels. For the life of her, Raven couldn't get her fingers to stop shaking as they grasped the cool steel ring. Passing into the entrance, she gave a silent prayer that her pathetic car would start. Halfway to it and in the middle of visualizing her worst nightmare of being stabbed repeatedly, the rumble of an engine broke through her delusions. It made her swivel around, heart flopping. *Stephen.* She shielded her eyes to the lights of his Yukon Denali. After being momentarily blinded, she saw the lady at the entrance of the parking structure. It was too difficult to make out her face because the cap was low over her eyes.

All thoughts pointed to Elise.

The woman stopped and stared. When Stephen cut the engine and the headlights clicked off, she vanished, as if… she was never really there to begin with.

"Raven, I told you to wait for me. Now, you're out here running like a crazy person," Stephen said through the window. He opened the door and got out. "What's wrong?"

"Nothing, I-I-" Well, she couldn't say she saw a woman with a– presumable– knife or that it had her thinking Elise and murder. It didn't make for a good explanation to the guy that you're really good friends with and kind of intimate with, too.

"I told you to park in the main lot, if there is an opening. If not, always wait for *me.*" He held her tight. Tension flowed away from her body as her head nestled in his chest. Stephen was about an inch shorter than Jon Dubois–yes, she still compared other men to her *first* and *only* love.

"It only took five minutes for me to finish talkin' with the deacon. We both know you're afraid of the dark. Why'd you have to get me all riled up?" he sighed, letting her go, so they could walk.

"I know, Steph. I'm *not* afraid of the dark…" *at least not all the time.* Raven gave him a soft punch on the arm to lighten the situation "I just wanted to go home and tuck Royael in bed. Being late gives her the excuse to stay up and watch cartoons all night while Granny is asleep."

They came to a stop by the front door of her car. "Tell my girl she's is a royal princess, and I'ma take her to Pizza Planet this weekend."

"Ok." She turned around to get in, biting her lip. *Should I continue this charade?* They'd kissed once on the cheek, and now, it seemed they'd jumped into the calm and serene pool of boyfriend and girlfriendness. But they'd been friends for three years, ever since she moved from Bellwood, so Grandpa Otis could start chemo therapy at a more equipped hospital in Dallas. Stephen was the first person that she called after having Royael and had been around for a while.

He looked down at her as she turned the key in the ignition. It made an awful screech.

Though he shook his head, that sexy smile was still on his face as he gestured for her to pop the hood. After doing so, she physically rolled down her window to hear him bark instructions that she didn't really care to listen to, because he liked to chastise her, also.

"When are you going to get a new car?"

"When I *gets* some money. Right now, I don't need one. I have you." She tilted her head with a smirk. Batting her long lashes, Raven let her baby blues give him the push he needed to work without acting like he was *somebody's daddy*. With furrowed brows, he resumed magic.

Voila, her car was in "working" order. It wasn't the purr of a super charged Ferrari, but it was telling her that she'd get home tonight and to her beautiful toddler.

Aw, shit. Royael was probably living the good life, watching adult cartoons while Granny was fast asleep besides her on the couch.

CHAPTER 2

One moment she was looking into the sweet honey eyes of her three-year-old daughter, and the next moment, Raven told her a bold-face lie. It wasn't that she meant to lie, but how could she tell Royael that her father had also turned out to be her half-uncle. That was too much information for a tot–too much information for *anybody*. Period.

"Your father was a good man," Raven began with a half truth, as she scooped the mocha girl into her arms. They sat at the park across the street from their townhome. A row of tiny beige homes, with brown shutters that needed to be replaced, cluttered one side of the street.

Royael's sandy-brown hair rained gold from the sun. It was a perfect Dallas summer, not a cloud in sight. Children ran around with water guns, terrorizing/saving their parents from the humidity.

"He served in the army." Raven kissed her daughter's rosy cheek and grinned as Annette rolled her eyes, sitting next to them on the bench.

"He was a lieutenant in the army, uh…a Tuskegee Airman," lies rolled off Raven's full lips so easily the more she explained this heroic father that Royael would never meet. She remembered learning about the courageous men in high school and because army-technical-ranks slipped her mind, the Tuskegee Airman story would just have to fly. A poetic, Royael loved to hear extravagant stories. So telling her a little lie made it okay. *That should do for now.*

"Tuggegge?" Royael tried to pronounce the word, heart-shaped lips spread into a grin. Her hot-pink Converses hit the ground with a thud. Two long, thick ponytails bounced around her shoulders when she went to share the news with her friends. They were all talking about how much fun they had with their daddies, the "my daddy this" and the "my daddy that" became a competition. Now, Royael was back in charge. Her father was *thee* hero.

"Well...*my* daddy is a Tuggegge Airman," Royael said with hands on her imaginary hip. Her friends seemed to be satisfied because they ran toward the swings and out of ear shot.

Raven scooted closer and put her arm around the big woman, with a short, graying afro. She kissed her granny's cheek, waiting to be reprimanded.

"Why'd you go tellin' that girl that lie?" Annette asked.

"Granny, I had to tell her something. Should I tell her that my *grimy father* is her father's father, also? Yup, that would make a lovely mother-daughter convo," Raven stressed under her breath. She hated saying "my father." Just saying Jonathan Dubois Senior and father in the same sentence sent chills of hatred down her spine. Thinking about his son, Jon, had the same affect, except the hair on the back of her neck stood to attention. She felt like a feline ready to claw, bite, and *kiss*.

"No, I suppose that wouldn't have been ideal...but in the army? And the historical Tuskegee Airmen! God forbid some kid tells their parent, and it gets back to Royael that your half-baked story isn't possible! When Royael gets older, she's going to want to know more. She's already a bossy, lil' thang and nosey as ever," Annette smiled as she talked about her haughty great granddaughter. Then wrath returned as her eyes went back to Raven.

"She won't remember this talk," Raven replied or so, she hoped. "I have to get ready for class. Do you want me to help start dinner before I leave?"

"Girl, naw. You begin work at the crack of dawn at the coffee shop then come home to play with Royael for a little bit, only to end the day at school. God forbid there's a beauty pageant; Royael always has to be the best. I don't see how you manage." Annette shook her head. "We'll go in now, though. It's getting hard to tear Royael away from her little crew these days."

It was the first indication that Annette was aging. Of course, she was climbing the ladder toward seventy. Raven pulled her bottom lip through her teeth. *Maybe Granny was getting too old to chase after a toddler?* She was still getting over her broken heart from Grandpa Otis dying of leukemia, but she hid that well. *Only smiles for Royael.*

"C'mon, Royael." Raven waved her daughter over.

Royael snapped her fingers and said "oh, shucks" before giving her best pageant wave to her friends. Running across the park, she sprinted ahead of them toward the sidewalk.

"Royael, slow down," Raven called.

The child glanced back, laughed and kept right on running into the street.

Raven didn't know which was louder: the echo of her own scream or the screeching of a Volkswagen's tires. All the sounds, children's laughter in the park, mothers talking on cell phones, dogs' barking—*all* of it stopped as if God pressed the mute button. Everything ceased, as did Raven's heart. Then, Annette was squeezing her arm.

"Raven, get that child!" A neighbor leaned out of the window, after swerving around the happy-go-lucky girl. There was anger and worry mixed in his eyes as he composed himself and drove away.

Safely across the street, Royael was oblivious to the ruckus. She'd just finished skipping onto the sidewalk and turned around, doing a flawless pirouette.

Bangles clanking and well-worn cowgirl boots clumped the sidewalk, Raven ran over to her child. She smacked Royael on her bottom. "What is wrong with you?"

Struck with fear, she pouted. "Oh, Mommy, what did I do?"

"You have to hold my hand, ok? You can't walk across the street by yourself." Raven fell to her knees and hugged her crying child. *You're the only real life piece of Jon I have left...* She closed her eyes at that thought, pressing back her own tears.

"Don't you love me anymore?" She sucked in a snuffle, drama at its best.

"I'll always love you." Raven felt instantly guilty for hitting her daughter. The child development class she'd taken warned against it. "I'm sorry, but you gotta hold my hand next time."

"In my day, that would have been a big ass spanking." Annette walked by the scene.

"Mommy's gotta go." Raven gave her child one last hug and hurried to the brown Ford Futura. She rounded the front of the car with its sunken in bumper and got in. It wasn't locked. Nobody stole in this neighborhood, but the car wasn't worth two quarters anyhow. Turning the key in the ignition, it made an awful screeching noise.

"Aw, shit!" Raven punched the stirring wheel, the horn honked. She looked at her watch and only had thirty minutes to get to class *and* find a parking spot. She turned the key again and commenced to sweet talking, "You know I love you. C'mon baby."

She leaned forward and backwards in the seat. Maybe the pull and tug would get it to go? Besides looking like a nutcase to neighbors who walked by, the car didn't budge. "Just another three years–okay–two tops! I should have a good job by then. Right now, I need you to..."

The engine started.

"Thank you, Jesus!" She patted the wheel and drove like a madman to the community college.

She hated to be late to her creative writing class. It wasn't in a big lecture hall where she could tip toe in the back. Body still pumping with adrenaline from road rage, Raven peeped into the tiny room. The professor sat on the edge of his desk, back to her, as he lectured to about fifteen students. With a sigh, she opened the door and walked in.

"Hello, Raven Shaw, thanks for taking the time out of your *busy schedule* to join us." He looked at the wall clock through wire rimmed glasses and added, "Wow, ten minutes into the class. We'll call that progress."

"Sorry, car trouble," she mumbled, taking a seat front and center. It was too difficult to walk to the back with the clutter of backpacks scattered in the aisles.

"Hopefully you were thinking about how to become a better writer while you were waiting for Triple A." He chuckled and some of the students laughed at his jokes–the ones he *gave* A's to.

Rolling her eyes, she dug into her satchel for a notebook and pen. Too bad she couldn't go into her own little dream world, but this professor loved to pick on people. So she stayed attentive.

"Miss Shaw, I want to talk with you a minute," the professor said after wrapping up class and the students were filing out of the small room.

"Yes." With the role of her eyes, Raven moved out of the line and toward the desk.

"Are you sure you should be in this class?"

"I signed up for it." Her eyebrows rose and came together. It was a couple weeks into the course, and he'd already painted evil red pen marks all over her first assignment with an all caps, "DO OVER!" and a scribbled smiley face.

"Of course, you did. Though, you don't seem to be excelling in this program and I noticed that you've jumped from child development, psychology, business, and nursing."

Instead of watching spittle move from his thin top lip to the bottom and back again, Raven looked up at bushy graying eyebrows.

"I think you need to take a trip to the counseling department." The spit stopped on his top lip.

"The counseling department?" she all but yelled, making him jump slightly. Taking a deep breath she mumbled, "You forgot sociology."

He gave her a peculiar glance, but she kept her eyes on his. She'd attempted to be polite and take his criticism with a dose of "I can do all things through Christ…," but he was crossing the line. *I'm not visiting a damn counseling department!*

"I'm just saying, Miss Shaw." The professor's voice was no longer stern. It had slight tremors. "I-I'm concerned that you'll be in school forever, if you don't chose a major."

"Huh?" She asked as he was just about whispering. Instead of waiting for him to continue, she smiled. "Okay, Professor, have a good evening." Shrugging, she walked out. No longer did he have a comment to throw back at her, he just sat there, eyes shifting. *Why would that big polar bear of a man be afraid of me?*

"Raven."

Still thinking about her squirming professor, she turned down the hallway to see a classmate. Wracking her mind for the first-day-of-class-ice-breaker, she recalled Sharon Riley. Sharon was the only one who hadn't laughed at all of the professor's jokes. Sharon looked to be pushing thirty and was more professional than the rest of the early-twenties and younger class, and wore suits with a *fashionista* flare. Always red, that matched her dyed bob. Already towering over Raven, the red stilettos made her even taller.

Letting go of the flustered feeling the professor left her with, Raven greeted her, "Hey, Sharon."

"Wanna go get a drink? You're old enough to go to a bar, right?"

"Yes," *just old enough.* "I should be getting home. I have a daughter to tuck into bed, who's probably watching adult cartoons as we speak." They walked through the hallways, with upcoming English department activity posters, and out to the parking lot.

"Well, if you ever want to talk." Under the streetlight in front of a cherry-red BMW, Sharon pulled a business card and a pen out of her bag. Leaning on the trunk, she scribbled on it. "My cell is on the back."

"All right, maybe later," Raven said, looking at the card before continuing on to her car. "Scandalous," she read the bright pink writing. Sharon worked at one of the most reputable celebrity gossip magazines in America. *Why the heck is Sharon coming to this community college?*

'The list…'

She stopped dead in her tracks. The thought hit her like a lightning bolt.

Sharon would be perfect. Just the person to tell her sordid story to. The list of vengeance she'd written after having Royael. Well, Sharon could help her get back at her mother, Charlene, and Jon! Hell, she'd already crossed his mother's name off the list. Shoving arm-hair-raising-thoughts of Elise out of her mind, she determined that she could ruin his whole family. And, Sharon was going to help with that, even if she just didn't know it yet.

With a half smile, she tossed her keys in the air and caught them. Opening the door, she got into the car. It "roared" to life as she turned the key into the ignition. *My luck has changed.*

CHAPTER 3

Wriggling her fingers and blowing air out of her mouth, Charlene's lips flapped. It was an acting exercise that she'd acquired long ago–being on the highest grossing soap opera, Loyalties and FamiLIES. The skill helped with nerves. A life-size ball of 'em, she sat at the table in her luxury apartment in L.A. She swiveled around on the barstool, at the kitchen counter, looking at the modern wall art. *Maybe it isn't time to connect yet?* Her brain flipped from topic to topic, instead of the-all-so-important-topic she'd been skirting around.

It still shook her to the core knowing she'd failed her daughter's only two requests. Raven had found her at the age of eighteen, wanting to see if she'd get tested as a donor while Otis suffered from leukemia. Charlene knew she couldn't help with that; he wasn't her father. Then there was the question about who was Raven's father. At the time Charlene was most certain that it was Roy Timmons the Truck Driving Rapist–for her child's sake, she'd hoped so when perceiving just how in love the girl was with *that boy–Jon. Darn, Raven got herself tangled in the enticing web of a Dubois.*

Sunlight streamed through the panoramic windows, giving one of the best views of downtown. She'd be leaving this place soon. After four years, it still didn't feel like home. Everything was perfect, from the Italian leather couch to the zebra rug, but she still didn't have family photos. No pictures of her daughter to put around. She swung back around and leaned her elbows on the granite counter, restarting the acting exercise as her thoughts ran back to Raven. After meeting Raven, she'd almost overdosed on valium and vodka. Damien had saved her in the nick of time and it landed her a stint at rehab. *Maybe, I've ruined her life enough–*

Her fiancé, Damien, tapped his fingers against the kitchen counter, giving her cue to respond.

"I'm getting ready to write Raven, now," she said, for the umpteenth time. Charlene pushed her hands through freshly pressed hair. She rubbed the scar that Roy had gifted her over twenty years ago. Thank God the scar was tucked away or else people could see how she'd hitched a ride from boring Bellwood, North Carolina with a handsome cowboy–who seemed like an unlikely savior at the time. That is, until the truck driver left her for dead in Iowa. It took years of self-torment to stop allowing him to permeate her every notion–asleep and awake. These days, she never thought about Roy. Except when nervous, the scar would itch.

Walking on the red carpet for the first time to receive–her first of four–Day Time Emmys for best actress in Loyalties and FamiLIEs, she had to force herself not to scratch it. The scar felt like it was being crawled over by a gazillion ants as if it didn't care that she donned a custom designed Vilonia gown. Right now, it was on fire.

"Charlene, you've said that a million times. Get to it." Damien rubbed his silky goatee.

"Maybe I should just send the wedding invitation and Raven can–"

"Write the letter, Char. Then you can add how much you *really* want her to come to our wedding and send her plane tickets. At the rate you're going, I'll be in Jamaica marrying myself." He laughed at his own joke, walking to the stainless-steel refrigerator, and pulled out a can of soda.

"You won't be marrying yourself, Damien Wright." Charlene got off the stool, stood on tippy toes and planted a kiss on his lips. "You're the best thing that has ever happened to me. Don't think you're getting off easy, I plan to lock you down."

"Have mercy on me." Hands around her tiny waist, he pushed her away lightly after sneaking in one more smooch. "I made too many promises to God to keep you alive and right now you're looking too *damn* good. One more week."

"One. More. Week," Charlene let her hips sway as she walked back to her barstool. That was another change she'd made after rehab, all those years ago. She decided to put God first. It was difficult…

"Now, what were we talking about again?" His brown eyes dimmed, in thought. "I can't believe it's been almost four years, since we've made love, I'm dying here."

"You're not dying and we're talking about my daughter."

"Right. Does she know you've been talking to your mom?"

"I don't know," Charlene said quietly, looking down at the lined paper. "Maybe I'll go to a stationary shop and get some pretty paper."

"No, Charlene, *do* it now."

"Maybe I should type it... No, typing signifies letters of an impersonal nature. I want it to be special. I want..." *to be forgiven.* She picked up the pen. "Maybe this will be just a rough draft."

"No, Charlene, *do it.*" Damien repeated and sipped his drink. "Write the letter once. Your first thought is always best. You do too much second guessing and it beats you up, so just *do it now.*"

"Okay," she giggled as he leaned over and kissed her neck. "Maybe I should call her?"

"Charlene! You haven't listened to anything I've said, have you? No wait. Give her a call." He pulled out his cell phone and held it out. "Then this will be all over."

"No." She glared at the phone as if it were a stick of dynamite. "I think I'll just write the letter."

He gave a smug I'm-not-backing-down look, to which she snatched the phone from his open palm and dialed Annette's house number.

"Annette?" Charlene still hadn't called her momma by that title yet, not out loud. They'd started talking after her rehab, off and on, but their relationship was in the beginning stages.

"Hi, darlin', how you be?" Annette sounded as sweet as apple pie.

"I'm fine." Charlene got the mannerisms out of the way. They chitchatted then Annette asked about the wedding and said she was so excited, since she hadn't been out of Dallas, since moving from Bellwood, let alone to a wedding in Jamaica.

"Is Raven around?" She finally asked.

"Well, Re-Re, I... haven't really told her that I been talkin' wit'cha. She hasn't taken Otis's death too well. She's been angry. Always frowning about somethin', 'cept when it comes to Royael. Right now, she's at school. I don't know what she's going for on the account that she keeps changing her major." Annette spoke in a long winded breath until asking, "Do you want her cell number?"

Charlene sighed. *Momma is trying to make sure she's not the middle-man.* They hung up.

After almost overdosing, she'd expected Raven might want to see her. Damien stayed in touch with her child ever since mentioning about Charlene being in rehab. They seemed to be on steady ground, but she hadn't had a conversation since that awful day. *For her sake, I hoped Roy was her father.*

"I can't believe it took me three years to get the courage to contact her again," Charlene said more so to herself, than to Damien. She thought about the anger she'd had with God, the loss of her best friend, and how God was able to heal her heart–from rape, depression, and everything else in between. Because of Jesus she was still standing and patiently waiting on Him to fix this mother-daughter relationship with Raven.

~~~

"I lucked out!" Raven waved around a glossy cream wedding invitation and tickets to Jamaica. She *didn't* have to sing Stephen's solo in the choir, and she had a *free* summer vacation.

Giving one last push of the swing, Stephen stepped from behind Royael and stuffed his hands in his baggy pants. "I'm glad you will get to spend time with your mom."

"I'm not going to experience anything with that *woman*! Hello, these are first-class tickets to a tropical island!" She waved the vouchers in his face. When he shook his head, Raven smirked in defeat. "Okay, I'm going to see *my friend* getting married. Damien has been really helpful over the years; always calling to see if I have everything that I need. A few times he sent diapers and baby clothes. He's like the father I never had–makes me not so sad when I think about Grandpa Otis." Raven took a seat on the bench, letting the sun warm her tanned legs.

"What about your mom?" Stephen walked toward the bench. When Royael's complained about not going high enough, it had him planted in the same spot, pushing the courageous child.

"Steph, do refrain from calling that woman my mother, mom, or momma. She's *neither*," Raven said rolling her eyes.

"Stop being so evil. Judge not, little Raven."

"Um-hum, *little* Stephen…" His words traveled through one ear and out the other as the list of revenge overpowered her mind. Though the list was tucked away in a compartment of her jewelry box, the paper felt tangible, the scribbling of the names were skimming over her inner eyelids.

CHAPTER 4

The orange and pink slushy swirls were tempting. The uncontrollable desire wasn't worth it. Charlene shook her head "no" politely at the Jamaican woman in a colorful sarong, holding two glasses of some fruity-alcoholic concoction as they exited the airport. She smiled, put the drinks down and placed a necklace with seashells around her neck and then Damien's.

"Welcome, Miss Shaw, Mr. Wright. This way please." Her hand a graceful wave, she led them to a Hummer. A man in a white uniform with a Paradise dolphin logo placed their luggage in back while she opened the passenger doors.

They rode along an unpaved highway overlooking white beaches with turquoise water. A boat waited at the docks to take them on a tour of Paradise Island's main resort, and finished off by heading toward the overwater bungalows surrounding the island. The guide pointed as he maneuvered through the waters. "The winding passageways lead to the main resort."

Minutes later, the guide steered near the dock, in front of a bungalow. A handsome Jamaican in a white suit, with bulging biceps, stood at attention. Brown pencil-thin dreadlocks graced his back and looked as if they were dipped in the sun.

Wow, Charlene stood as he held out his hand. He would do so well on a soap opera.

The butler had a deep, soothing as he enunciated every word, "Good day, Mr. Wright and Miss Shaw. We have made the arrangements. Tonight, Miss Shaw, you'll be staying in the bungalow with an Annette and Raven Shaw, while Mr. Wright is taken to one of the villas at the main resort. I shall be your personal butler." His pearly whites were swoon-worthy, then he turned to Damien and in his perfect English asked, "Sir, would you like to take in the surroundings, or are you continuing back to the main resort?"

"Don't want to get too excited, babe," Damien said into Charlene's ear. To the butler, he replied, "I'm traveling back."

"As you wish, Mr. Wright." He helped the boat keeper unload Charlene's designer B' Jori luggage. He backed away so they could finish their conversation.

"Are you ready to spend the weekend with your daughter?" Damien asked.

"I guess...." Charlene sighed, breathing in the smell of his cologne as he kissed her neck.

"I'll see you on Sunday," Damien said.

"Okay," she whispered. Like a lost child, for a moment, she thought about Raven. *Time to change subjects.* "Don't have *too* much fun at your bachelor party."

"Who said I'm having a party?" He winked, settling as the boat keeper presumed his position.

"Miss Shaw, you'll find that everything for the wedding has been arranged according to your request," the butler began as they walked the short distance to the bungalow door. "Tonight's dinner will be prepared on the docks overlooking the sea, massages promptly at eight in the morning for your party, followed by a relaxing evening in the bungalow. On Sunday morning a stylist for hair and makeup will come by and the wedding activities will commence," he concluded, placing her duffle bag on top of the rollaway luggage and opened the door.

The ambience left her breathless. The living room was a wide-open space, with a glass-panel wall that exposed a view of the blue-green waters and lush emerald mountain backdrop. A fluffy khaki sofa with royal-blue accent pillows was in the middle of the large room. Nautical canvas paintings of sea shells were placed against the bamboo walls.

The butler led her around, extending a hand while explaining every accommodation in his calming, enticing accent.

He led her into a bathroom with a glass tub, surrounded by glass tile displaying the ocean underneath her feet. Colorful exotic fishes swam below. She followed him from bedroom to bedroom. They stopped at the room that would be hers for the weekend.

The butler positioned her luggage just inside of the entrance. "This is the largest room; it has a private terrace, with an outdoor shower." He concluded his tour with, "is there anything I can do for you?" in the Jamaican accent she was loving and growing accustom to.

Charlene took a quick shower. When she came out of the bathroom, her clothes were already folded and placed into bamboo drawers or hung in the closet. She put on a bathing suit and a floral caftan that swayed in the breeze as she walked to the sun lounge out back. Sitting on the bamboo couch with thick cushions, Charlene said a quick prayer, "Dear Lord, thank you for my blessings. Please, please, please make Raven understand me, and help me understand her. Strengthen our relationship. Thank you for being a gracious God. Amen." When she opened her eyes the butler was standing before her, with a bamboo tray of colorful fruits.

"Would you like something to drink? We have everything, anything that you desire."

"Thank you," Charlene said as he set the tray down. "Green tea would be nice."

"No, you don't want Green tea. Go to China, get green tea. Come to Jamaica, get Jamaican tea. You try Hibiscus tea, it's very good–will make you feel calm. Hot or cold?"

Her eyes brightened at his quick suggestion, his charming smile was contagious. "I guess I'll take it cold." Being calm when her family arrived was for the best. Especially if she took heed to her momma's advice about Raven being so angry lately.

Charlene savored the sweet taste of the magenta liquid. She'd finished her first glass when she saw Annette and Raven get off the boat, through the open living room wall. *Where is Royael?* Charlene wanted to see her granddaughter ever since she'd heard about the baby and had sent three tickets. Sighing, she put on a smile and arose as her mother, in cotton Capri pants and a tourist tee, walked up to her.

"Momma," the word flowed out before Charlene could even thinking about it. She hadn't seen Annette in over twenty years, not since hitching a ride with Roy. Tears wet her cheeks; Charlene smiled, cried and hugged Annette. It was amazing how a hug could have a person feeling truly loved.

"I miss you so much," Annette said slowly, letting her child go.

Charlene noticed the tears in her mother's eyes. She looked around for Raven, who'd been standing directly behind Annette a moment ago. The sound of Raven's laughter traveled, causing Charlene and Annette to turn toward the living room. Raven was talking with the butler. Charlene followed a few steps behind as he led Raven into one of the rooms, placing her bags on the floor.

Charlene stood just outside the door, poised to enter. *One, two, three…action.* Ears perked, she heard her daughter's "giggly" voice. *Wow! Raven's flirting with him?* Folding her arms, Charlene walked into the bedroom.

"Hello, Raven." Charlene's smile was shaky. With one last look at Raven, the butler walked out, leaving them alone. The sea air that was welcoming when she arrived began to clog her lungs.

It was so quiet that the waves crashing into the pillars below were IMAX theatre quality. She couldn't even remember the taste of the hibiscus tea or how soothing it had been. Standing eye to eye, Charlene looked into her daughter's captivating blue ones, her own eyes smiling, Raven's not.

Raven's hair was pulled into a fish braid and pulled to the side, almost to her waist. Her maxi dress looked cute with its cultural cucu beaded neckline. For a moment, she visualized Raven as a child. *What would life be like if I were the mother I should've been?*

"Hi, Charlene," Raven finally said, looking her up and down, as if creating her own assessment. Her plump lips were pulled into a thin line. After breaking contact, Raven's eyes dimmed in total comfort as she sank into the mattress, laid back.

"How was the plane ride?"

"Great, I wish I could *afford* first-class. I'd do it all the time." Raven flipped onto her belly, leaning on her elbows and looked at Charlene with empty marble eyes.

"We'll have dinner in about an hour," Charlene said. She didn't know how to communicate with her own child. *Should I do like the butler and explain the itinerary for the weekend?*

"Um-hum, Charlene." Raven grabbed a feather pillow and placed it under her head, leaning it against the reclaimed-wood headboard.

"We're having massages in the morning," she added, noticing the brick wall between them could compete with the Great Wall of China. She opened her mouth to add another activity for the week, but thought against it, and backed out of the room, wondering how to talk with this young woman in the future. *Well, if that cold attitude gets any worse, then...*

CHAPTER 5

Raven smirked as Charlene closed the door. *The woman is acting like a mouse.* Walking to the dresser, she dug through her purse, took out her cell phone and called Sharon Riley. When the call connected, she said, "I'm here."

"Great. You have the camera. It'll take pictures and you can use it for videos. If you choose to take footage of the wedding, you must be near the subject," Sharon replied. Raven didn't know if it was the fuzzy reception or if Sharon was nervous.

"Got it."

"I know she's your mother, however, if at any time you want to back out of this, fine by me. I don't know your whole story, but, what we're doing won't mend fences," she warned.

"I understand."

"Okay, see you soon," Sharon said and the call disconnected.

Raven rolled her eyes. Sharon wasn't as cut throat as she expected a person working for the paparazzi would be. Guilt tugged at her heart, but Raven needed money. The money that Jon Dubois gave her over three years ago had dwindled. She needed to be prepared for hard times. Royael was taking dance lessons and beauty pageants weren't cheap. Just last week, Annette wasn't feeling well and Raven found out it was because she cut back on her expensive blood pressure pills.

"Don't feel bad," Raven told herself as she picked up the camcorder that Sharon had provided her with. *Granny needs her medication and Royael deserves a good life.* Thinking of her daughter, Raven dialed Uncle Oscar's number and called to check on her. "Hey Unc."

"Raven, you sound down? What's going on?"

She sighed, he could peg her easier than a cowboy could hog tie the wildest boar. He filled the gaps of her heart that were always saved for Grandpa Otis. "Just checking on Royael."

"She's fine. We're at Rover Valley like we use to do with my big brother," Uncle Oscar paused as if mentioning Otis's name was too much to bear. "She's down at the lake, catching fish with your cousins. They got me fixin' up the campsite."

Jon use to come with us to camp at Rover. Tears blurred her eyes as she told her great uncle she loved him and hung up.

The feeling of being alone dug its frosty talons around her abdomen. *I'm not doing anything wrong. Charlene deserves it!* Raven sank back into the bed and put her hands behind her head, pursing her lips, still at war between what to do.

'Charlene's on her fourth year in that tacky show. She's been in a blockbuster this summer! What kinda life will you provide Royael when your savings runs out? Get your trigger finger ready!' The voice boomed in her ears. Raven almost put the pillow over her head, but the voice simmered down, *'Dumbass, she's a private woman. All her fans want are a couple of pictures. Do this for the fans…'*

~~~

Candles flickered off drinking glasses. A white-clothed table on the deck was set for three. An array of exotic flowers added color to the middle of the table, downplaying Charlene's somber mood. Being the first to arrive for dinner, she took a seat and the butler pushed the chair in. He seemed to be good at reading body language, because he kept the talk to a minimum and she was content to watch the resort lights from a distance. She peered at the glow of bungalows scattered across the sea all around her and wondered how other guests were enjoying the tropical escape. Next to the railing of the dock, there was a long table with all kinds of Caribbean food. It was doing a great job at tantalizing her senses, trying to lighten the heaviness of her shoulders.

"Hello, darlin'," Annette said as the butler pulled the heavy khaki chair out for her.

Charlene plastered a smile on her face and greeted her momma as Raven walked onto the deck, wearing a halter floral dress. The butler didn't take his eyes off of her as he pulled out the chair across from Charlene. Raven was all smiles as she took a seat and thanked him.

"This smells heavenly." Annette broke the silence as a chef set the first course in front of them.

The chef explained the magnificence of the spicy dish, adding to the artistic visual and aroma appeal. He made them want to eat his words. Next, he sat down a plate of Jamaican jerk-chicken and shrimp kabobs. Except for the sound of the waves hitting the pillars below, they ate in silence. Only the bold flavors of fresh seafood and vegetables screamed in their mouths.

"Where's Royael?" Charlene asked; the lack of sound was suffocating. "I really wanted to meet her."

"Shouldn't I get to know you first?" Raven began. "Royael's too young to be taken advantage of. Don't you think—oh never mind, you wouldn't understand, Charlene. You abandoned me as an infant." Raven popped a plump piece of curry crab in her mouth.

"Raven, please," Annette said through gritted teeth.

"Sorry, Granny," Raven gave a weak smile.

Annette shook her head, and got up from the table. "I've had a long day. You two need to talk."

Charlene's eyes brightened, pleading for Annette to stay as she made a retreat back into the bungalow. Shoulders slumped; she was alone with her daughter—the butler and chef didn't count.

"I need a drink," Raven signaled the butler, "something sweet, *strong*."

"Raven, can we get along tonight? I'm getting married on Sunday and I just wanted you and Momma here," Charlene begged, knowing that at some point she wanted to bring up the big elephant in the room, but not immediately. Indecision was a whip to her back.

"Yes. Life is perfect for you, isn't it?" Raven took the sugary potion that the butler presented and downed it. Putting her palm to forehead, she tried to get the brain freeze to subside. When it did, she whispered, "It's always about you, isn't it?"

"No," Charlene stressed. "I wanted tonight to be about *us*, about forgiving."

"Forgiveness? I'm a throwaway child," Raven's voice lowered in disgust. "I was in love with my half brother. If only you could have stayed around, I would've known Jon was off limits. He was my best friend. He loved me since…since I could walk. I guess that doesn't matter now!" Her voice rose again as she stabbed at a piece of lobster, dunking it into the hot butter. "I came to you, needing help with Grandpa Otis–he's dead because of you! And you just go and make every-*freaking*-thing about *you*. 'Let me try to kill myself and see how much attention I can get,' waawaawaa." Raven pretended to rub her eyes as if she were crying. "It worked! You got a *good* man. I have nothing."

"I'm sorry." Charlene's eyes glossed over with tears.

"That's years too late." Raven got up, leaving her mother to her own sorrows.

Charlene watched her walk into the living room and out the front door. Her body shook and for the life of her, she couldn't stop that damn scar from itching! Underneath the table, she let her nails dig into her thighs. *I'm not going to scratch it!* She vowed to be stronger.

~~~

Hands placed on the wood railing, Raven stood on the winding pathway, glaring at dark water. Not enjoying the fresh air or the bright stars above, she walked swiftly in her sling-back sandals. *I didn't even run my morning five miles today.* When she heard the sound of quick, heavy footsteps, she remembered the lady in the trench coat from church a couple of weeks ago, and spun around.

"Where are you going? Miss Raven?" The butler asked.

"Away from here."

"Miss Charlene told me to keep an eye on you." He picked up pace besides her. She gave a wry smile. He was short. Not as short as she, but a lot shorter than Jon.

"Take me somewhere private." Raven commanded. It was kind of fun to boss around the handsome, sweet butler that relented to her every whim. *I'm acting like Elise did with her maid.*

"As you wish." His voice was silk against her ears as he led her to a row boat on the side of the dock. "Paradise Resort owns many smaller islands, so there are some very quiet places around here that you can sit and think, away from the main resort."

"I don't want to think." Raven held his hand as she climbed into the boat, steadying her heels, before taking a seat.

She watched his biceps constrict and relax as he rowed. Surrounding bungalows became fireflies in the distance, and she began to second guess her decision of going alone in the dark with a man she hardly knew; teetering on a tiny boat into black water, black nothingness. Well, at least Charlene would know that the butler was the last one to see her if something happened. *The butler!*

"What's your name?" She asked quickly.

"Marley."

"Are you serious?" Raven giggled, feeling somewhat tipsy from the drink. It wasn't funny, but he made her think about the late, reggae artist.

"Yes, ma'am."

"Don't call me *ma'am*," she ordered. The rich, bossy type was becoming easier by the minute.

He guided the boat next to a rocky isle. "Be cautious. Even though it's the most beautiful, secluded area, it can be dangerous." Marley stood up and got out of the boat. He helped her out, before grabbing a blanket and lantern.

Her body felt like it was swaying on the rocky ground. Hoping her wedge sandals wouldn't falter, she took his hand and followed him, guided by a lit lantern.

They walked to a smooth, sandy shore. She watched him spread the blanket out. Raven took a seat Indian style, careful to let the dress fall around her legs. "You come prepared."

"One must always be prepared for the *bossy* guests that stay at the resort," he replied.

Raven smiled and patted the ground next to her. He took a seat.

"So you mad at your mother?" Marley asked.

"Charlene is not my mother in any sense of the word," Raven gazed at the waves as they pulled into the shore.

"You've got to forgive."

Forgive. The word, a prickly thorn on a beautiful rose. "What if I don't want to?" When Marley arched an eye brow at her childish reply she added, "It's not that simple. I just met the woman a few years ago and…" Raven didn't know how to proceed. Marley leaned forward, giving her all his attention, a nudge in the right direction. Still, she was tongue tied and emotionally drained.

"Anger only hurts you; it doesn't hurt her as much as it hurts you, Raven. She can try and try, maybe one day she'll stop trying. If you never forgive her, where will that put you?" Marley took her hand in his. "Anger turns into hate. Then, you get old and ugly instead of old and beautiful. Hatred kills beauty. You're angry because you love her."

"I do *not* love her." Raven lowered her head and watched as sand ran threw her fingers.

"Yes, you love her or you wouldn't be angry. Hatred is the opposite of love's continuum." Marley lifted her chin, looking directly into her eyes.

She felt like he was challenging her to deny love…and as far as her mother goes, well, love and Charlene didn't belong in the same sentence. Instead of replying, she laid her head on his shoulder, and they watched the tranquil waves roll in from the sea.

CHAPTER 6

"Where is she?" Charlene stood outside of the resort's day spa with Annette and her soon to be mother-in-law, Daniela.

Daniela met them at breakfast, earlier. They'd eaten slowly, not mentioning Raven's disappearance or the butler, for that matter. When it came time for their spa appointment, another butler was waiting at the dock and took them to another island that housed the tranquil sanctuary.

"I don't know," Annette said, visibly embarrassed.

Charlene gnawed at her bottom lip while Daniela chattered about the different spa services on the menu trying to ease the tension. She stood with her arms crossed and finally took in a deep breath when a boat guided to shore with the first butler and Raven. Raven had on the same printed maxi dress from the night before. Charlene thanked the Lord under her breath as she ran through the sand while the butler was pulling the boat onto the shore.

"How dare you run off with *my daughter*? I could have your job for this," Charlene threatened.

"Cool it, Charlene. The time just simply ran away from us and you better not have Marley fired." Raven took Marley's hand as he helped her out of the boat.

Marley! Charlene felt like slapping him as Raven brushed past her. "How old are you?"

"Twenty-nine, ma'am." Marley's perfect English made her want to slap him even more.

"Way too old to be gallivanting with my child," Charlene spoke under her breath. "We have a *new* butler, so I better not see you near my bungalow. Do you hear me?" Charlene wagged her finger at him, wishing it was equipped with bullets.

"Yes, ma'am. My apologies." Marley bowed and turned back toward the boat.

~~~

Charlene inhaled the coconut oil fragrance that had just been rubbed into her body. She glided over fragmented multi-colored stones in plush slippers to the Jacuzzi. Raven and Daniela were chatting with misted, content faces. She was surprised by how well they were getting along.

"Royael is a little fashionista. You'd love her," Raven said to Daniela as they lay back on the jets bursting with hot, bubbly water. "She loves dressing up in my clothes and wore high heels even before she could walk. I mean that literally, she crawled around with shoes on her hands and knees."

Charlene smiled as her daughter lit-up while talking about Royael. Having never experienced that joy, she listened to them talk about their children.

"I know you're going to have more kids?" Daniela looked to Charlene.

Hesitating to respond, she noticed a slight flicker in Raven's eyes even as she tried not to wonder about having children with Damien. They were in their mid-thirties so she had a few years. He'd talked about having babies and deep in her heart, she, kind of, wanted to do the mother-child-thing right for once in her life. But she had to do it right with her *first* child.

~~~

During dinner, Charlene breathed easy as the man who went by the title of "butler" only, with a hook nose, kept the conversation to a minimum. Daniela chattered, and then she and Annette disappeared into the bungalow, leaving her alone with Raven, once again. Tonight, Charlene determined, wouldn't be déjà vu. She and Raven took a seat on the lounge chairs. While Raven enjoyed a cocktail, she sipped hibiscus tea, the only recommendation from Marley that she'd heed.

"Can we start over?" Charlene asked. *Stay strong, and push on.*

Raven was quiet for some time. Charlene's breath caught as Raven's tense shoulders relaxed. Her heart drummed as she listened to Raven's response.

"Okay," her daughter whispered. "Let's get to know each other from this point on."

"Oh-kay…" Charlene felt almost hesitant as if she was agreeing to something she had never dreamed would come true. Her mouth opened to question her daughter's sanity. *This was just too easy…* However, it was exactly what she needed.

Raven talked about moving to Dallas, working at the coffee shop, and Charlene learned firsthand just how wishy-washy her child was at declaring a college major. For the first time in her life, she found herself laughing and *joking* with Raven. *Don't cry,* Charlene chided herself.

"So is there anyone special in your life?" Charlene asked.

"I don't know. I have a friend, Stephen, that I guess wants to be more than just a friend," Raven spoke softly. Charlene saw the distance in her eyes as she proceeded, "I like him so much, but I'm not sure I want to cross that line. We've kissed, but it was more like kissing… a brother."

Charlene didn't know what to say. Obviously, kissing Jon hadn't resembled kissing a brother. Royael was the byproduct of what she assumed started with a kiss. *Maybe I stirred this conversation into the wrong direction?* She didn't know if she should say sorry, carrying a lot of the blame.

"Have you talked with him?" Charlene asked. She couldn't bring herself to let the three letter word, "J-o-n," past her lips. Raven frowned as if she knew just who *him* was.

"Not since he found out I was pregnant."

"Is he helping you with Royael? Financially, I mean." Charlene asked. The man's family was as rich as sin. *He's a billionaire's grandson, for goodness sakes. But, I should've sent my daughter money, also.*

"So I kissed Marley last night…we didn't go all the way," Raven said, smiling at her mother, a fresh, youthful glow back on her face.

Why's she changing the subject? All right. I do want to know more about this Marley. She still wanted to have a chat with his boss. At her daughter's previous request, she didn't. Instead, she listened as Raven smiled and giggled about the night she had with Marley.

37

"We had a great time, but I don't know if I should go back and tell Stephen. I'm certain he thinks that we're dating. We met three years ago when I joined the choir. He's great, but I know if we continue I'll feel guilty for kissing Marley. On the other hand, how do I tell him I don't want to continue, that I just want to stay friends?" Raven downed the daiquiri.

At a loss for words, she felt almost privy to her daughter's personal thoughts. The words were on the tip of her tongue to tell Raven to "cool it" on the alcohol, yet that would be taking a motherly stance and their relationship was in limbo or like a person without balance jumping into the double-dutch. She didn't know how to answer her daughter's issues.

"You're young, beautiful. You have your whole life ahead of you. I don't think you owe Stephen an explanation. If you still want to, and it hurts his feelings, just tell him that you have to kiss a bunch of toads to find the right one." Charlene felt satisfied with her response.

Raven laid her head on Charlene's shoulder. It was their first physical contact since her daughter was six months old and she'd hightailed if for a Hollywood dream. She smiled and silently whispered "Thank you, God" into her daughter's hair. Her mind became a slideshow of imagining her daughter growing up and them sitting together over the years. Images of Raven's first step, graduating from kindergarten, the first heartbreak, prom flew through her mind…then Raven arose.

"You need to get a goodnights' sleep to be a beautiful bride in the morning," Raven said, stirring Charlene out of her imagination. They walked into the bungalow and to their separate rooms.

For the first time since seeking her daughter, sleep came easy for Charlene.

A shriek slammed her out of that peaceful, dreamlessness. Eyes popping open to pitch black, Charlene almost forgot she was staying in a resort in the middle of the Caribbean. Then she heard the soothing water below. The screams exceed the terror of her own when she used to have nightmares about going in and out of consciousness in the trailer of Roy's big rig, at the age of fifteen. She hopped out of bed. Bare feet planted on cool glass tile, she glanced toward the alarm clock. The neon lights indicated that it was just past three in the morning. She rushed out of her room, running into her momma in the hallway.

Annette put a finger to her lips as they listened to another piercing cry from the closed bedroom door. "No, Raven doesn't want to be bothered. She's just having a nightmare."

"A nightmare? It sounds like someone is trying to kill her," Charlene's voice was a hard whisper.

Annette signaled Charlene to follow. They went into the kitchen. Still worried about Raven, she watched her momma poured two glasses of water. With hers in hand, they took a seat on the dining chairs.

"What was all that about? And why doesn't she want anyone to comfort her?"

"I don't know why. Raven's headstrong. That's the way she and Otis always were. If she had a nightmare, he'd go to her and I could hear her talking to him, something about killing and green eyes. After he… passed, I went to her, once. She told me that she was okay and to just go to sleep."

"When did the nightmares start?" Charlene asked, still very concerned.

"Oh, I don't know. After…" Annette looked down at the floor, racking her fingers through thick hair. "It was after she came back from finding you and learned that she and Jon were related. It stopped when Royael was born, but started again a little while after Otis died."

Charlene fidgeted with her fingers. A sharp scream made her bolt up, she rushed toward Raven's door. *There's nothing like a mother's comfort…*

"I'd wait 'til I know her longer before asking about the dreams." Annette passed by to her room.

Charlene's hand grazed Raven's door knob. She stood there for a while, try as she might, she couldn't hear a sound. No more deathly cries in the night, no movements.

~~~

In a goddess wedding dress with flow fabric and a halo of exotic flowers, Charlene smiled at Damien, who looked equally tantalizing in a tan linen suit. They sat at a sweethearts table, decorated with candles and seashells, facing the crowd. The sparkling azure and shoreline made for a magnificent backdrop as they listened to speeches. There were about fifty of their close friends and family–mostly Damien's family. She'd only invited her mother and daughter, rehab friend Teresa, and a few costars from Loyalties and FamiLIES–only one of which didn't come–rounded off the exclusive guest list. She tried to stop her shimmery eyes from continual riveting toward Raven's table. When guests would clank their glasses, she'd relax and kiss Damien, after which her eyes would go right back to her child.

Stop stressing, Raven's here. That's all that matters, right? A mixture of joy and confusion overwhelmed her. Aloof all morning, Raven had seemed more interested in taking pictures of the guests and the wedding scene. All the progress they'd made last night, had done a 180. Not so much that Raven began to act like she hated her guts again. Yet, a hesitance weighed Charlene's heart. *Maybe the girl woke up on the wrong side of the bed. She did have that awful nightmare…*

During speech time, Raven stood up in a knee-length chiffon dress, hair in curly cascades down her back. Charlene smiled at her daughter's almost-angelic-flower-girl-look. Hesitant about their renewing relationship, she hoped Raven planned something eloquent.

Raven clinked a silver fork onto the crystal goblet. Everyone clapped, some chanted "speech…speech..." Glossy pink lips curled into a beam, she began, "I'm Raven Shaw, daughter of the bride. Most of you don't know who I am. That's okay, because I've only known my mom for four years. In case you're wondering, I'm not four though…" A champagne-feel-good-chuckle erupted from her throat. "I guess you wonder how that came about…but that's another story unless you take into account that Charlene use to run away from all her obligations." Raven used her index finger and middle finger as legs to indicate run away and almost stumbled. "Damien, what were you thinking?…okay, she's gorgeous. Everyone raise their glasses to Damien and Char."

Warmth crept up Charlene's neck as her daughter hiccupped. Most of the guests stared at her instead of raising their glasses, uncertainty clouding their faces.

"C'mon people, raise yo' glasses. Let's take a sip." She paused to down her entire glass of champagne, but there were "reinforcements" on the table. Holding up another flute, she said, "I hope the two of ya have thought about this because there's a 50% chance you'll have to do it again. I won't say it's a bad thing. I've enjoyed myself so much today. Hopefully, I get invited to *both* of y'all next weddings. Take a sip," slurred words ended in a hiccup and bottoms up to the new glass.

The guests gawked, still holding up their first round of flutes; eyes shifting back and forth from the sweetheart table to Raven. Charlene looked around for Annette. *Dang, she must have gone to the restroom or something. Good time for Raven to show her true colors.*

Damien started to rise when Charlene touched his shoulder.

"…Hey, we have to drink enough for Charlene. She deserves a drink, but can't because she's a recovering alcoholic, among other things. Hehehe. Let's take a sip…" Raven downed the third glass and tossed it over her shoulder into the sand. She looked down at the table ready to pick up another glass, fingers moving around, she frowned at all the empty flutes. Sighing, she half smiled again, "Okay, I'm all out. So here's to *that woman* and Damien."

Charlene inwardly cringed as Raven began clapping and waved an empty flute in the air. Holding in her embarrassment–Academy Award worthy– she watched her daughter walk toward the evening sun. She wanted to cry, yet guests were looking at her like they needed permission to breathe. She had to get it together… *Now, what to say?* Damien beat her to the punch. He stood and apologized about his stepchild's behavior. Seconds later, the band began playing an upbeat song.

~~~

Sand soothed the soles of her feet as Raven meandered through the shore. The pop of fireworks speared the twilight. Grateful that the main island was so large, she walked until the music faded and stars began to appear. With no vacationers in site, she was alone, just the way she liked it. About a half mile later, a figure came into view a few yards ahead. Positioning herself closer to the edge of continuous waves, she continued. The water chilled her feet at first, but that kept her at a better distance from the silhouette of a man sitting in the sand as she passed by.

"Hello, Raven."

The familiar voice made her lick her lips. Marley. Fireworks painted his face with green and blue and purple glows. Salty sand caked her feet as she walked toward him.

"What have you been up to?" His deep voice caressed her bare shoulders as she sat next to him.

"Did I get you in trouble?" Raven didn't want to think about how drunk she had to get to be able to ruin her mom's wedding at the moment. The guilty conscious would have to come later.

"I was suspended for a week." He turned the subject back to his initial question by asking, "I have a couple of friends that work the wedding scene. They said you were acting, uh…crazy. You didn't heed my advice."

"I tried." *You don't know how much I want to forgive her. It's the Christian thing to do, but I just can't!*

He caressed her cheek with his knuckles, and then his thumb traveled to the corner of her lips, "You're frowning."

When his mouth sought hers, it was just the way she'd imagined it. Helpless to his touch, she let his arms wrap around her as he deepened the kiss. For the first time in years, she felt a connection to the opposite sex. Falling back into the sand, her hands roam around his biceps as he climbed on top of her. His fingers traveled under her dress, blazed over her hips, grabbing as much butt as he could, continuing on to tug down her panties.

Raven stopped him, with her hand over his.

Stephen. Her good friend deserved loyalty. She sighed. She *needed* this, but was it worth it, since she'd never see Marley again come Monday.

CHAPTER 7

Words stumbled out of Raven's mouth as she wrung her fingers, "Stephen, I have to tell you something."

He leaned in for a "welcome back kiss." She inhaled the scent of his cologne as he pulled away and took a step back on the porch. Maybe she could blame her tension on the long ride home or how Royael had bounced off the walls when she picked her up from Uncle Oscar's. No matter the truth, the simple phrase had that sexy, playful dimple of his fading away.

"You don't look like you're going to tell me *somethin'* good." He sat down on the porch swing for a second then got back up, looked at her with searing questioning eyes.

"I'm sorry," was all she could say as she looked down at cement.

"Yeah, I bet you are, Raven. I bet you are." He marched down the steps.

"Aw, Steph, we were really good friends first." *That's all I wanted.* Raven huffed at his heels. *I haven't even told you what I've done!* He made no point to stop and listen to reason. If only he would look in her eyes, so she could plead his forgiveness for kissing Marley, but he took out his keys instead, walked around the car and hopped in. Raven got into the front passenger seat.

"What do you want?" Stephen stared at the steering wheel, jaw tense.

"We shoulda just stayed friends and…" An imaginary fist wrapped around her throat.

When it became evident that the invisible titanium shield between them wouldn't dissolve, she got out of the car. How could she explain that friends made the worst lovers, when she couldn't even think straight? If only she could tell him about Jon.

She ambled back into the house. Annette kneeled in their tiny living room, putting luggage in the compartment underneath the stairwell.

"Re-Re, you could be happy if you wanted to." Hand to her knee, she straightened up.

Taking a seat on Grandpa Otis's favorite chair, Raven didn't reply. Her hands ran down the cracked leather as tears pooled at the corners of her eyes. *Grandpa, wish I could talk to you.* The living room was already small enough with one loveseat and the coffee table then Annette came to hover over her. *I'm damn near suffocating.*

"Now, I'd never say to lie, because that's a sin, but you didn't do anything with that butler that would make Stephen so angry…"

Pursing her lips, Raven looked up at her talkative granny. The last thing Raven heard was Annette saying that she sabotaged love. *Oh, Granny. I'm not in love with Stephen. I just wanted us to stay friends. It's safer that way.*

~~~

Eyes roaming around the dark environment of Serene Lounge, Raven looked for Sharon that evening. Having never been to Serene, but suggested by Sharon, she knew it was the kind of upscale bar that served sky-rocket pricey drinks. Raven had spruced up by applying makeup to match the gold shimmery wrap. Weaving by leather-studded high-back stools that matched the tall chrome tables, she gave a quick smile to a few guys in suits who attempted to flirt. After convincing one particularly confident pock-faced guy that she wasn't interested, she found Sharon seated, legs crossed, sipping on lemon schnapps.

"I got it," Raven said over the live jazz music as she had to almost climb up the tall stool across from her. Allowing mixed emotions about Stephen to crawl toward the most dormant parts of her heart, she rubbed her hands together and focused on the vital task.

"Great, do you want to order anything? My treat…"

"Hmmm…" Visions of her drunkenness the entire weekend made her stomach go momentarily sour, that is until her eyes zeroed in on a cold strawberry mojito that a server had just walked by with. *I do need to get Stephen off my mind…* She gave into temptation.

"What have you got for me?" Sharon's stilettos tapped against the footrest of the stool.

"The wedding ceremony and some of the reception. I did get

pictures of a few actors that attended." Raven pulled the camera out of her purse and slid it across the table top.

Sharon pressed the power button and viewed the saved footage. She placed the speaker to her ear to zone out the music. "Classic beachfront wedding, I like. The sound is a bit fuzzy from the wind though. The pictures are clear, great. I've never turned anything in this good. Honestly, I only got the job because my uncle is the head editor."

"Yup," Raven replied, sipping a mojito, ready for Sharon to place the money in her palm.

CHAPTER 8

Charlene and her assistant, Barbie, walked into the front door of her new Malibu home. They'd gifted themselves with a day at the movies after having such a busy week, working with the interior decorator and attempting to get Damien to agree with some of the more frilly designs.

Barbie flipped her pink braids and clicked her gum. "Girl…that movie was good!"

"I know." Charlene sat down on the purple horsehair couch in the living room. Closing her eyes, she took a deep breath. When she opened them, Barbie handed her a cold bottle of water.

"Thanks. This summer heat is killin' me!" She opened it and chugged down the water. "I need to drink *twenty*, with all that junk food we ate today, or I'm gonna look like a hot mess when I channel my inner Meagan," Charlene sighed. The new season for Loyalty and FamiLIES was a month away.

"Stay little in the middle, you'll be a'ight." Barbie moved her hands in the shape of a coke bottle.

They were laughing when Damien walked into the room in basketball shorts and Nikes. Sweat glistened down his chest. If it hadn't been for the flared nostrils and his wide stance, she would have told Barbie to go home, *right now!*

"Hey, babe, you missed a good movie." She smiled, trying to regain some of that lighthearted mood they were in. *What's up with him?* He was usually tired, hungry, or both after exercising. Never angry. Even Barbie felt the tension as she mouthed about getting to work and walked down the hall toward the office.

"What's wrong?" Charlene patted the seat next to her.

He didn't make a move to sit down as he put a Scandalous magazine in her face; their wedding graced the cover. Mouth open wide, she grabbed it and flipped through the four page spread of them exchanging nuptials and the reception–it *almost* looked professional.

"I'm surprised Raven didn't include a picture of her drunk self."

"How do you know Raven did this?" Voice barely above a whisper, she fidgeted with her fingers.

"She apologized the last time I spoke with her." He seemed to soften for a fraction of a second, and then continued. "We let that speech-fiasco pass. I didn't say *anything*. Do you know how she made us look? Now, she's profiting from it!"

She cringed when he stormed out of the room. Even though she'd always felt a little at odds with him keeping in touch with her family, he'd been the go-between after she'd been released from rehab. *Is he going to stop communicating with Raven? He's been a great help.*

The sound of a door slamming down the hall made her jump. She hugged a silk decorative pillow, hoping that he'd always be there for Raven even if the girl didn't want to have anything to do with her. After a few cleansing breaths, Charlene read the story. *My own daughter used me... I deserve it.*

Eyes burning from her hundredth scan of the words and pictures, Charlene finally rolled the magazine up, stood, and tossed it into the wastebasket. She went through the halls of her new home looking for her new husband. As she suspected, he lifted weights on the bench in the exercise room. Throat constricted, trying not to cry, she whispered, "I want to move to Dallas."

He stopped mid-lift, put the rack on the holder and rose to a seated position. Wiping the sweat of his forehead with the back of his hand, Damien looked at his wife.

She never had to beg him in the past, but watching him stare in silence was maddening. Clearing her throat, she added, "I know we're trying to have children. I just can't do it. At least not until I make amends with Raven."

"What if she never forgives you?"

Doubt escaped her lips in a long winded breath. "Okay, we rent a house in Dallas when the show is off season. I Raven and I...if it works out, we have a second home."

He nodded slowly, "I wouldn't expect anything less from you,

Char."

She grinned as he got up and gave her a soggy hug.

~~~

Charlene's eyes bugged out as she looked at the list of extravagant homes with multimillion dollar price ranges that her assistant handed to her. "Barbie, this house is ten million *damn* dollars. We just got married and moved here."

Chewing on a wad of gum, Barbie exaggeratedly read the flyer. "This extraordinary home," SMACK, "features an open floor-plan," POP, "with *soaring* custom ceilings–"

"Barbie, I'm serious. If you come back with another house this expensive, you're in trouble. Try and find a mini version with '*soaring* custom ceilings'." They both cracked up at that. She could afford a few of the homes on the list, but Damien–being a conscientious accountant–wouldn't dream of them spending their money like that. After coming home from rehab, he'd taught her a hard lesson about maxing out credit cards.

"A'ight, here's the other list." Barbie had a sly grin. "I just wanted to stay somewhere *nice*, since you're taking me out of L.A. to some dusty place with dirty cowboys."

"I swear, I've never met someone so in love with L.A." Shaking her head, she scanned the paper. Some of the homes offered rental agreements. *We can make it permanent later.*

CHAPTER 9

Raven awoke to a marching band in her brain. She grimaced, reflecting on her night out with Sharon. Most of her words were static in her brain, but the "spilling of guts," now *that* was clear as crystal. A couple of mojitos and she'd blabbered her whole life story; everything from fishing to playing in the meadow with her childhood friend, Jon. "*It was us against the world. Jon was so fat. And, hell, in a small, Christian town, I was the talk of it! My grandparents had appeared with me, a baby, about a year after my fifteen year-old mom disappeared.*" Grimacing, she recalled saying how Jon's mother, Elise, sent him to France at the age of fourteen when finding them kissing–rather him kissing her. "*I was at the mall shopping I think it was for the winter formal. I was a senior and the finest guy in the world stepped up to me, claiming I knew him...*" She'd been smiling as she told the story. Now, she felt like suffocating herself with a pillow as she recalled mentioning how he'd saved her from a crazy boyfriend. The love story all ended with the heartbreak of learning that she was having a love child with her half brother.

Two clicks on the Internet by Sharon would show that the black and French, Jon Dubois, from North Carolina was the heir–on his mother's side–to the Devereux Corporation, a multibillion dollar company ran by his French grandfather, Pierre Devereux. Hand to temple, she willed the lil' drummer boy to finish his "grand finale." Grabbing her cell phone off the chipped wood nightstand, she dialed Sharon's number and paced the bedroom floor–more like five steps in each direction. She waited.

"Call me back ASAP," Raven said after the automated message ended. *Sharon seems like good enough people.* At Serene Lounge, she'd blabbed about taking the creative classes at night to become a novelist in order to tell her life story.

'*Dumbass, that might've been a ploy for more info about Charlene and YOU opened up Pandora's Box!*'

Grumbling at the voice's logic, she didn't notice Royael in her bedroom until she felt tugging on her pajama pants. Lost in thought,

Raven thumped her forehead and said, "Aw shit!" remembering the creative writing final due tomorrow.

"Aw *shit!*" Royael screamed, holding up her teddy, Mookie, shaking him around.

~~~

"We kept playing phone tag," Sharon said closing the door behind her, after their evening class. She'd called that morning while Raven worked at the coffee shop.

"Sharon, what did I tell you the other night?" Raven closed her eyes and rubbed her face.

"You told me all about your mother, Jonathan Dubois Senior, and your relationship with his son, Jon Junior." She whispered the next part, "Heir to the Devereux fortune."

Raven opened her eyes, tilted her head and groaned. "I need to explain. I was drunk–"

"And you're not ready for the world to know what happened," Sharon interjected, palms out. "Look, Raven, I understand. I told you my story last night, about my parents abandoning me for drugs. If it weren't for my uncle, my life would be totally different. I wouldn't be blessed with a job or a family. I used to be mad, but I've gotten over it."

She sighed, not really interested in Sharon's ability to overcome her sob story.

"I won't tell the story until you're ready," Sharon spoke softly. They shook hands, and then she linked arms with Raven as they headed toward the exit. "What's with Professor?"

"What do you mean?"

"He's scared of you now." She smiled. "He's given you a hard time the entire semester. When you went up to his desk after class, he looked ready to crap boulders!"

"I don't think so." Raven shrugged and pushed through the doors.

~~~

Attention-hungry Tiwanda leaned back on the high notes and moved around the pulpit like an Olympic gold medalist. Raven shook her head at the mess and lipped the chorus when necessary. Sadness chilled her heart as she watched Stephen stroke the piano keys. They hadn't had a real conversation since he came to see her after the wedding, over a month ago. *Am I really sabotaging my chance at love? Why is it so bad that I just wanted to keep things uncomplicated?* Every time he wanted an explanation, she'd go mute. Determined not to do so today, she called out to him as he walked to his car after church.

"*What* is it?" The bite in his voice simmered away, as if he realized this was still holy property.

"Can we talk?" Raven twirled her silver-feather necklace.

"I'm meeting Melody for lunch. You know how crowded restaurants are on Sundays," Stephen replied and kept walking.

Fanning her face from the thick heat, Raven turned back to the giant church, heading to the children's ministry to pick up Royael. She wove past the exiting crowd. In the corner of her eyes, she saw a familiar face and called out, "Bill? *Bill!*" For the second time today she called a man's name as he walked away, but this one turned around with a smile on his face, and she ran into his arms.

"Raven Shaw, what a delight to see you." He lingered before letting her go.

"Bill Mack." She grinned at the guy she'd taken chemistry with at Bellwood High. As far as she knew, he'd gone off to a university in Dallas. She'd never called him back when he'd finally gotten the nerve to reach out to her after graduation—heck, she'd been pregnant and discarded by then.

"Where are your glasses, Bill? You are knockin' the girls dead now." Raven winked, imagining the thick glasses that once made his eyes tiny dots. They were, now, framed by thick eyelashes. Gone was the nappy bowl-cut. Skin no longer scaly, Bill's brown arms were smooth with some definition, not too muscular, but not *too* shabby. She often felt guilty because her ex- in high school, 'golden boy' Chris, had given him the name "Alligator Bill." Poor Bill used to scratch the scales on his arms when nervous. He'd scratched them raw when he asked her to dance during senior prom.

"I'm not doing well in that department." Bill blushed. Evidently, the *almost* handsome guy was still shy. "We should go out sometime, though."

Raven's eyes brightened. It seemed asking her out was quite difficult the way he stuffed his hands into his jean. Thank the Lord he didn't scratch.

~~~

It took a few weeks to align their schedules. Bill received a Bachelor's in less than three years and was now busy working on a Doctorate of Biophysics. They met at a restaurant in uptown Dallas. Modern Japanese art adorned the walls, and music played as diners chatted.

Bill's jeans were tight–not-skinny-jean-style-tight–but at least they weren't "Capri-ish." That didn't stop the guys, who sniggered at his buttoned-all-the-way-to-the-top polo shirt, from giving her an "I can save you look" while they sat in the cramped waiting area on a crowded Friday night. Thankfully, a hostess in magenta kimono dress whisked them toward a square table with open grill.

Seated with six other canoodling couples, Bill leaned in close to Raven. She attempted to watch the hibachi chef juggle succulent shrimp as he confessed, "I really like you. I'm so glad you came here with me today."

She'd known as much when he'd gotten the courage to try and save her from Chris at the prom. *Jon had saved me…* A draft of emptiness chilled her heart. Bill took her hand. Trying to push away dormant, heartbreaking emotions for Jon, she noticed the other patrons at their table were wearing that is-he-about-to-propose-mask on their faces. Raven's cheeks warmed as the chef made a heart shape with the rice and said something about being in love in a thick Japanese accent. She tried not to be startled by all the claps and raised sake bottles that they were getting. *Bill's my "safe" man, but he's ruining the safe-zone!*

After an awesome meal of Surf and Turf, they took a walk along the promenade. Raven's heels clicking on the flagstone. The sound of the streaming waterfall made her senses mesh back to normal. She felt his hand take hers, yet again. Groaning inwardly, she hoped he wouldn't slather on another round of sappiness. They stopped under the moonlight, twinkling stars mirrored in his eyes. A sunflower, Bill was all open up today.

"If it weren't for you always being so nice to me in school, I would've run away. I thank God you're back in my life."

Her eyes glistened. How could she shut down his notion of them being together, when he told her how beautiful she was? Taking a chance, she gave in and let him kiss her. Saboteur? Maybe not.

CHAPTER 10

A New Year's Eve baby, Royael was ready to bring in her fourth year like a diva. She'd made a mile-long birthday list as if Santa Claus was hosting the shindig. That self-confident smile faded when she found out that they would be at church for her birthday.

"Are you crazy?" Royael's hand planted on imaginary hip, her bottom lip jutted out.

Ignoring her child's miniature 'tude, Raven lifted Royael up and put her in Bill's car. It was going to be a packed event, and she had to get ready. She couldn't very well appear late on the stage. *I'm not Tiwanda.*

In between singing and smiling at Bill, who was sitting front and center–grinning like the happiest man on earth–Raven noticed Charlene and Damien. *What the hell are they doing here?* Too angry to continue, she lip-synched. Her voice was drowned out by the dominating force, Manna choir. Tiwanda sang all extra hard, sweating, running on the posh purple carpet, and stomping–*getting skinny must be her New Year's resolution?* Stephen was playing the piano just as hard. A pang of sadness overtook her. They still hadn't had much of a conversation since summer. *Men really can hold grudges.*

At the end of the midnight service, Raven sought Stephen out, wanting to start a new year with her closest friend–since Jon–by her side, but Bill was waiting. Royael sure was waiting. Charlene and Damien were waiting, also.

"Mommy, look what Stephen got me for my birthday!" Royael held a box with a ballerina doll as she ran around the gathering headed toward the exit. Bill at her heels, tried to keep up.

"Wow!" She looked around through the swarm for Stephen. *He must've gone to children's church before service.* She gave Bill a hug as Damien and Charlene neared them in the busy aisle.

"Happy New Years, Damien," Raven gave her stepfather a hug. She'd apologized to him, over the phone, for her wedding outburst and was reprimanded by him like a father would. Icy-blue eyes turned to Charlene, "What brings you to our neck of the woods?"

In a white Dior pantsuit, Charlene was all smiles when she said, "We bought a house!"

Breath of life escaped Raven as Charlene hugged her. She couldn't very well say "Aw Shit" because Royael would've loved mimicking that. Besides, they were still in church. Stiff handed, she patted her back. "Congratulations," Raven mumbled, then made introductions to a goggle eyed Bill.

He used a church pamphlet for Charlene's autograph. "You're more beautiful in real life."

"Thanks." Charlene added a heart to her signature.

"See ya'll around," Raven replied, when her brain finally registered the fact that her mother was a local to the Dallas area. She tried to grab Bill's arm, but he chattered about movies.

"We're having a barbeque Saturday," Damien said to Raven as Bill talked his wife's ear off.

"We'll be there." Bill nodded and took down their information. He chatted a while longer as Raven stood back, arms folded, watching. Even Royael mimicked her stance.

"You and Raven have a safe night." Damien said, finally cutting off the happy guy. Bill shook his hand vigorously, hugged Charlene like they were related, and when he seemed satisfied, linked fingers with Raven so they could leave.

"Why did you do that?" Raven's voice rose as they left the now empty building. In the few months that they'd dated, he'd never seen her angry. Being with Bill was like having an alternative life, where she didn't have to think about creative ways to pay the bills or how to help Granny buy medication. She didn't have to think about her mother, or that idiot Jon. However, right now, he attempted to weasel Charlene into their happy, *simple* relationship.

"Do what?" Bill blinked as he stared at Charlene's signature as they walked.

"Why did you *agree* to the barbeque?" Raven peered into the backseat as Bill put on Royael's seatbelt. The little chicken played possum. Knowing her daughter was awake, she had to be careful with her choice of words about Charlene. When he got in the front seat, she whispered through gritted teeth, "I don't want to be anywhere near *her*."

"Char's your mom," Bill's eyebrows crinkled. This was one of those places where their thought processes diverged. Bill grew up with a negligent foster mother. It was evident when he came to school with lips that looked like they'd been scraping asphalt and arms and legs that weren't any better. He'd love to have a mom, so he just didn't understand.

"Of all people, you know what *Charlene* put me through. I was popular in high school, but you remember elementary and middle school. You remember those kids taunting me, gossiping about Charlene! You know firsthand what being teased felt like," *because you were taunted all the way through.*

~~~

Wrought-iron gates surrounded the complex. Raven mashed in the code Damien had provided and drove through.

"This is fancy," Annette stressed the words, looking at a golf course to one side with rolling, vibrant grass and picturesque cascading ponds.

"Uh-huh," Raven replied, driving past three-story homes. She parked across the street from a vast stone home with glossy black oak doors. Fragments of a lake peaked through the backdrop of woods.

Famous peach cobbler in one hand, Annette got out of the car. She held Royael's hand, and they started across the street, stopping on the sidewalk. "Are you coming?"

"Go ahead, Granny. I have to leave Bill directions." Raven forced a smile. She never lied to Annette, but she was waiting for Sharon. For some odd reason, she'd gotten the notion to call Sharon the other day. The lady was her first real female friend, outside of church, work and not being a neighbor. They didn't plan to do anything scandalous, though she couldn't see herself at her mother's home without an ally.

"Charlene's having a barbeque, come with me," Raven had said over the phone.

"I….don't know, Raven," Sharon sounded hesitant. "What happened to that nice guy?"

"Bill's coming late. He's working on a computer program…that accurately detects the chance of heart disease." Raven gave a half truth. Bill did work on something astonishing, always talking about analyzing the heart with computer thingamajig, during their meager time together. When Sharon hadn't replied to seal the deal, she added, "He's trying to save the sick."

Sharon sighed. "Give me the address. I'm driving in my own damn car in case I get kicked out."

A glance at her phone read that Sharon was a few minutes late. Then Raven noticed her bright-red BMW pull up through the rearview mirror. The vibrant dyed redhead popped out of the car, dressed in her signature color: red designer jeans, red sweater, and some badass red boots. Raven looked down at her own outfit. She always wore jeans and bangles, but today she'd pulled on an oversized sweater and had on big, fake gold hoops. *Not too shabby.*

"I thought you flaked." The door squeaked as Raven shut it.

"Slap some fried-chicken grease on that thang and to answer your question, I should have." Sharon gave a smug look, then a full blown grin as they walked across the street.

Raven's jaw dropped when a girl about her age opened the door and introduced herself as Barbie while smacking on Bubblicious. They introduced themselves.

"C'mon," Barbie's grin exposed a gold tooth. Pink braids flipped in the air when she turned.

"Barbie…" Raven mimicked the girl's voice. Her top lip curled as the girl swished down the crystal figurine and glossy African art decorated hallway with a wiggly-spandex-wearing-butt.

"Girl, quit!" Sharon shook her head and they chuckled quietly.

Their senses were met by the sweet tangy aroma of barbeque as they entered the open, informal living room and dining area. Exotic pots of flowers and plush couches were aesthetically placed between the open areas. A stone fireplace, near the dining table, was aglow. Gauzy eggshell draperies were pulled back, and sunlight spilled upon more people than she had anticipated. A lot more.

Through the lively gathering, Raven didn't see Charlene anywhere, but was surprised when Damien introduced her as his stepdaughter to a few of his friends. *Seems he didn't hold grudges.*

~~~

Charlene's shoulders tensed as she lied to Annette when they first arrived. She hadn't meant to say they'd actually *bought* the house. It was magnificent–luxury meets nature–and just what she needed to get away from L.A. Sitting at the vanity, she stopped blending nude eye shadow as her eyes cut to Royael's bouncing on her bed; *wearing shoes.* Shaking her head, she continued to primp.

"People are down stairs, Char. You look beautiful. Are you ready?" Annette asked. When Charlene didn't reply, she smiled and added, "I brought peach cobbler, your favorite."

"Oh, Momma you didn't have to bring anything. We had everything catered." Holding back the terseness in her voice, she snapped the makeup shut.

"Chile, you know I don't care about eating no food from somebody I don't know. What if they don't wash their hands? God forbid we eat some barbeque sauce surprise."

Applying mascara, Charlene chose not to roll her eyes. *Same old Momma, always complaining about anything and everything.* "You didn't have to get married in Jamaica" and "You're wasting money on…." The times she'd called and offered Annette money, there were complaints about that, too. After awhile, she'd stopped asking. *My prideful Momma.*

One last assessment, her face was perfect. She sighed as Annette and Royael left, but was surprised when she heard a knock at the door, a few moments later, as she arose from the vanity. "Come in…come in…I SAID come in!"

"Char, I think we have a problem," Barbie said, clicking on a wad of gum.

"Barbie, take that gum out of your mouth! I'm *not* in the mood." Charlene fidgeted with the French tip of her finger nails.

"Sorry." Barbie pulled a large clump out of her mouth. "Raven brought company—"

"And? That nice, harmless boy?" His name slipped her mind, though he'd been so...sweet.

"No, a lady by the name of Sharon Riley. She sounds familiar. I don't trust her."

"Barbie, you're just being paranoid," Charlene snapped, brushing past her. Not normally brisk with her assistant, she didn't like the implication. *Didn't I go through enough during the wedding incident?* She walked down the stairs and, of course, Damien had to gush about his lovely wife. He acted like–well, a man married for six months, which he was.

Her nerves took a nose dive when the waiters brought out the first course and placed them on crystal chargers. Southern edible art. The chef explained his inspiration for each meal. The baby-back ribs were stacked like a pyramid in the middle of a small, square plate over a bed of the creamiest mashed potatoes she'd ever eaten.

"This isn't enough food," Annette grumbled, sitting next to Charlene.

"Just try it," Charlene whispered through gritted teeth, looking around at the guests to see if they noticed her momma pushing the cloud of potatoes.

Annette sighed, "All right, but at least we got my peach cobbler if anyone's still hungry. It seems as if the chef wasn't expectin' *all* these people."

Charlene pursed her lips at the last comment. There were well over twenty people at the large table. She watched the look on Annette's face when taking a bite of the potatoes. Priceless. *Momma loved it!*–wouldn't admit it, though.

Continuously eyeing Sharon, who sat with Raven on the opposite side of the large oak wood table, Charlene didn't feel any bad vibes. Not enough for Barbie to have been so paranoid. After the main course, being a lovely hostess, Charlene flitted around from guest to guest. She watched her daughter and Sharon play dominos with some of Damien's clients and enjoying a conversation with a few friends when Barbie signaled her.

They stood in the kitchen while the servers cleared silver chafing dishes off the granite counters.

"What?" Charlene seethed. *Raven's foolery had to be over, right?*

"Sharon Riley, niece of the head editor of Scandalous magazine." Barbie rolled her neck as she spoke. Fresh wad of gum in her mouth, but she didn't chew.

Charlene's mouth tightened then relaxed as giving the drama to God was best. She had to take it to John 14:27 and chanted, "Peace I leave with you… Let not your hearts be troubled..." in her head, when she noticed Barbie still waiting for an answer.

"Discretely kick her *ass* out," she replied.

~~~

Raven didn't get comfortable until she and Sharon were in the middle of a lively domino game with two handsome men who were attempting to lay on the charm.

"We should raise the stakes," the main charmer said.

"Why? Ya'll gonna lose anyway," Raven slapped down a domino and got a 'dub.'

"Maybe we're letting you win." The other one winked.

"Um-hum, boys. Keep telling yourselves that while adding up the scores." Sharon arched an eyebrow.

He came back with, "I bet if we start playin' for some phone numbers, ya'll gonna lose."

"Yeah," the other one agreed, "If we win the next game, ya'll give us your numbers?"

Raven said, "Pah-leez, what do *we* get when ya'll lose?"

Before the men could retort, they started laughing. Then Barbie came near the table, smiled and whispered into Sharon's ear.

"Well lady," Sharon gestured to Raven, then to the men, "and gentlemen, I have to be going."

"We hate to see you leave, but *love* to watch you go." He eyed Sharon's behind as she arose.

"I'm not even going to reply to that tired line," she smirked.

Raven followed Sharon down the hall toward the front door. "You don't have a life outside of me, work, and school, so where are you going?" Raven laughed, stopping when Sharon turned toward her as they stood at the front door.

"They know who I am. Guess they think we're on a scandalous mission." Sharon shrugged.

After she left, Raven sat in the corner of the living room. Her eyes turned frosty as she sent blades of ice to her mom.

~~~

Charlene excused herself from her current group and went to sit next to her daughter.

Raven looked straight ahead, asking, "What–growing bored with your *fan club*?"

"Why are you mad at me, Raven? You had *that* woman in my house after taking pictures of my wedding." Charlene stressed every word. *Should I even start on how you acted during the reception?*

"We weren't going to do anything. Sharon's my friend."

"I don't trust her!"

"Do you trust me?" Raven folded her arms, glaring at her victim.

"The thing is," Charlene began slowly, thinking about everything they'd been through. "I don't think you trust me. I'm asking more than I should, but can you forgive me?"

"For what? Me being taunted while I was young, when kids gossiped, saying you ran off to be a prostitute. Or for you not trying to help *your* own father when he was dying of leukemia? How about, you not being there when I fell in love with my half-brother! You coulda stopped me, if you'd stayed around or called sometimes. You coulda called in between your stupid movies and said, 'I think you should leave that boy alone, he's your effing brother!' That woulda helped." She stopped ranting. Eyes nailing her mom to the couch, she asked, "Now, what else do you want me to forgive you for?"

Grateful that Raven whispered, Charlene looked around as embarrassment crept up her throat. The pain coming from her daughter left a tangible void in her heart. "Please…" she began. Words jumbled together, she didn't know how to continue. Her eyes shifted again, there were no spectators. Raven stood up and walked away.

Three-two-one, action! Charlene got up and pretended to be as sweet as her momma's *unnecessary* peach cobbler. Not fifteen minutes later, Barbie gave her another we-need-to-talk look. She rolled her eyes, ready to hear about more scheming from Sharon when Barbie spoke, "Ya ma in the kitchen tryna clean up. She's been arguing with the chef about not putting her dessert on the menu."

"Did you tell her that the caterers were cleaning up?" Charlene stressed.

"No need. Annette wouldn't listen."

Kneading tension in the back of her neck, she walked toward the kitchen.

~~~

The fully equipped kitchen was quite like the ones Annette dreamed of. Oh yes, she often dreamed of cooking with a passion. She watched servers putting away appliances and taking catering supplies out the back door. The head-chef had long ago shaken his head at her commanding tone and walked away. If he had any brains–brains besides the ones that made that jamming mashed potatoes and ribs earlier–he'd have stayed and taken notes.

"You aren't using enough soap." Annette looked over a young man's shoulder.

"Okay," the worker said, grinning as he rolled his eyes.

Annette bit back her tongue from saying something unchristian-like as he took the soap off the counter and slowly poured a long stream of the lemon-scented liquid into the lack-suds water.

"This still got stains." Annette held up a stainless-steel chafing dish on the drying rack next to him and pointed to a smudge of barbeque sauce in the corner.

"Momma! Come enjoy the party."

At the sound of her daughter's voice, Annette slowly turned to see Charlene at the archway of the kitchen. She grimaced. "I got to help these people. They don't know what they doing."

"Everyone out!" Charlene ordered.

Annette moseyed toward the back door, planned on giving the chef her pearls of wisdom. She had the perfect ingredient that would rock those sweet potatoes he'd made…

"Not you, Momma."

Annette stopped, lips pursed, she watched the crew leave. The door shut behind them. Charlene spoke, "You don't have to help, Momma. I paid more than enough to cater."

"I'm most comfortable in the kitchen." Annette entwined her chubby fingers around a cup towel. "If you don't remember, I can stay in the kitchen all day long."

"I understand, but not today." Her eyes pleaded. When Annette didn't make a move to do as suggested, she added, "Let's go back and enjoy the company."

"Why'd you have to go and have all these people here today? You wasted money on fancy catering when I could've cooked. Besides, you said it would be just *us*."

"These are our friends."

"Not all of 'em. Some are Damien's friends, but you're just entertaining a bunch of folks."

"Momma, they're *my* friends, too. I just didn't want it to be…"

"Just us? Me, you, Damien, Raven, and Royael?" Annette questioned. *You stayed away so long? Was it so hard to come home after you were raped? Or just call your own momma?*

"No, Momma. I just thought we…"

"I'll go sit down somewhere so your fancy caters can clean. I won't bore all your fancy friends." Annette walked out of the kitchen.

Awhile later Raven came up to her with a stack of cards. "Can I interest you in a game of gin rummy, Granny?"

Annette smiled at her granddaughter and couldn't help noticing Charlene give them a sad look.

CHAPTER 11

Springing out of bed, Charlene dashed to the bathroom and fell to her knees on travertine tile. She leaned over the porcelain base and freed chunks of last night's Thai food. The restaurant they went to wasn't in the best part of Dallas, but rivaled any place in L.A. *We should go back home.* The temporary move was a mistake. Over the course of three months, while traveling back and forth from L.A. for the show, they hadn't spent much time together. More times than not, her daughter would flake. When Raven did show up, she'd play on her phone or talk with Annette. It was evident that Raven and Annette were close, mother-daughter close. *Where does that put me?*

"You okay, babe?" Damien yawned as he padded into the bathroom.

"Seafood curry is swimming in the toilet. Other than that, I'm just peachy," Charlene mumbled. Sunrays from the picturesque window warmed her cheek as she peeled the other side of her face off the toilet seat. Ugh the toilet seat. '*Gotta feel real crappy.*' Charlene put her hands to her ears. Marcus Webber? Roy Timmons? When was the last time she'd heard their voices mix together?

"…all right, you don't have to listen to what I'm saying, but I don't think it's the Thai food." Putting his hands underneath her arms, he lifted her up.

"What?" With the back of her hand, she wiped her mouth, still thinking about the man who raped her over twenty years ago and Marcus Weber. Weber was one of Damien's best accounting clients, a creepy casting agent that reminded her of Roy the Rapist. She'd been drowning in her sorrows of failing as an actress and abandoning Raven, when she met Marcus. His porn-star girlfriend had introduced her to valium, which could only be *perfectly* coupled with vodka, of course.

"Your ass is getting fatter." Damien smacked her behind. "Maybe you're pregnant."

"What?" Charlene sat on the stone ledge of the whirl tub. *I need to call Teresa.* Though she frequented the drug and alcohol meetings, she found that her relationship with a fellow addict had evolved on more levels than she'd dreamed of. She remembered their first talk at a coffee shop after a meeting. She'd been overly dramatic; Teresa had been as mellow as the rich chocolate coming from a steaming cup in front of her.

"You don't understand, Teresa. When Raven was eighteen years old, she came and found me! What type of mother has to be searched for by her child? To make matters worse, she only wanted two things from me. I couldn't help her with Otis. How could I tell her that the grandpa she loved so much wasn't my father? Then she wanted to know who her father was..."

"Charlene, we're talking about forgiving ourselves..." Teresa leaned her elbows on the scuffed wood counter and reached over to take her hands.

"No. I can't—"

"Look, Char, how in the hell are you gonna seek forgiveness of Raven, when you're unable to forgive yourself?"

"I said you might be pregnant. I'm sure as hell happy about it. How about you?"

Her eyes met Damien's for a fraction of a second as he watched her through the mirror. She quickly looked away. Eyes locked on the vase of white tulips, she brushed her teeth. Arms folded, he waited. She spit minty foam into the sink, rinsed, and replied, "I'm not pregnant, it's too soon."

His "logical explanation" to her throwing up, left her on edge. Dressed in a cloud of confusion, Charlene rummaged through the refrigerator for breakfast when she heard footsteps.

"What's on the agenda today, boss?" Barbie walked into the kitchen. She had a key to their house but stayed in a hotel.

"Hi, Barbie." Charlene rinsed off a Fuji apple. "Nothing today, take a mini-vacay. I'm going to the nail shop with Raven. It's the first time she's agreed to go somewhere with me alone. Pray for me." She gave a wry smile. Noticing the frown on Barbie's face, she asked, "What's up with you?"

"Well, it's my birthday." Barbie took a seat on the stool. Looking hopeless, she shrugged. "Guess I don't get a present?"

"I forgot." Trying to win back her daughter equaled oatmeal brain. "You should come."

She traced the granite countertop and said, "I don't want to intrude…"

"C'mon, Barbie. I appreciate you. We can even go shopping afterwards."

"What about a B' Jori purse?" Barbie perked up, with a half smile.

"Barbie, I thought Charlene give you the day off when you left yesterday?" Damien asked, walking into the kitchen. He made a beeline for the coffee maker.

"It's her birthday and we're going to have a girls' day out!"

"What about Raven? Did she cancel?" He rubbed her shoulder.

"We're all going." She grabbed her keys, but not before noticing a look of confusion on his face.

~~~

Adjusting the camera lens, Raven took a picture of dew on vibrant green grass and a gray Dallas morning sky. *Perfect.* She took a few more snapshots and got up.

"Mommy, take my picture!" Royael did a push start with the merry-go-round, grabbed on the rail and hopped on. Her ponytails swung in the air underneath a beanie that framed her face.

The leather toes of Raven's cowboy boots dug into the grass as she kneeled down to capture a couple of candid shots. When finished, she got up and pulled on her beige leather jacket and readjusted a cream infinity scarf. "Okay, time to head inside."

"Aw, Mommy, more pictures. I'm buuutiful!"

"No." She pulled the bar to a stop. "I can't use all of this film on you. My instructor let me take this camera home for spring break week." After taking those Scandalous wedding photos, Raven had found that she enjoyed photography and decided to take a class at the college.

"Just a couple more…" Royael's bottom lip protruded. Though hard to say no to that pout, Charlene's Escalade pulled up across the street in front of their home. She took the child inside, adding a bribe for more photos later. Stepping outside, she ambled up to the passenger door and *noticed Barbie*. She received a gold-tooth-smile and a subtle nod toward the back.

"Hi, Charlene. Hi, Bimbo." A tight smile formed on Raven's face as she put on her seatbelt, glaring into the side window at Barbie's expression.

"It's Barbie. Remember?" She turned and glared. When Raven's searing gaze didn't falter, she faced forward. "I saw you with that camera. Were you taking pictures of your mom, again?"

"Barbie, quit that." Charlene gave her a friendly punch on the shoulders.

Relax, Raven recited, but her jaw was set to rigid-mode. A subtle throbbing began by the time they made it to the nail shop. Finally as she stood looking at the prices, her mouth turned into a relaxing 'O' shape. Following the manicurist past crystal vases of orchids, and glossy paintings, Raven knew where the money went.

When Barbie tried to sit in the middle chair, Raven stuck her boot out and tripped the twit. Charlene chatted with the manicurist about a nail color, so anything goes. War.

"Gosh, Bimbo, I'm sorry!" Raven held out a hand to help her up.

Barbie's face twisted. "It's cool, Re-Re. I got it."

No, this chick did not use my nickname. Charlene hadn't made that mistake. Raven sunk back into the cushiony leather chair and pressed the massage remote on the armrest; stopping on 'max'–she needed the extra relief.

"So Raven, I'd love to see your pictures," Charlene said as their pedicurists got to work.

Raven hesitated, her voice sounded genuine, but the photos were intimate. She'd given a lot of thought to the composition and message of each photo. It would be like sharing a piece of herself to a mother she didn't know. "Maybe later."

Charlene smiled. Raven felt like smiling and was about to when Barbie broke the moment.

"Char, this feels gooood." Barbie purred as the corns on her toes were being scrapped off.

"Yeah, this beats the place we go to at home."

"We." Raven shut down. Barbie carried the conversation and each time her mother tried to reel her in, Raven would shrug. When they got to the car with fresh mani- and pedis-, Charlene said, "Raven, you can sit in the front with me."

"I'm comfortable in the back," was the longest string of words she'd said in awhile. Noticing Charlene sulk, she added, "It's not every day that I get chauffeured around," with a smile.

They talked. Invisible, Raven listened with imaginary masking tape over her lips. She stared at her neon-orange fingernails; her favorite color did nothing to brighten her mood. When she looked up, Charlene had passed her freeway exit. *Where are we going? I only signed up for the nail shop.*

Raven's heart sunk as Charlene maneuvered around a busy mall parking lot. Still in a daze, she didn't even feel the sun beginning to warm as they walked past trimmed planted palm trees, going from store to store at the expensive outdoor mall. Her mother would show her a beautiful scarf or a pair of designer jeans and she'd reply, "That cost too much" or "I hate that color" or "Not my style." After a while her mom stopped trying. *That's just fine by me.*

The spring break crowds waved at Charlene, occasionally asking her for autographs and pictures. It all made Raven's shoulders tense as she held the celebrity's many shopping bags.

"Hey, let's go into B' Jori!" Barbie said as they stood outside of the glass doors. Clothing and accessories were fashionably displayed in the windows.

"I forgot. Ghetto bitches love B' Jori." Raven replied. "Get a real one, and then you can swap it with all your fake ones. Coordinate it, girl!" She snapped her finger with a smile.

Barbie and her mother stood stark still, mouths open wide.

"Raven, don't talk like that!" Charlene voiced like a mother reprimanding a toddler. Her eyes flitted side to side making sure nobody noticed the altercation.

"Or what?" She dropped the paper bags with colorful tissue and folded her arms. "Are ya gonna take me over your knee and spank me? How'll that look with all of your fans around?"

"You would like that, huh?" Barbie's eyes moistened and she sniffled. "Is Sharon lurking in a bush, wa-waiting for Charlene to blow up? Is that why you've been so cr-cruel today?"

"She didn't mean it." Charlene patted Barbie's arm, then turned to Raven, "Say sorry."

Barbie stood behind Charlene with a come-back-to-that smile.

Raven rolled her eyes and turned away from her mom's request. Barbie was a worthy adversary. *I guess I underestimated you and your gold tooth…*

CHAPTER 12

Charlene sidestepped a trail of rose peddles that led from the front door to the kitchen. A glow flickered from tapered candles, highlighting a bottle of apple cider. All she wanted to do was go upstairs, take a bubble bath, and end the day with *dreamless* sleep. *No lovin' today, please.*

Damien stood at the island in the middle of the kitchen, booty playing peek-a-boo beneath an apron. He held up a carton of chicken marsala. "Damn, I was getting ready to put all this food into these wooden bowls and pretend like I cooked. How did it go?"

She took a seat at the white-and-black paisley stool and poured a glass of the cider, hoping it had a little kick to it. "Raven acted awful! She was *so evil* to Barbie."

"Maybe it should've been just you and Raven." He shrugged as he set square plates with burgundy peonies on the table. "Bonding time."

He chuckled, while she told the horror story of the day. When finished, her almond eyes narrowed and she asked, "Why are you laughing?"

"Sorry, it's a funny story. I'm a guy, with a guy's sense of humor."

"Raven's not a *guy*. She shouldn't be running around saying the b-word!" Charlene speared romaine lettuce and crunched on it. The tangy Caesar salad dressing, her favorite, did nothing to lift her mood.

"Maybe Barbie should've stayed at the hotel today. I heard you give her the day off yesterday. The girl's always stuck under you and needs to get some friends."

"She's my assistant and is stuck in a different state. She only has me." When her husband gave a blank stare, she further clarified, "Today is her birthday!"

"What's more important Barbie's birthday or having a relationship with Raven?"

I just don't think Raven wants to be bothered with me. Charlene pushed her food away. With a gulp of cider, she downed the lettuce suddenly lodged in her throat. Not allowing her insecurities to reign, she took on a defensive stance. "Why are you taking Raven's side?"

"She's my stepdaughter. I could care less about the other kid." He shook his head. "There you go, acting like Meagan. That dramatic mindset of yours needs to be left in Hollywood where it belongs. With family, there are no sides."

Frowning, she watched Damien near the kitchen island with the bag of takeout food. There was another bag next to it. Picking up the white paper bag, he set it in front of Charlene, and then walked to the hallway leading to the den. Huffing, she opened it to see a pregnancy test.

~~~

The next morning, she stirred him awake. "Get up."

"What?" His voice was thick, groggy.

Leveling her voice so as not to display her irritation, she said, "I just peed on a stick, and you're going to be with me when I read it."

Stretching, he got up from bed and followed her to the pee-stick. She picked it up from the granite counter. The sconces on the walls gave off just enough light when she held up the stick. *I'm 36. I'm too old to start over. I'm...*

"I'm pregnant," she murmured. In his embrace, she mimicked his happy demeanor. When he seemed satisfied, she went into the upstairs office and called her agent. Tony paused for a moment after she told him the news.

"All right. We're just going to have to work around your schedule," Tony voiced heavily. "I'll run that by the production team for The Eradicator. The crème de la crème of action flicks have created a role just for you and...."

She sighed as he mentioned the impending blockbuster that was set for the end of next year. The hype, the anticipation from the writer/director of The Eradicator was already the biggest buzz. He ended his lecture with a resounding question of her acting ability regarding both the soap and the blockbuster to which she assured him of her competence.

"Now, the bad news," Tony sighed, "it may void the Meagan *Loyalty and Fam* contract."

Groaning, she hung up. *I've invested five years on the soap opera. A pregnant, oversexed vixen? Pah-leez! Pregnant women were only sexy to the men that had got them that way—if that.*

CHAPTER 13

Stephen had stopped Raven to talk after choir practice, and that was all she could think about as she sat on a futon in Bill's studio apartment. Their conversation laced through her brain as she watched curls of smoke from incense sticks. *After all these months, Steph wants to know what happened in Jamaica.* Her phone rang; Charlene's ringtone. Instead of answering, she pressed the mute button like she'd been doing since going out with Charlene and Barbie. She tried to focus on the photo samples on the coffee table. Bill rapidly typed on his laptop. Their–*study*–date suited Bill, but her mind kept travelling back to Stephen.

He's seen me at church with Bill. Melody tells me all about their dates. It's too late for us. That thought wasn't fuel enough to stop the image of his dimples disappearing as she confirmed kissing Marley earlier. *"Yes, Stephen. A butler, named Marley, who I most likely will never see ever again…"*

"Raven, are you listening?"

The sound of typing stopped. He wasn't using that excited voice and words she didn't understand when explaining the dynamics of a heart-monitor. All she could see was the look on Stephen's face and how he'd walked away right after her admission of kinda cheating with Marley.

"Hey, let's go bungee jumping this weekend?" She asked. Maybe one day she could get Bill to want to do things she liked–things she and Stephen liked. Fear momentarily flickered in his eyes and her heart deflated. Getting ready to ask him about going dirt-bike riding, he spoke.

"I just said that my program is having a seminar this weekend," he replied.

"Oh-kay," she tried not to sound disappointed. Stephen would've been all for her ideas. Instead of thinking of him any further, she tuned into Bill. Her safe man.

~~~

"Wow, you're three months pregnant. Aren't you almost forty?" Raven's upper-lip curled as she looked at Charlene. They sat around the formal dining table at her mom's house for Sunday dinner.

"C'mon, Raven. Let's make nice," Damien chided from the head of the table.

"Well, congratulations, Damien," she replied, knowing she should say so to her mom, also. Naw, she didn't feel like it. As if a light bulb turned on in her head, she turned to Charlene and added, "Since you really haven't raised children before, I want to give you some words of wisdom."

"Okay…" Charlene leaned forward as if the long dinner table had stretched a mile wide.

"Don't forget to come home."

She echoed Raven's words, eyebrows creased together.

"I'm sure you don't understand that one." Raven cackled. Taking on a lecturing stance, she added, "Don't forget that you have a baby. You don't want to have him or her tryna find *you*."

While Charlene's head dipped a notch, in shame, Raven downed a glass of wine–the cheap stuff that creeps in quickly. Her mother didn't keep alcohol in their home, but was always inviting her and Annette for Sunday dinner. So she was…obligated to bring something.

"Yeah, Grandma. Don't forget your baby!" Royael's wide eyes were serious. Seconds later, she burst into tears, "I forgot Mookie at home. Mommy we gotta go and get my bear!"

They ate in silence after Raven and Annette calmed Royael down who sat between the two. Later, Raven placed her sleeping child in a guest room and went to watch television in the den.

When she heard a knock, she said, "Come in," expecting it to be Charlene. All her mother did nowadays was apologize, so she never let up on the criticism.

Instead of Charlene appearing, Damien entered. "We need to talk."

Raven muted the television as he took a seat.

"If I didn't feel like you loved Char somewhere deep down inside, I would've told her that we should go home a long time ago."

Yes. You've been intruding on my life for months...never mind that she comes back and forth for that tacky soap opera. That's still time wasted!

"I love you like my own child." Damien gave her a stern stare, the kind she assumed bad kids get from fathers who *actually cared*. "Are you going to try to work things out with your mother? Will you forgive her? Because, we can go back to L.A. and never bother you again. Is that what you want?"

"I..." *Never bother me again...*

"You're angry, but she's trying hard. There's a child growing in her stomach. I want that child to be nurtured and not feel stress." He put his hand on her shoulder. "You deserve to be loved by your mother and your mother deserves to be loved by you."

"Aw, Damien." Raven unmuted the TV and began flipping through channels. *Dang, I hadn't thought of the baby...*She rubbed the back of her neck, hating the way she'd acted–for the child's sake.

He grabbed the remote, turned it off. "Stop this pity-party. Charlene loves you."

Raven looked down at plush white carpet, tried to count the strands but they blurred together as tears stung her eyes. Feeling his eyes on her, she turned away from him and looked at the crystal mermaid figurines on a build in shelf.

"You don't want to feel the hurt, because it means going back to why you're mad at her."

She didn't save grandpa. All she had to do was go to the doctors and see if she was a potential donor! She didn't save me from falling in love with Jon...

"You push away all your pain and punish her. Somewhere inside, you want to be loved."

Tears started falling. He held her tight. Limbs numb, Raven pushed herself to hug him back. She closed her eyes. In her mind, Damien became her father.

~~~

"Okay, Momma. Just clean it all!" Charlene put her hands in the air as she walked away. Besides, she needed to call her agent. In the past couple of weeks, they'd done a few scenes for the show, ending with

Meagan being kidnapped for a hefty ransom. Luckily, her belly just began to round, hardly showing wonderment of the gift it held. The stylist had worked magic with Meagan's skimpy ensemble. She'd have to do voiceovers every once in awhile, but she was free to be pregnant.

"What happened?" She asked into her cell phone, sitting in the office, staring at the intricate weaving of the Oriental rug.

"The writers were…reasonably angry at first. They had to edit half a season of script to include Meagan's kidnapping. Good news, last week's ratings were fire. You get to rest until the beginning of next year. The catch," he paused, "the director wants a killer mid-season finale. We need you fresh, sexy and in the right mindset before the holidays to wrap up one episode? Can you do it?" Tony's breath caught. He seemed livelier today than when she broke the news to him.

"The baby will barely be a month, then…yes. Yes, I can do it," she spoke with the confidence she had when acting. But, the same mentality failed her when it came to Raven. Going downstairs, she dreaded the next verbal boxing match.

One, two, three…action! Hyping herself, she turned the knob to the den. Hormones were a whip to her back as she walked inside the cream colored room with crystal mermaid figurines.

"Charlene, wanna watch TV?" Raven asked.

A trap? *No, I did just get her into an impressive photography school, with so much more to offer than the city college.* For a moment, Charlene felt like her bribes were ashes. Grinning back, she finally nodded. Bare feet sinking into carpet, she sank into the suede cushion next to her daughter. They watched stand-up comedy. There were words, curse words, that she didn't prefer to hear, but the comedian had her sides aching. It didn't hurt that her child was laughing, too.

CHAPTER 14

When his secretary said that Nana was on line four, Jon remembered his first day of work. He mentally went back to it. *The skyscraper was a dominating force. The mirrored windows of the building mimicked the clear, blue Dallas sky as Jon strode into the USA branch of the Devereux Corporation. He had on his big boy pants, literally—a virgin-wool suit tailored to perfection on his six-foot-four, athletic frame. Caramel complexion popped against the black suit. A briefcase in one hand, and his cell phone glued to his other.*

"I must apologize for being absent on your first day. I'm stuck in London for an important board meeting." Grandfather Pierre referred to the decreased sales of the newspaper aspect of Devereux Communications. "You are my legacy…" He chanted, giving Jon the pep talk for the umpteenth time, the poise needed to manage the creative design for a new chain of D Hotels springing up across the world.

After hanging up, he was surprised to get a call from Estella Devereux, his Nana. Grumbling, he gave her the same courtesy as he just gave his grandfather. Answering, he expected to be congratulated, but that was just wishful thinking on his part. She was Estella, of course. A French supermodel. When she'd stopped modeling, her money began to dwindle. Pierre had turned the little bit of money she had left into a multi-billion dollar fortress.

"Hello, Nana," Jon said as he stepped onto the elevator. His cheeks automatically began to ache as he remembered her pinching them with disgust when he was fourteen and fat. Banished from home after his mom caught him kissing Raven, he was heartbroken and alone. He had to succumb to Nana's hatred of his weight and how she'd forced him to speak in French.

"Jon, I've been told that you've started your first day of work. How does it feel to be your grandfather's **Legacy**?*"*

He rolled hazel eyes as she spat the words. She'd been within earshot of the university where he received a Bachelor in Business and was calling now. "If you'd have come to my graduation, you would've heard the speech," he replied. Estella never left France; a place where she was still revered. Where people remembered her as a model and not just the face of her perfume "Stellar by Estella" or cosmetic line

77

that ripped the counters of pricy department stores. God forbid she just be remembered as a billionaire's wife.

"Your grandfather didn't invite me." *Her soft, hesitant voice made Jon wonder if it was because he'd just gotten off the elevator.*

"You didn't read it in Devereux's publications or some competitors broadcasted in mass media." *His throat constricted as he had a hard time controlling the anger he felt from being mistreated by her as a child. It took a mental mantra to remind himself that he wasn't the fat boy from Carolina anymore. He could now speak French fluently—being multilingual was a great asset—as if she hadn't beaten that in him enough during his visits. He'd exceeded the expectations of the affluent, just not her expectations.*

"Of course, I knew! I wasn't invited." *Her voice rocketed then flattened.*

"Grandpa didn't invite you? I find that hard to believe."

"Please forgive me for hurting you. I've something of the upmost importance to inform—"

"Nana…" *something in her voice was different…sincere. He didn't trust it. Her new mannerism shut him down. He rushed his words,* "I have to call you back. Love you, bye." *Jon hung up and walked to the door of his new office.*

He shuttered thinking about how he'd never called her back and it was months later. He'd sent gifts for every holiday—his secretary, Patricia, had bought and had them wrapped. He'd sign a card. Either way, Nana got them. She'd send back a thank you note and that "we need to talk" line.

"Jon *I said* your grandmother is on line four." Patricia cut into his thoughts. Her voice reverberated around the large room.

"Tell her that I just walked into a meeting. Whenever she calls, give her another excuse. Oh, and be creative. Cut all my calls. I'm going home, Camille is in town." The name rolled off his tongue like honey.

•

CHAPTER 15

The click of the camera was constant as Raven looked through the lens at the lake behind her mom's house. The stream's continuous murmur always gave her a sense of peace. The moss and clear green water took her back to the meadow in Bellwood. She snapped shots of dragon flies rippling over the water and ducks quacking as her brain replayed the first counseling session that she went to. The headaches and bickering with Barbie had reached a boiling point; she'd finally taken the creative writing Professor's advice. She hadn't hallucinated about Elise Dubois—or what she presumed was the green-eyed phantom of Elise, in the trench coat and cap—stalking her since she'd seen Dr. Stanton. Nor had she dreamt of Jon's mom.

'Find yourself at peace and make amends,' Dr. Stanton had said. Tranquility had unraveled the yarn of nerves in her abdomen. Boots clumping through tall grass, she inhaled dew. Her annoyance of Barbie began to washout as remorse set in. She realized why Barbie *always* weaseled her way into her relationship with Charlene. With a sense of hesitance, she went into the house.

'Concentrate on your anger. Release. Forgive,' the psychiatrist's masculine voice was a distant memory as she climbed the stairs. The black oak shutters in the office were closed on such a beautiful sunny day. She twiddled with the camera around her neck and asked, "Barbie, can we talk?"

A tense "yes" was Barbie's response, face glowing green from the computer screen.

Okay, now what? One session with a smooth-talking man and it has me tryna make amends with an asshole. "How's…your mom, I've noticed that you've never mentioned her?"

"Why are you so interested in me all of a sudden, *Ray*-ven?" Her eyes never left the screen.

"I know that you're going to be around. Maybe we should try to get along?"

Black marbles turned to glare at Raven. The left side of Barbie's crusty lips curved into a sneer.

Raven huffed, retreated. She walked down the hall to the guest bedroom where Daniela unpacked her luggage. Charlene was about eight months and Daniela had come to stay. The older woman filled the void of not having a grandmother on her father's side. *If only I could fill that grandfather void...* She reminisced about Grandpa Otis for a second. Besides, Daniela could sooth her bruised ego. *That doctor was wrong.*

'You only went to one session, Dumbass. I would love to see what the future holds with the intelligent Dr. Stanton,' the voice said. *'It was quite funny. Do go back. Maybe you can really open up about Elise Devereux-Dubois.'*

Disregarding the voice's laughter in her ears, she gave Daniela a hug. She glanced at a cracked-leather Bible on the oak nightstand. The patchwork quilt on the bed couldn't have been Charlene's doing. It was well worn, had character. "Grandma, you settling in?"

"Char told me that you've started a new photography school. Is your four-year associates' degree quest coming to an end?" Daniela grinned.

"One of my professors, Mr. Tinker, says I have raw talent. Maybe I'll graduate." She winked.

"I want to see your photos," Charlene interjected, voice traveling from the walk-in closet.

She hadn't known that her mom was in the room. As if her hesitance to answer Charlene was tangible, Daniela jokingly said, "You know you in trouble, right? I haven't received any pictures of Royael lately."

"I'm guilty." Raven straightened an old photo of Damien on the dresser as they chatted.

"I'm just about done in here. We should go shopping for the baby," Daniela said.

"Okay..." Charlene exited the closet. She looked into her daughter's eyes as if she needed approval and added, "I suppose I could send Barbie home–back to her hotel room."

She waddled around, holding her belly, having blown up after the producers of her soap opera had agreed to change the scenes to incorporate her pregnancy. Their agreement was cosign to eat everything on her plate, Damien's plate, and any of the leftovers, too.

~~~

They stepped inside a couture baby boutique at the same mall that Raven had argued with Barbie. Daniela pulled out items right to left, trailed by an eager sales associate. Raven and Charlene linked arms and followed.

"My ankles," Charlene grimaced, trying to keep up, but her mother-in-law was far ahead.

They took a seat on a cobalt sofa with pastries placed on an end table. Raven could tell her mom wanted to talk and watched as she took a bite of a purple macaroon. After a few bites, she spoke, "You never really told me if Jon helps you with Royael."

"No." Raven placed a lemon Danish in a gold napkin with the boutique's moniker.

"Why not?" Her puffy face contorted with anger. "Children are expensive. Royael *is* expensive. Dance classes and pageants, your tuition. How is Momma doing with Royael while you're in school? Oh, and Momma! I know she's taking diabetic pills, still trying to cook all those dang cakes, too."

Raven picked a piece off the pastry. "I work at a coffee shop. Granny still gets some money. We've been survivin' off the money from…those pictures. I'm so sorry."

"It is okay, Raven."

Tears formed in her eyes as she put her uneaten Danish on the end table. Having never genuinely apologized to Charlene about the Scandalous wedding photos, she turned to look at her mom. "No, I let you and Damien down." *Wow, okay, maybe Stanton was right. This does feels good.*

They hugged in the middle of the store, and for the first time, Raven noticed that her mom wasn't looking around in embarrassment "How were you surviving before that article?"

"Jon se-sent me," she paused feeling the force of a punch to her heart. Shifting in the seat she said, "He gave me fifty thousand dollars not to have Royael."

Charlene's eyes bugged out, bigger than her swollen nose and lips.

"We were gonna run away when I found out that I was pregnant," Raven started, staring at a white-canvas-enclosed baby carriage with triple-digit price tag. "Then we found out that we were related. Jon sent me a letter." Her eyes glued to the gold post of the carriage, sliding down to the large wheels. "He let me know it was incest, wanted me to have an abbbboortion." A sob chocked her throat. *I'm crying in the middle of a beautiful baby store.* She almost smiled at that thought. It felt so good. They connected hands as if the mere act strengthened their relationship.

~~~

A week later Raven, Daniela, and Charlene ate a late breakfast while looking at her photography. She blushed as they complemented her work.

Daniela's eyes widened. "Oh, I gotta show ya'll Damien's baby pictures."

"He's gonna flip," Charlene said, biting French toast, noticing her sly grin.

"What? I'm just going to show you how handsome he was *and* how big his ears were," she replied to a round of giggles. "Besides he's out-of-town."

They got up from the table of half eaten omelets and an empty bowl where cut up fruit had been. Charlene downed her OJ, and said, "Ya'll go ahead, I have to clean."

Raven scolded her, "Mom, let the dirty dishes rest a while."

"Okay." She chuckled. "I'll place everything in the sink and be upstairs by the time Daniela finds the photos *in all her luggage*." She shooed them away. Having become even more of a neat freak while pregnant, she placed dishes in the sink and grabbed a dishrag to go over the granite countertops when the phone rang. Jogging through the house to the sound, it felt like one false move and the baby would pop out. Phone wedged in the couch, she picked it up to see Damien's cell on the screen.

"Hey, Char, I've been calling all morning. Weber's coming by. I need you to give him a file."

"Do you want me to fax it," Charlene tried to keep the urgency out of her voice. She didn't want to see the man with steel-blue *evil* eyes.

"It has to be an original. He's in town and will be by in a couple of minutes. Just grab a manila folder out of the office."

"Oh-kay. How was your flight?"

"Good, honey, I gotta go. I'm meeting a client in less than an hour, and I'm reading files while stuck in traffic."

Charlene clicked the OFF button as the doorbell rang. She padded to the glossy black door. One glance out the peephole showed a crater face. She cracked the door. "Hello, Mr. Weber."

"Hello, Mrs. Wright." A buttery-yellow-toothed-smile was plastered on Marcus's face.

"Hold on, I just spoke with Damien." She cracked the door, hurried up the stairs and down the long corridor into the office. Breath jagged, she stopped to lean on the edge of the desk.

"Are you alone?"

Charlene's body shook. His voice was right behind her. She turned around, wedged between the desk and the mountain of a man. Shutters drawn, his big body blocked most of the door frame, though shadows of light from the hallway didn't mask the sex in his eyes.

"I miss seeing you on television, Meagan. Why'd ya go and act like that, but wouldn't be in any of my films?" He referred to the pornographic films that he cast.

"It's cable TV, Marcus. It. Is. Not. Real." The words trembled out as her hands shielded her belly. *Her baby. Should I scream? What if he tries to hurt Raven, and Daniela is old...* Mouth gone dry, tongue feeling like it had carpet burns on it, she could *not* scream.

"C'mon, Meagan, do me like you did the guy. The one that you meet in Milan."

"My name is Charlene. I'm pregnant. We were *acting*..." She didn't know if the words passed her lips. His expression reminded her of Roy. Trying to shake her head and decrease the dizziness, she didn't want to be unconscious. *Raven was in my womb when I was raped by Roy!* She cradled her stomach tighter as he came closer.

"Meagan," he purred.

Darkness seeped through the swaying of the room. His rancid breath indicated his nearness. *Jesus help*...She blacked out.

Time beyond grasp, Charlene took a sharp breath and looked into Marcus's empty blue eyes. He lay inches away. Pieces of shattered glass surrounded them on the Oriental rug. Blood trickled at the side of his temple, into pale lashes, into his eyes. Turning her head slightly, she saw Raven's knees pressed into his gut. Her daughter's eyes were a gray storm, not a hint of a calm sea, not one hint.

Spots of blood sprouted as Raven pierced the fat folds of his neck with a shard of multicolored glass. She whispered in his ear and his head bobbed up and down in sheer terror. Red tears began to stream down the side of his face and cheeks.

"Raven," Charlene found her voice. Her daughter continued to use the glass like an ice pick. She spoke louder, "Raven."

Sincere blue eyes turned Charlene's way, as a confirmation that they were safe, and Raven hopped off of Marcus. Then Raven's attention went back to Marcus as she stomped down on his balls, twisting the heels of her favorite cowgirl boots. The sides of her mouth were skyward in contentment. The vibes, the aura around her, denoted that she relished every movement, every groan of agony while Charlene grimaced, perceiving his pain.

"Get out, sick bastard!" Raven kicked him swiftly in the ribs.

Charlene watched as the pig grunted, rolled over. Marcus crawled out of the room, holding his privates with one hand and clawing at tile with the other. Raven followed, kicking him every couple of steps. He must have toppled down the stairs, because she heard a sound that mimicked a spoof comedy. Then she heard what she could only assume as the front door slamming.

Less than a minute later, Raven came to her side, breathing easy. The girl hadn't broken a sweat. Hoisting Charlene into a standing position and eased her onto the leather couch, saying, "Watch yourself. Sorry about your fancy vase… well, I'll go get you some water."

"I'm coming with you." Legs regaining their strength, she followed. Nestled on the barstool in the kitchen, Raven handed her a glass of water. *The girl moves quick*. She gulped it down and it filled her burning belly. Finally, getting the nerve, she asked, "When you came in…w-was he, d-did–"

"I heard you fall. When I came in, he was standing over you, cupping your breast. I slammed the lamp on his head," Raven shrugged, leaning against the refrigerator door.

Slowly, the air seeped back into Charlene's lungs. Blood surged through her body as she told Raven how she met Marcus Weber. How she'd always felt something "off" about him.

"Why haven't you told Damien? He'd never do business with such a creep!"

"Yeah, well he was Damien's biggest client when we first met and sent more leads his way." She shook her head, recalling the first time she met began Marcus. "He always reminded me of Roy."

"The truck driver that raped you?" Raven twisted her index finger through her leather wristband.

Charlene nodded, but couldn't read her child's expression.

Raven walked to the sink and turned on the water. "I was almost raped once."

She hadn't expected Raven to be open and so…calm. She tried to get up, go to her child, but it felt like a giant had taken a sledge hammer to her back. "What happened?"

"Jon's mother, Elise, sent him away before the start of high school. You don't know how we met, huh?" With hint of longing in her voice, Raven poured soap into the sink. "Grandpa Otis always told me the story. Jon and I were two. We were in the church nursery during snack time. A three year old took Jon's snack. I smacked her silly. After that, we were an unlikely pair, until he moved away before high school. Anyway, back to the story. I started going with Chris. He was very popular, too popular."

She winced, watching Raven put the clean omelet skillet onto the rack. Some part of Charlene wanted her daughter to stop cleaning and just sit down, so they could talk. No, Raven kept cleaning.

"It was my fault, really. I saw the warning signs, but being with Chris erased all the gossip, every link to you. All the cruel stories that kids would say about you had disappeared, because he was revered–respected. Then Jon came back during senior year. Chris thought I was cheating. Truthfully, I was starting to fall in love, but Jon and I had only been best friends…so I wasn't sure what I wanted. Chris flipped. He expected us to have sex and… One night I went out with Chris, and… he, and C-Chris pinned me do-down on the back of his truck. When I got my chance, I *took it*."

Charlene watched pink liquid and soap suds drip as Raven rinsed a glass cup. "Your hand?"

Eyebrows knitted together, Raven looked down and noticed blood mixed with soapy water.

Guilt gnawed her heart. She hadn't been that concerned with her daughter's wellbeing after kicking Marcus out. *I've a lot to learn about being a mother*. Hurrying to the bathroom, she came back with a first-aid kit and started bandaging the cut. Charlene winced at the long slit. "You're brave. You might need stitches."

"I don't need stitches. Guess it happened when I picked up that shard of glass and started poking Marcus," Raven gave a weak smile. "So have you tried finding Roy?"

Charlene's face shook, cheeks trembled.

"We should find him. He needs to suffer." Voice monotone, her

beautiful face finely contoured in gold marble again. So unreadable.

CHAPTER 16

His velvety brown skin captivated her. The tremor of her fingers indicated just how much Raven willed herself not to reach out and touch the strength in his arms. Just a slight graze would do. Licking her lips, her eyes roamed over white boxer-briefs, a thin barrier. His body, a canvas. Fortunately, she was safe behind her tripod. Switching position, she looked through the lens freely. From neck to toe, tattoos covered the muscles of his lean body. The angles contorted perfectly underneath the ultra bright lighting in the studio. His body contrasted with the crisp white backdrop. Except for the click of the camera, silence was thick as she captured the model a few feet away. Gone was the nervousness–a slight hesitance–she'd felt when Tattoo Man came into the studio. He'd unwrapped from his robe exposing artistic beauty. *Exciting. Black beauty.* Her energy sprang to life. Heavenly moments captured. Raw, gritty moments. A bold approach, but the instructor said anything goes for the final exam which would grace the folds of her professional portfolio. She hadn't dreamed that an *almost naked* man with paraphilias–tattoo fetish–would be her choice for a final at the exclusive photography school.

"Raven, you're not acting like you were when we began." Tattoo Man gave a sly grin.

"I'm focused," came her in-the-zone-mumble. Kneeling, she took a full scale shot. *Perfection!*

"Comfortable enough to go for drinks?" The curve of his lips indicated that "drinks" were just a ploy.

Instantly, she knew her cheeks turned a deep raspberry, the same color of the popular shake at the coffee shop where she worked. It was hard replying while eye level with the bulge, which was pretty darn happy at the moment. At least, all of the light was on him and he wasn't close. Close enough to smell her desire. Arising in a hurry, the bangles around her wrist jingled. She twirled her index finger for him to turn around to which he gave her an answer-the-question wink. Finally, she replied, "I have a boyfriend."

"Who?" He went into an angular motion, displaying length and superb back muscles.

A giggle of happiness almost escaped as she discovered the gem to her portfolio. The tiger on his back would appear to pop out of that picture when developed. *Pure genius.*

"Raven, I asked who he is." Tattoo man faced forward for a split second.

God, this man is fine... "Cooperate, please," Raven scolded. "His name is Bill. He's a biochemical major at Dallas University."

"Sounds boring." He faced her again, thick eyebrow lifted.

"Not boring...intelligent," Raven stopped talking. *I don't have to explain my relationship to you!* Her heartbeat rose at the same rate that the muscles of his legs tensed and relaxed. He stepped off the platform, sauntered over. His pace and the look in his eyes reminded her of the tiger–she had been so intrigued to capture–on his back.

Tattoo Man was too handsome, too suave; too self confident just like...Jon–that instantly turned her off. She slapped his hand away as he undid the top button of her flannel shirt. His searing stare dared her to re-button it and hide the exposed bit of her lace bra.

"I'm celibate." She smiled, knowing that would turn him off.

"Um-hum. That just means it's been awhile since you had good–"

The sound of her phone ringing snipped the sexual tension. The ringtone was her mom's song. A new song she'd programmed about a month ago, after they'd bonded at the baby boutique. *Thanks to Dr. Stanton.* Rushing past him, she picked up the phone.

"Hey, Mom. I just looked at the time when you called. I'm going to be a little late for our Thursday lunch." Her eyes flicked to the man before her. "Time got away from me. Let's meet–"

"Well, don't you sound flustered. It's me, Daniela, we on our way to the hospital."

"Oh, I'm on my way!" In her excitement, she hung up quickly and turned back to Tattoo Man. "My mom is having a baby, gotta go."

She didn't wait for his reply, but his exquisite face was just as disappointed as the sad side of the Gemini-mask tattoo on his calf.

A jumble of nerves, Raven grabbed her everyday–less expensive–camera from the cracked dashboard. They would need semi-professional pictures of the new baby. Stuffing it in her purse, she sprinted inside the hospital. Barbie stood in the hallway of the labor unit. They looked at each other for a second. She offered Barbie a quick smile. Heck, she was meeting new family today.

All the adrenaline simmered when Raven saw Charlene in bed. Beads of perspiration dotted Charlene's face. She had that get-this-damn-baby-out-of-me look. Damien, Daniela, and Granny surrounded her, each trying to do their part to encourage. Raven slowed through the threshold into a room that smelled of disinfectant and slight notes of the array of roses by the window.

"You can do it, Mom," Raven added her bit of persuasion. "How far along is she?" Raven looked toward Damien. He paced back and forth like a worried kitten.

"About six centimeters," Daniela replied.

"That can take awhile." Annette rubbed Charlene's back as she lay on her side, gripping the rail.

"Did you get an epidural?" Raven asked, wishing she'd got one with Royael. Having babies wasn't an easy business. "Don't tense Mom, it amps the pain."

"That's what I told–"

"Shut up, Damien," Charlene cut him off through gritted teeth. She stopped talking as a hiss of breath exited her mouth and labor pains tormented her body. "I don't give a *damn* about those Lamaze classes!"

"You were born when she was in a coma," Annette whispered to Raven. "Char wants to make sure she sees this one. Even though I told her an epidural won't make her go unconscious."

~~~

Charlene's body wavered from the pain. Her eyes burned from lack of sleep. Body timid as a feather, but her spirit strengthened. She held her arms open as Daniela placed the baby girl inside. It had been momentary torture letting Trinity be cajoled by her family. Even Damien seemed softened by the experience as he'd held their child. She reinspected itty-bitty hands and spiral black hair while big brown eyes stared back at her. Holding Trinity as tightly as a baby could be held; she made promises to keep her safe. *I'm going to be the perfect mother. You will have a perfect life.* Hand behind Trinity's head, she rubbed and supported her, trying to cease the tears that were on the verge of forming. She just had to be perfect for this child.

"That's the most beautiful baby I've ever seen," Damien said, next to her shoulder.

She let him pat her arm, though hours ago she considered bludgeoning him to death with the camcorder he had the nerve to turn on. Daniela and Annette hovered over the other side of the hospital bed, taking turns saying who the baby looked like. It was just like old folks to compare new babies to their great-great-insert-distant-relative-here.

Raven clicked away at her camera, and softly bumped shoulders with her stepdad. He pulled his arm around her as she said, "My baby sister is a doll."

"I keep thinking that if I blink this will all go away." He had an energetic aura about him. Something in his stance read that he would keep this baby safe.

"Enough mushiness," Charlene said to her husband, wiping at her own tears of promise. "Now grab that camera and take a picture of me and my two beautiful daughters.

CHAPTER 17

With shaky fingers, Raven took off her choir robe and sat in the middle of the stadium-style church, watching a mass of people greet and leave together. She wondered what Stephen wanted to talk about this time when he asked her to wait. Maybe he wanted to get back to being friends? Go to the shooting range, hop on the quads? *Go back to being uncomplicated.*

Stephen took a seat besides her. They both stared at the cathedral stage and the plush purple choir chairs. After awhile he spoke, "It's getting serious with Melody."

"Great. Melody's the sweetest person I've ever seen on that stage." The smile on her face was hard as stone. It was easier to hold it that way. She wasn't jealous that he could never be the love of her life. She *was* jealous that his life had transformed, blossomed. She had Bill and their budding relationship, but there was a void.

"I wanted you to know because we were so close."

Something in his voice that made her look away. She replied, "Well, I wish you and Melody all the happiness in the world."

"Raven, you're so nonchalant. I was *in love with you once.*" Stephen searched her face, but she kept her eyes on the spray of roses lining the stage stairs. He continued. "I loved everything about you–love at first sight. You were beautiful–you *are* beautiful. Sweet–when you wanna be." He grabbed her hand. "Fun. You're like having a very hot homeboy–naw just kiddin'. I've come to realize I was in love with saving you."

"Saving me?" She whispered, finally looking at him. At last, noticing that he didn't look at her the way he used to, but like they were friends, *just friends. Why is he telling me this?*

"When I first met you, I saw sadness in your eyes. I thought it was beautiful, a subtle longing. I've learned that I can't feed that emptiness. Something is missing."

Instantly, she knew he wanted what she wanted, for them to get back on track and just be friends, but he also needed an explanation. She looked around the empty auditorium. Their voices wouldn't reach far enough to expose her sins and God knew all. This was golden opportunity to get her friend back and let each other in, but she just couldn't tell Stephen her story. Not about Jon, and most certainly not about Elise Dubois. "Stephen, I have to go."

~~~

"Raven look at these old hoots," Charlene giggled, burping Trinity's back as they stood just outside of the kitchen. Every Sunday Annette and Raven would come over her house after church to help cook and it would always end with Annette and Daniela in the kitchen.

"I know, Granny won't let anybody cook, even Daniela looks like she's about to give in," Raven giggled as they peeked around the corner. Annette stood over Daniela's shoulder as she added spice to the yams to which Daniela was supposed to be in charge of.

"Look here, Daniela, we gonna make that the 'North *Caroliner* way'," Annette said as Daniela seasoned the cabbage. Her famous pot roast was already in the oven, the juices making magic and the aroma from the pot of greens enveloped the kitchen. Her eyes narrowed, unsure about the amount of salt Daniela shook into the cabbage. "Let me see if you did it right."

Daniela huffed as she grabbed a spoon from the drawer and dipped it in the pot. It was clear Daniela had yet to understand that Annette was in her zone. Cooking was Annette's battle field. Hand on hip, Daniela watched Annette blow on the hot cabbage. "Look here, you ol' battleaxe, I'm not that much younger than you."

Without replying, Annette took a bite. "Well, this *is* pretty good!"

"Good enough for it not being 'the North Caroliner way'," Charlene mimicked.

Raven stifled the laughter threatening to erupt.

"I can hear ya'll," Annette yelled.

Giggling, they retreated back into the den. Trinity cooed while they took a seat on the couch.

Royael hopped up from her cross-leg position in front of the flat-screen TV. "What's so funny?"

"Poor Daniela, they don't get along much in the kitchen," Raven leaned back on a decoration pillow, sides aching as she laughed.

Not understanding, Royael went back to the cartoon.

"Yeah, that's because Momma is always tryna take over. All week Daniela cooks and cleans like the world is going to end. She's so happy to finally have a grandbaby," Charlene said.

"I'm sure she is and I'm sure you're taking advantage of all this southern hospitality. Do know that we'll be back to exercising soon." Raven pinched her mom's thigh.

Charlene picked up a decorative pillow and swatted her hand away. "You're the one that runs five miles every morning. Maybe I can bribe you to be my body double and I won't have too."

Raven went to help in the kitchen and Charlene watched as Royael placed a blanket on the floor, sitting with Mookie. When she fed Trinity a bottle, her granddaughter followed by feeding Mookie an empty bottle, and then burped the bear's furry back. "Softly, Royael…like this."

When she did so, Mookie's fuzzy head stopped bobbling. "Grandma, can I play with Trinity. She keeps going to sleep."

Charlene's heart melted at her granddaughter's frown when she shook her head and placed Trinity into a woven bassinet. "We have to be quiet, the baby is sleep. Mookie's asleep. Why don't you place him next to Trinity? Gently."

She'd just finished helping her grandchild position the bear next to the baby when Raven walked back into the room and the aroma of spices followed, teasing Charlene's nose.

"We'll be eating soon, Mom. I have something to get your mind off the wait." Raven opened the pink, velvet bound book and handed it to her. "I've got a picture for every day Trinity's been born."

Charlene looked through them, stopping on day 14 to trace her thumb over the photo. Trinity had been placed in her bassinet, wearing a silk pink-and-white dotted dress. Tears brimmed at her lids. "Taking pictures really makes you happy, huh?"

"Yup. When I look through a lens, it's because that moment in time was well worth it."

She nodded. "I've been meaning to ask, today you looked a little down after church."

"Stephen wanted to talk, again. He wanted to know more about me before I moved to Dallas."

"I don't know Stephen, but when I see him at the piano every Sunday," she paused, feeling the pressure weighed down on her daughter's shoulders. *What type of advice does a mother give?* "I think he'd understand that your past is a touchy subject, if you just tell him so."

"I've tried speaking to him every since your wedding. We even did a double date, because Melody blurted it out after church, and it would've been awkward for him to decline. It was awful; he looked at Bill and me like… we didn't belong." Raven stopped and sighed. "Ever since then, he's been slowly wanting to talk and he finally wanted to speak now of all days–after church."

"Isn't that a good thing?"

"Well, yes, but," Raven paused, "he's just being stubborn."

Charlene perceived the fluster all over Raven's face, clouding her eyes. Her daughter wasn't telling her everything. After the Marcus Weber incident, she'd assumed they'd be as close as any normal mother-daughter relationship. *My child saved me…* The way Raven had opened up afterwards, well, that had to be the ultimate bond? No, maybe her child wasn't like any other. Maybe all families were different, because getting closer to Raven occurred in baby steps. Raven was like a rose with layers of beautiful petals, shielding her from…the love Charlene wanted to give. *Is it too soon to probe more into what Raven's been through?* All musing aside, Charlene went back to the current conversation.

"Men can be stubborn. Sometimes you just have to look the bull in the eye and tell him just what you have to give." Nodding, she felt confident in her advice. "A good friend will understand."

~~~

In shorts and a tank, Raven sank to the dirt in total freedom. Her head tilted back as a hearty laugh came from her soul.

Stephen took a seat next to her, his hand grazing up her calf muscle. "How does this feel?"

"I'm sure I'll live," the words bubbled out of her mouth, still in that hyped-up-state-of-happiness. When his hands applied pressure, massaging and roaming upwards to her thigh, Raven's blue eyes turned into slits. "What are you doing?"

"Comforting you," Stephen said. She smirked. Head cocked to the side, he added, "I thought you sprained your–"

"My ankle," she interjected. *He's as crazy as I remembered.*

"Oh, I thought you…said your thigh was–"

"Uh-huh, sprain my thigh, Steph? You're too cute." She rolled her eyes, standing up and could feel his eyes on her shorts. Maybe he was reading the orange punch line on her bottom? Maybe not. "Let's get back. I gotta meet my mom in less than an hour."

He helped her pick up the 250-dirtbike. Clumps of muck caked the dinted orange frame. She swung a leg over it, not in the least bit hurt. Despite all the games Stephen played–he'd seen her take worse falls–she was grateful that they were friends again. After not being able to open up fully when he'd admitted to getting closer to Melody, she'd taken her mom's advice and called him. Back on the trail, tendrils of black hair escaped the helmet as she accelerated on the dirt jump. The hard sound of the engine and the rush of cool air was a relief. She'd missed this while being with Bill. In her mind Bill and Stephen were the makings of the perfect man. Bill was intelligent and kind. Stephen was outgoing and funny. That's all she needed.

When Stephen pulled in front of her home a while later, he said, "Wait."

Her eyebrows knitted together as he walked around the SUV and opened the door. Before she could protest, he scooped her in his muscular arms and took her up the steps. She wriggled, trying to get free. She pinched his shoulder. "If you don't let me go, I'll kill ya!"

"Stop being so stubborn, Re-Re. You hurt yourself." He smiled down at her and the dimples were back.

"You're being bad! I'm telling Melody," She joked. The smile on his face disappeared. *Wow, I was just kidding,* she thought as he set her down on the sidewalk. Then she noticed what he'd straightened up about. *Country Boys,* she shook her head.

"Hi," voice edgy, Charlene was at the top of the steps, hands on hips, eyeing them suspiciously. When he shook her hand and introduced himself in that sexy southern drawl, and that all so sexy dimple appeared, her mom could do nothing but smile back.

"Bye, Stephen." Raven walked past him to give her mom a hug.

"No 'byes,' Raven." He backed off the steps slowly, still grinning. "See ya'll later."

With a confident smirk on her face, Charlene watched Stephen's SUV pulled away. Then she sucked her teeth and said, "I got two questions. Why are you cheating on poor sweet Bill with that man? And damn he's fine–oh, I guess that's just one question."

Listening to her mom's giddy chuckle, Raven took a seat on the porch swing, the heels of her combat boots digging into the planks as she rocked back and forth. "I'm not cheating on Bill. That's Stephen, remember? He's a little confused, right now. He's in love with Melody but not ready to take the plunge." Her mind went to Chris and Jon for a second. *No, this is not the same thing. Stephen is and always will be just my friend. I won't ruin this one...* "Let me put on some workout clothes."

"Aw," Charlene folded her arms. "We should just do lunch like usual."

"Your six weeks are up. Let's go to the gym, then lunch." Raven walked into the house.

Charlene trailed behind her, "But Damien and I haven't even had six week sex, yet!"

"Ughhh, I don't need to hear about all your post baby romps–"

"Hush yourself." Annette put finger to lip, cradling a sleeping Trinity from the couch.

"Sorry, Granny," Raven whispered. She softly pinched a fat leg that had unwound itself from Trinity's blanket. "Thunder Thighs is getting fat. Mom is heading in the same direction."

"Ya'll get outta here. This baby is asleep and we getting good and tired of the both of ya. You over here tryna wake her up, and Charlene keeps acting like I ain't ever raised a child in my life." Annette mimicked her daughter's voice, "Make sure you test the milk before you give it to Trinity."

When Raven jogged back downstairs, dressed in spandex shorts and a tee, Annette still halfheartedly argued with Charlene. "I only get to keep Trinity two days a week, so ya'll get on, shoo. Go lose some weight, chubby. It doesn't make any sense, you been eattin' at them restaurants…"

They laughed, shutting the door behind them, to the sound of Annette muttering about restaurants and food poison. With a half smile, Charlene said, "We should bring her a doggy bag after we work out."

"Um-hum, if you want Granny to kill us." Raven mimicked Annette's words about eating out. "Okay, Mom, let's get serious. We have to get you ready for the mid-season finale. I'm going to make sure you look good."

"You're just as bossy as that ol' lady," Charlene cocked her head toward the house as she pressed the unlock button to the Escalade.

"Aren't we all," Raven winked getting into the car. Before turning on their favorite Mary J Blige song, she added, "We're Shaw gals."

CHAPTER 18

Gray clouds zipped by the windows as the plane headed toward Dallas. Chatter filled the space. The plane was crowded with Thanksgiving vacationers. Charlene snuggled in her much larger first-class seat with Barbie next to her. She wondered how much "welcome home food" Annette would cook, and how she'd have to work at losing weight *again* after the holiday season.

She'd just completed the mid-season finale. Meagan was found. Ransom paid. Twists and turns in the plot bolted down, leaving fans on the edge of their seats. The story ended with a cliff hanger so severe, she bet viewers were gnawing on their fingernails waiting for more.

Leaning back, she tuned in and out as her assistant chatted about her impending celebrity appearances. She had Raven to thank for looking good as Meagan on the show and the load of red carpet events that her PR scheduled during the soap opera downtime. *All I want to do is spend time with my girls, but I have to say in the limelight.* In disinterest, she noticed the top of a gossip magazine in the pouch in front of her. Frowning at the symbolism of anti-freedom, she leaned over to push it deeper into the pocket when she noticed her name.

Snatching up the magazine, her jaw dropped at the title. She instantly flashed back to a week ago. *I picked up Raven for lunch and exercise like usual, but her car wasn't in front of the house.* "She said she was getting it fixed," Charlene mumbled.

"What?" Barbie's question broke into her thoughts.

"Nothing," her words were barely audible. *Raven had car trouble. She said that Stephen would fix it as soon as she bought the part. I'd offered the money, pulled a stack of cash out as we sat in a restaurant.* "If it's not enough I can write a check," *I said.*

Ping. The sound of the seatbelt light turning on slammed her back to present. Looking out the window, she saw pieces of lush green earth through misty clouds.

Raven refused the money. Oh my gosh! The day before I left for L.A...

"…We are now descending into Dallas…the weather is overcast, foggy for the remainder of the a.m…" The chipper male voice on the intercom seeped in and out of her memory.

We were supposed to do lunch in uptown Dallas the day before.

"…I want to personally welcome you to…"

Out of all the times, we did lunch on Tuesdays, Raven never missed. Except for that day!

Brain fuzzy, she couldn't recall what she'd told Barbie while exiting the airport, but she was sure she'd pointed to a line of taxis. Charlene gripped the magazine in her hand, climbing into her Escalade at the airport extended parking. She tossed the magazine on the passenger seat. There were *stolen* pictures of Trinity from the maternity ward and the 14 day old picture Raven took that she'd been so proud of.

Tears blurred her face, black mascara smeared on the sleeve of her crème silk sleeve as she wiped her face, driving down the street. *Raven was too guilty to see me before I left! Just like a Shaw, too proud to take money! But…family?* Hands gripping the steering wheel, she felt like the Hulk and had to force herself to slow down while turning down the street and skidded to a stop in front of her family's' townhome.

Getting out the car, the sound of shattering window glass phased out as she stomped up the sidewalk. Neighbors on their porch or jogging by had that I-know-you look, but her stance deterred them from an autograph. She didn't feel the chill, but her knuckles burned as she beat on the door and waited.

Face clouded with concern, Annette opened the door. Bacon sizzled in the background and the smell of homemade waffles—that wonderful, sweet smell did nothing for her.

"Hi, Momma. Where's Raven?" She strolled past and into the tiny living room.

"Upstairs getting Royael ready for dance class. How was the show? Are you all right?"

Charlene looked toward the stairs as Raven bounced down and tried to give her a hug. She pushed the magazine in her daughter's face.

With narrowed eyes, she watched her focus on the pictures of Trinity in a basinet with pink and white polka dot dress and matching hat.

"Awe, my baby sister is so adorable."

"Really, Raven? I've offered you money. Paid for your photography school. But, you can't help being conniving." Instead of concerning herself with the wet-works falling down her daughter's cheeks, Charlene turned to see Royael padding downstairs. She tuned out her grandchild's warm hello. Like a tornado, she went through the house. Picked up a flower vase, "This looks new. Did you buy this with the money you got for effing me over?"

She slammed the vase into the floor. The sound of it shattering on to vinyl in the kitchen caused Royael to cry hysterically.

Annette shielded Royael, and pointed up the stairs, but the child froze. "Go, now!"

Charlene torpedoed toward a picture, snatched it off the living room wall. "This frame looks new." She tossed it over her shoulders. In a confusing-state-of-madness, she ended back into the kitchen, as a new toaster oven caught her eye. It looked out of place with the rest of the outdated appliances. She snatched the plug out of the walls, scrapped it over the peeling green counter. It CLANKED to the floor. "Did this come from the money, too?"

"Mom, I didn't do it." Rooted in the same spot, Raven turned the bangles on her wrist.

"*Do not* call me mom, ever again." Stilettos clicking on the vinyl, she picked up Royael and pulled at the girls clothes. "When did your momma buy you this *new*-looking tutu?"

Eyes roaming for more items they'd bought by *effing* her over. She stormed to the bookshelf that also doubled as a TV stand. When strong arms snaked around her waist, she screamed. *When had Damien arrived?* Front door opened wide, the neighbors could see her foolishness if they wanted to–*great*.

"Calm down, babe," he said.

Dang, Barbie had to have called him. She wriggled free of her husband's hold. Body shaking, snot and tears rolled down her face, Charlene looked square into her daughter's eyes. "I won't take this. P-putting my baby's picture on a gossip magazine. It's manipulative!"

"Mom, I didn't do it!" Raven's body heaved as she spoke.

Damien tried to grab her arm. She popped him with the rolled up magazine.

"Charlene, you best be leaving *now*." Annette pointed toward the door.

In a few swift steps she stepped in front of Annette, eyes pleading. "Momma, I said Raven tried to pimp out my family. Don't you care?"

"Get out, now!" Annette's lips were mashed together.

Her head cocked to the side as she nodded. "So you're on Raven's side?" *I knew it!*

"I'm not on no sides. Listen here, don't you *ever* come in my house acting all foolish, got the devil in ya. Well, he does *not* belong here!"

"Momma?" Charlene tried to take her hand, but she moved away. *The devil is not in me it's in Raven.* She couldn't move for sobbing. Damien touched her shoulder, said something in her ear while rubbing her back. She wiggled away from him. "I get it. I never even had a chance! You *two* are always together. Raven is the child that you wished I had been–just because she sings in the choir *don't* make her Christian. You're still mad at me for running away and not coming home even after I was raped."

"I'm not mad at you but disappointed that you'd come into *my house* and terrorize your child. Did you see your granddaughter crying a minute ago?" Annette pursed her lips. They mirrored each other's bewilderment.

"You don't have to be disappointed in me again." Charlene stood tall, shoulders squared.

"Char, don't say something regrettable. We'll figure out who did this," Damien promised.

"I already know *who*." She turned to her child, "Raven, I don't ever want to see you again. You're a jaded child that's been through so much that you can't truly forgive people. That depression will eat you up, one day." Glancing at Annette, she added, "I don't want to see you either."

She walked out, slamming the door behind her. The neighbors on their porches and families at the park stared. Realizing she still had the magazine in her hand, she gave them the show they'd been dying to see; her acting fool. She tossed the magazine at the closed door with such force that her body swayed. And with a tight lip, she stalked down the sidewalk. *I'm never coming back.*

Daniela was probably at home consoling Trinity. It was time to go see her daughter.

Her *only* daughter.

CHAPTER 19

Though large storms do not occur often, they always trail smaller ones. When you think you've hit rock bottom, you're at your lowest, but no, a tidal wave comes along. There's always an ebb, and then BAM! It wipes you out…

Raven lay in her bed, staring at the cracked stucco ceiling. She lived the storm. Only, she'd thought the hurricane had come the day before her mother went to L.A. *She awoke, clutching at her throat, attempting to breathe. Like many times before, she'd dreamed of killing Elise. She sunk to the floor in between her dresser and bed, heart beating rapidly and snatched up her phone to call Charlene.*

"Hey, Mom. I-I can't meet for lunch today. I'm so sorry. Good luck on the season finale. See ya soon." She thanked God for getting her through leaving a message without gasping in between words. It took strength from the depths of her being to get up.

There was no noise in the house. Raven thanked God for Annette, knowing that she must've taken Royael across the street to the park. Raven's "black mood" was an unwritten understanding between them. Stuffing on sweats and a crumply shirt, which may have come from the laundry basket, Raven went to see Stanton.

"Hello, Raven. The therapist's voice reached out and caressed her—not strong enough to stop the storm that raged in her heart, yet, just enough for momentary ebb.

"D-Dr. Ssstanton," the words swished past her lips as she wheezed. The man with a wisp of thinning hair before her became a blur. Headaches and blurred vision always accompanied the "black mood." Using her hands for support, Raven sunk down into the suede seat.

He arose, walked around the desk and handed Raven a paper bag.

"I dreamed…I-I dreamed of Elise." Throat so dry, she started to cough.

"Raven, I need you to stop trying to talk. Just breathe into the bag. Go ahead, cry if you need to. Let it out. Then we can talk." Stanton patted her back as Raven doubled over.

"I don't want to cry." Without warning, sobs flooded. The paper bag crumpled within her grasp.

"We need continuous sessions for more permanent results," he chided, reclaiming his seat. Leaning over the piles of paperwork on his desk, Stanton snatched tissue from the Kleenex box, handing it to Raven.

"I watched a movie last night. Then I dreamed of Elise again. I woke up so angry! My mom is leaving for L.A., I was su-supposed to meet her. We should been at lunch, right now! I shoulda been telling her that she'd do a good job on the mid-season finale," she blubbered, rubbing her face with the tissue so much it started to break apart.

Raven assumed that day was the storm—the all consuming hurricane. Winds. Rain. Waves. Surge. No, it wasn't the big one but a precursor. A dense fog, merely a drizzle. Then Mom came back and accused her of selling Trinity's photos. It took two weeks for her to get out of bed. Two weeks after Charlene's outburst—the *real storm*—for Raven to finally open her mouth and utter strings to form sentences. Staring at the ceiling, she called Damien.

"Hey, what happened? Your Dallas house phone is off?" Raven's voice was soft, weak from nonuse. She'd wanted to come and see baby Trinity, talk with Mom. Sooth the storm.

"We moved back to L.A.," he replied in a sincere tone.

"It's almost Christmas. I thought the Dallas home was for your vacation?"

"We…were renting. Char was determined to see how things went…with you." Sounding more determined, he added, "I've been talking to her and will keep at it. She's breastfeeding and extra hormonal. I'll call you back."

While waiting, she'd shoveled down a cup of yogurt, her first real meal in a while. She ran only three miles and would have to work back up to her usual five. And, hey, that was okay, because he'd be calling back with great news. She was dressing for work when he did.

"I'm sorry, Raven. She needs more time. I'll keep working at it."

In zombie-mode she'd went to work and for the life of her, couldn't figure out how she ended up at school that evening. She'd planned only to do her shift at the coffee shop. The photography lined shelves of the best students' work—work she'd always stopped to admired–dulled before her eyes as she thought about Damien's words. His call had slammed her back into dejection.

I'm already here; might as well make the best of it. Looking at the highlighted photography on the hallway shelves, she attempted to get into the right zone. Her breath caught as she stared at one photo in particular: a black and white of a bum sitting in the grass. Everything about him, from his matted hair, down to a large fly perched on his weather-beaten forehead, to his big toe sticking out of his tennis shoe, made her soul cry out in sadness. She knew he hadn't been sad that day–she'd taken the picture. He'd been free; that much was evident in his facial expression. And a moment in his contented life only cost her 99 cents, the cost of a hamburger.

Wow! My photo is highlighted amongst the school's "greats." Mr. Tinker had to be behind this. She hadn't known that her work was on that level yet. *I'm worthy of this?*

She walked into class where her Professor Tinker and his tiny afro were already getting ready for class. He stood at the podium pulling out projection photos and a coffee-stained smile lit his face. "We've missed you these past couple of weeks."

"Sorry," her eyes cast downward to the checkered floor. "Family problems."

"Okay," he glanced at the clock as students trudged in. "We gotta get started, come to me if you have any problems. Oh, and the financial aid office needs to see you after class. Urgent."

Catchy phrases were tacked on the padded-cubicle walls in the financial counselor's office. The Asian man looked up from his computer and smiled. "Good afternoon, Ms. Shaw. I've attempted to call you on several occasions and have also emailed."

"Sorry. I was having family troubles." *I was depressed.*

He nodded sympathetically. "I don't know of any other way to tell you that the services you were using for financial aid has canceled. You're welcome to finish this semester, of course, but the winter semester is coming up. You've already selected courses," he paused to sigh. "I'm afraid I'll have to place them on hold until we can determine..."

Raven sat stumped. Charlene had stopped paying for school. She felt small when asking, "How much are the classes?" Having always paid for her own classes at junior college, her mouth went wide in shock as the counselor gave a quote per unit.

"Ms. Shaw, we have a Financial Aid program available for students in need. Unfortunately, the deadline has passed for winter term. How about we try and apply for a loan?"

The word sent tremors down her heart. *What if I never get a good job? How would I pay it back? I shoulda stayed at the junior college!* "I'm sorry but I don't think so."

"Please do consider coming back..." his voice rushed as she headed out the door.

~~~

Sports commentators gave enthusiastic predictions on flat-screen TVs bolted to brick walls. Chatter and drunken cackling was as consistent as the cheap cigarette billows being dragged out of just parted lips. Empty shot glasses scattered the scuffed bar counter and Raven laughed with her new friend, Jose. He gave a chip-toothed grin, and they tossed back another round of double shots. She rolled her eyes when hearing Sharon's authoritative voice as her friend came along side her.

"Raven, you've had enough." Sharon tapped the guy Raven leaned on, "Excuse me. I suggest you stop buying her drinks. You're not getting the *cookie* tonight."

"Jose, don't listen to her. She's tryna fill this mommy void that I have. Hehehe," she leaned closer to him and waved her empty glass. "Hey! Are you related to Jose Cuerbooo?"

"If you want me to be," he replied with a wink.

Sharon rolled her eyes away from the lustful, burly man and said, "Give me your phone, Raven. I can't carry you out by myself. I'm calling, Bill."

"Ya can't. Bill's phone is off tonight. He's got a paper due tomorrow. Last week, it was some big project. Don't worry, every week it's something new." She signaled for the bartender and turned to Jose, "Cuerrbbbo, ya got this?... Good looking out. Another round and get one for my mama."

"I'm not your mama!" Sharon grabbed Raven's purse.

"What you doing? You know I ain't got any damn money!" Trying to get up, she fell into Jose's lap. Brain on a merry-go-round, she stayed put. If he didn't mind, she didn't mind.

"I'm looking for your phone." Sharon jiggled the orange case in her hand. "I'm calling Stephen. I hope he remembers me from that one get together. It's loud, I'll be back."

"Bye, Mama." Raven waved from Jose's lap. She turned back to the bartender who had just placed three shots on the table and tossed one back after another. "Bottoms up, Jose!"

Warm breath tickled her ear as Jose put his arm around her, whispering all the things he'd like to do with her once they left. His Spanglish was funny. His imagination was hilarious! She didn't plan on leaving with him, so she giggled some more. It took a while to notice her giddiness spurred him on as he mentioned more outrageous, acrobatic sexual activities. Then she felt her body being lifted up and out of his lap.

"What the—" Raven said, being planted down on her own two boots. Earth ceased its spinning as she looked up into warm honey eyes. His full lips were teasing her to kiss him. "Jon..." Putting her hands over her mouth in disbelief, she gawked at the only love she'd ever known. Here, standing so close. She would, if she could, get on her tippy toes and plant a big, fat kiss on his lips.

"I know you're not that drunk to have forgotten my name!"

Soberness slammed into her. Her *intact* heart crumpled back into pieces again. No, it wasn't Jon, but Stephen standing before her.

Jose stood up, looked Stephen up and down. "Step back, *cabrón*. Chica is coming with me!"

Stephen stepped closer and glared at the shorter, weaker guy. Jose glowered; chin held high, fluffy chest puffed out. He was living proof that drunken people didn't know their limitations. Stephen's hands balled into fists at his sides. "You better sit yo' ass back down."

"I don't want trouble!" The bartender tapped a dual-pump shotgun in his hands.

Jose did a double take, grunted, and sat. Stephen turned to Raven, swooped her in his arms like she was his to take. He passed a fake Christmas tree and out the door. She shaded her eyes as he strode into the cool night. Through long eyelashes she saw Sharon leaning against her BMW.

"Thanks for calling me. Raven was acting like a fool. I'll just take her home. You won't be able to take her up the stairs anyway," Stephen voiced assertively.

"Oh, okay. Thanks for your help," she hesitated and backed toward her door.

"No thanks needed," he replied over his shoulder. He opened the passenger door and placed Raven in the seat, then leaned over her to latch the seatbelt.

When he pulled in front of her home, Stephen said, "Raven... I'm going in your purse to get your keys." She didn't reply, just let him think she was smashed. He left the car, opened the front door and came back. Taking care in getting her out of the car, he carried her into the house and up the steps. In her bedroom, Stephen laid her on the bed.

"Raven," he tried to stir her awake. "C'mon, Re-Re. You don't want to sleep in tight jeans."

Sighing after a moment of waiting for a reply, Stephen pulled the sheet over her and put his shaking hands underneath, he unattached the button on her jeans. Raven let her body go limp and be pushed and pulled with every move. He was even more bashful than Tattoo Man had been while she was fully sober. She peeked at him through her curled lashes, but when he finished, she closed her eyes. Warm and snuggly is what she felt when his eyes roamed over her body.

"Re-Re, you're gonna to tell me about Jon," he finally said.

Raven's chest rose and fell gently. She pretended to snore. A soft, sweet snore. His knuckles tenderly caressed her cheek. "I love you," he said before walking out.

I practically gift wrapped this good man and gave him to Melody. I'm a damn shame…

CHAPTER 20

A humdrum of college-student-coffee-fanatics philosophized while sitting on fluffy couches. Others got their fixes in solo-mode, typing on laptops at black and chrome bistro tables. The aroma of ground coffee beans, spices, and pastries infused the industrial-style building with high ceiling beams.

"Thanks for changing my shifts, Cassidy," Raven said, removing an empty pastry rack from the display. She took a look at her friend, with tight corn rolls that perfected her arched eyebrows.

"It's the least I could do," Cassidy replied. In the next moment she called out a customer's order then turned back to Raven. "I know my dad hasn't been able to give you many hours, we do appreciate you. But why aren't you at school this evening?"

The redbrick-framed windows became a camera lens as Raven looked at an orange ball of fire dipping over the Dallas horizon. "I'm over that phase of my life."

"Hmmm," Cassidy began with an I-can-see-right-through-you look. "My dad said Stephen came by at the beginning of the week when you were out sick, then again while he opened this morning."

Raven nodded, walking around the glass display to straighten the bagels. Cassidy knew when to continue asking questions and when to let her simmer in her own thoughts. After the crowd trickled, she went into the back to place the empty pastry racks in the dishwasher. Taking a break, she pressed her cell phone's voice mail for the first time in more than a week.

Stephen called numerous times. First, he wanted to know who Jon was and why she'd missed choir practice, then again when she missed church. Sharon called, "Girl, we need to talk about your drinking..." Raven pressed delete to her concerned voice. *I'm not an alcoholic. I've drank on less occasions than I can count on one hand.* She deleted the call from her financial aid officer as soon as he said hello, though she paused to hear Mr. Tinker's message. *Why do you have more expectations for me than I have for myself?*

~~~

On her day off, Raven woke to a quiet house. *Granny must've taken Royael to the park.* Out of routine and a whim that God might just hear her plea, she knelt on the floor to say a quick prayer. "Please help us with the bills..." Her throat knotted up just thinking about their financial situation and she couldn't continue. The doorbell rang. Raven grumbled. Steel rods for legs, she got up from the bed and paced downstairs. Looking through the peep hole, she sighed, "Stephen."

"Open up, Raven. I spoke with Annette across the street. I know you in there."

Back leaning against the door, she imagined the last time she'd seen him. Stephen had reminded her of what Jon used to be. *My rock...* She wished he hadn't saved her the other night.

The door bell rang again. Biting her lip, Raven turned around, unlocked the bolt and turned the knob. Stephen and rays of December sunlight entered the dark living room. Her eyes closed momentarily. She squinted, readjusted. *God, I hate the sun right now!*

"Nice to see you, too." He brushed past her and took a seat on the couch. "Who is he?"

"Hey, Steph." She sank down into Grandpa Otis's lazy boy.

"Don't play with me, Re-Re. Now, who is Jon?" Stephen asked. When she rolled her eyes in disinterest, he added, "I'm your friend. I thought we were going to sidestep our little issues?"

She noticed the tension in his sexy lips as he skirted around the "Marley fiasco."

"Jon is Royael's father, isn't he? The man that made you empty inside. He's the reason you think you can't be loved. Then you go wasting time with Bill, who's nothing like you and—"

"Stephen, please." *I don't need the drama today.* Her finger traced the cracks in Grandpa Otis's leather chair, and she glanced at him as he nodded his apology. Placing his hands behind his head, he leaned back and waited. She sighed, hoping that she could trust this man. Oh, how she wanted to tell someone about Jon, about Jonathan, and most certainly a memory of Elise clawed her heart...

She licked her lips, and then tugged the plump bottom one through her teeth as she felt Stephen's gaze piercing into her soul. Hands on the armrest, Grandpa's chair gave her the comfort to tell him the truth. The whole truth.

~~~

Sitting on the side of Royael's pink ballerina-shaped bed, Raven sang. Her daughter's eyes drooped, ready for a midday nap. She slowly arose and tiptoed toward the door. The soft voice calling her name made Raven turn back around. Lips pursed, she knelt back on the floor.

"Are you still sad?" Royael yawned.

"No," Raven replied as the doorbell rang. "Go to sleep and I'll take your picture later."

"Okay, Mommy. I'm glad you're happy." She turned over and pulled up her fleece blanket. "I have to do my job and make Mommy happy."

Her daughter's words moved her heart as Raven descended the stairs. She closed her eyes to still the tears that were beginning to form. Composed, she opened the door to Sharon. *Is this be-truthful-to-a-friend-day?*

"You look like a hot mess." Sharon sat on the same spot Stephen claimed.

Raven looked down at her comfy slippers. She had on her hoodie and sweat pants. *Hey, at least I got dressed.* "Well, thanks, Sharon. You look as beautiful as ever."

"Thanks." She rummaged through her purse and smacked a business magazine down on the coffee table.

Raven legs went momentarily weak as she took a seat next to her friend; magazines were scary, horrid monsters now. *Self inflicted karma?* Familiar hazel eyes at her...Jon Dubois on the cover. Her gaze traveled over a blue tailored pinstripe suit, cufflinks twinkling with diamonds.

Handsome. Muscular arms folded. Confidence. Chin high, perfect lips curved into a smile. Arrogance.

"Read it," Sharon said. When Raven didn't make a move to take the magazine, she snatched it and opened it to a page that already had an ear-fold. "Jon Dubois, *Legacy* to the golden umbrella, Devereux Corporation...Opens D Hotel USA corporate branch...new sky rise in Dallas...*multi*billion dollar mogul, Grandfather Pierre Devereux has handed him the key to the D Hotel kingdom!" Sharon paused. "Must I continue?"

"Sharon, just go home and take that with you." Raven stood up. "We can get together some other time, but don't come back with *that*."

"Girl, sit! We're gonna get his slimy ass."

"Get him how?" Her eyebrow rose as she sat. Curiosity triumphed over annoyance.

'Think of the list we made the day Royael was born.'

Raven stuck her index finger in her ear and scratched, hoping the voice would shut up. *He was only a maybe...I-I can't ever see him again. I can't—*

'Confidence fails you, oh so easily,' the voice spat in disgust.

"You're going to tell him that you know somebody who works for Scandalous. Jon can confirm it's me." Sharon pointed to herself. "However, he won't know that I already know about his family secrets. He'll give you enough money to pay for your school, Royael's school–hell, enough for her to attend college, Annette's bills. Whatever you need, and honey, *ya'll do need*." Her eyes stopped at the small box TV on top of the bookshelf make-shift TV stand.

"What if he doesn't give in?" Raven thought about Royael's dance classes. *Renewal time is coming up. I still have to buy her costume for her Christmas recital and that's less than two weeks.* Her eyes flitted to their scrawny "Charlie Brown" Christmas tree and the few gifts underneath.

"What if, what if, what if! He's rich. The affluent only recognize reputation. If it gets out that Jon Dubois had a baby with his half sister, it would be the talk of the town. I mean all the way from the US of A to France. So it would behoove him to act like he *got* sense!"

CHAPTER 21

"Help you out…" rung in her ears the entire night and all the while she watched Royael open her measly Christmas gifts. The voice sang the words while Bill held mistletoe over her head and drenched her with kisses. It shouted out the words by Royael's fifth birthday as she popped Tylenol. The New Year didn't start off any better. No magic wand would place enough money in her hands to pay every utility. With that thought in mind, Raven ran her morning five to the voice mimicking Sharon's words. She showered, put on a gray pencil skirt and cowl-neck blouse. In the bathroom she curled her hair and added just enough makeup to look professional. *I need earrings.* Raven stopped at the jewelry box on her dresser, opened the fake cherry wood door. She placed cubic zirconia studs in her ear. Before closing the box, her hand reached past all of her trinkets to the back. She felt for the silver spoon ring Jon had given her and the piece of paper underneath.

'Damn time that little brain of yours gets to work!'

Brushing off the voice's words, she twirled the spoon ring in her hand.

'Don't get teary eyed about the ring, Dumbass! Obviously, Jon never kept his promise to you and Royael.'

A long sigh was her agreement as she placed the ring down and picked up the paper.

'Feed off of this, Raven.'

Astonished by the voice's correct use of her name, she slowly unfolded the crinkled paper. After bonding with Charlene in the past year, she'd forgotten about it. *I never crossed Mom off.* She sighed. *Where has revenge gotten me?*

'Oh, please, we won't even go into the joys of vengeance on Elise, but with Charlene, you enjoyed yourself. Those wedding pictures couldn't compare to her terrorizing our house! She would not save Grandpa Otis…' Raven sniffled as

the voice continued to weave a web of encouragement. '*Let her actions be your inspiration.*'

Inside the car the engine shrieked in response to her turning the key in the ignition. She shook the steering wheel and screamed. *I just had enough courage to go confront Jon.* Seething, she called Bill. His phone was off. She dialed Stephen and he answered on the second ring. While waiting, she peered through the windshield at the morning fog. Determination shaken. The sound of music blaring across the street tore through her mindset. Stephen pulled up with Melody's Honda behind him. Raven got out of her car and gave them both a hug.

"Look, if ya scratch my car, I'ma kill ya." That sexy dimple came out to play as he held up the keys.

She tried to grab them, but he had them in a death grip. Batting her eyelashes, she smiled nervously, feeling apprehensive with Melody watching. He let go, then he and Melody walked toward her car. Raven got into the SUV. No way was her five-foot-two frame going to ride in his car without adjusting anything, she scooted the seat up. Concentrating, she slowly pressed on the gas and it lurched forward.

"C'mon, Raven," he said from the side walk. "At least *look like* you can drive."

Raven leaned out the window and said, "I got this."

Melody smiled and her stubby arm snaked around Stephen as Raven drove away.

~ ~ ~

A stream of workers flocked in and out of the Devereux building. She reviewed the lobby directory and saw Jonathan Dubois Junior as the director of hotel creation, whatever that meant. Clutching her briefcase, knuckles becoming ashen, she blended in and trailed onto a large elevator. The noisiness decreased a notch at each level as employees exited. Alone, Raven stepped off at the top floor. Her heels clicked on the floor, mimicking the beating of her heart as she past rows of French doors. Scanning the gold signs, she stopped at the right door, Jon's door.

Her hand went to the knob and after a cleansing breath, she opened it. A vast display of orchids and star gazers added a touch of femininity to dark marble statues in the receptionist area. A gray haired woman sat at the desk. A photo of the secretary and a younger female version of her almost brought Raven to tears. *Mom...* Smiling, she shoved away all emotion. "Hi, I'm here to see Jon."

"*Mr.* Dubois is a very busy man." Patricia looked Raven up and down, impression evident by the frown on her face. "You'll need an appointment."

"Look lady, I need to speak with him now," tossing a reply over her shoulders, she headed toward the double doors. *I might never come back, if I leave now!*

"Ma'am, I said you can't go in there!" Patricia ordered. "I'm calling security!"

Raven could almost feel the secretary spit the words as she grasped the doors with both hands and opened them. *Remember to breathe.*

Yards away, Jon stood at a full window, back to her, talking on the phone. When he turned around, she stopped walking. He was taller than she remembered. Intimidating. The business magazine hadn't done him justice. She'd stared at it for hours, hoping to find a flaw. Now, as she stood just in the doorway, she didn't know what to do or say. She watched him round the corner of his desk. The bridge of his nose complemented a face of perfect symmetry. Biceps bulged under his shirtsleeves–powerful, like he could pick her up and toss her out. Hell, out of the universe!

Dang, I looked into his eyes... Jon's amber gaze held Raven captive, insides trembling, soul shaking like a leaf. *How long have I been standing here?* Brain on crash-mode, she still couldn't believe that she stood in his office. Their eyes magnetized, his leaving her speechless and lost. *Stop, Raven. Take a breath and stop looking into his eyes! Damn you–*

Two suited men stood at either side of her, tugging her arms. The connection she had with Jon snapped as she was being tugged away. She screamed at the security, "Get your hands off me!"

"Raven?" Face cocked to the side, Jon stepped closer. He had to know if this was real.

"You don't remember me?" Raven asked. The men stopped, all three looked at Jon, brows raised. The security wondered what to do. She wondered if she was *just that forgetful.*

"Let her go," Jon said, coming to his senses. Looking into those blue eyes had him back in Bellwood, North Carolina. He was instantly captivated by his childhood best friend. Ex-lover.

"Mr. Dubois…allow me to just pat her down," one of the guards asserted.

"Like hell!" Raven kneed him in the groin. The scrawny-chinned twit had wanted to cop a feel.

"Just let her go. She'll hurt both of you if you don't," Jon said to the other security guard. He wanted to smile at the way she handled the guard, still holding his privates in pain, but that was against the bro-code. Endeavoring not to give into the twitch at the corner of his mouth, he took on a serious stance as he rounded the desk to his chair. "Lil' Raven always so feisty."

She watched the guards close the door behind them. Turning back to Jon, she disregarded his request for her to sit, needing the height factor to make five-foot-two feel…bold. Jutting her chin, head held high. *Domination.* The only way to get through to people like him. Her commanding tone made her feel five-five. "You're going to help me with my—*our daughter!*"

"Daughter?" Jon sank into his seat.

"Yes, *our* daughter. I want you to help me with her," Raven started again, stepping past white couches. She cut her eyes at him, and added, "Financially."

"Financially?" He rubbed a hand over the waves in his fade haircut.

"All that education and you don't understand, I want help with Royael." His inquisitive face made her lose momentum. Five-two again.

"Royal, what? You're crazier than I remember."

"Her name is *Royael.* You wouldn't know that, though." She let her fingertips rest on his desk, leaning forward as spirals of hair framed an icy gaze. "I've been paying for dance classes, clothes, food, *everything*! I guess I gotta get crazy with you," she warned as her words didn't seem to penetrate.

"You look pretty crazy standing there." He knew those words would cause him hell, but it was true–and a grin came with it, too. Jon looked at her balled fists, eyes twinkling. He placed a hand on the phone and added, "Should I call security?"

"That's how it gotta be?" She took a seat on top of the sleek desk, crossed her legs. She felt five-ten and had seen this stance in a movie. No, this wasn't like leveraging in a film as his eyes scorched her skin. Keeping up calm appearances, she pulled back a silver ball from the swinging pendulum, watched it clink back and forth. She breathed through her mouth. His scent already embraced her. Calming. Teasing. Angering.

"We can go there if you want, Jon. Before you dial that number, I should warn that I am *great* friends with one of the editors of Scandalous magazine." Voice soft as satin, Raven peered into Jon's eyes. It was okay, now that she had all his attention. She breathed in the scent of fear. Inside she was well over six-feet and had the upper hand!

He took his hand off the receiver.

She smirked, "Thought so. I'm sure you don't want anyone to know our lil' secret."

"Hmmm..." Jon laced his hands behind his head and leaned back for a second, taking in that pout of hers. Then his hazel eyes narrowed. "I do not like *threats*, Raven Shaw."

"Oh, yeah. Well, I didn't like your letter saying our baby is a freak of nature. You suck! You thought I would *abort* my child because you didn't want her." She hopped off the desk, putting her hand on full hips with all of the confidence of a giant. "Royael is the most beautiful, fun, loving, energetic…She's everything that any father would want in a child. Except. For. *You*."

She fed off his guilty-as-sin façade. He no longer had that cocky allure. He had that little-fat-Jon-from-the-seventh-grade-look about him. Uncertain, out of control.

"Royael's deserves a better life." Looking around the marble flooring, she remembered leaving her briefcase outside. Instead of losing momentum, she snatched a sticky note off his desk. Scribbled on it, flicked it in his general direction. "Put some money in that account for Royael."

~ ~ ~

Jon sat in *his chair*. A chair made by a luxury Italian car design firm. It always made him confident, helped him handle business associates who attempted to play hardball. The fabric molded to his body. It was a million dollar chair for Christ sake. Right now, his chair did nothing to ease his anger from watching a perfect rose with thorns make her grand exit.

Jon let her name roll of his tongue. Not convinced that this was real, he glanced to the cognac snifter at the bar. *I haven't had a sip today.* Standing, he went to the window and watched the hubbub of people below. He waited. Then he gazed at Raven as she got into a SUV that was too awkward for her. She backed out slowly, as if that brazenness she'd just used on him had already deflated.

Jaw tense, his mind flashed back to her time-stopping beauty. Her blue eyes had turned into a gray storm as she ranted. *In my office!* At first, he'd been amused, hypnotized at her forbidden golden-toned thighs when she sat on his mahogany table. He could care less about her attitude. He almost laughed when she'd mentioned Scandalous magazine. If she did her homework, she'd known that Devereux Communications owned it and the complementing television station.

The letter almost made him snap. "I'd never infer that my child was…" Those awful words she'd used wouldn't even pass his lips. He'd loved Raven, proposed to her–so it was with an antique spoon ring, but he promised to get her something better later.

"I was going to leave my life for her and our baby. This is the thanks I get!" He walked to the silver cart, picked up the drink and downed it. Liquid fire seared his throat, warmed his body as he remembered *the cold letter she wrote*! "I just can't have a baby with you…"

Each word wove through his brain like a disease as he picked up the crystal bottle and poured another glass. Hell, she'd even added some biblical scripture and finished the story with she was *sorry*, but she wasn't keeping it. About to pour his third, he stopped. He didn't want to be drunk. Drinking wouldn't help him forget how he'd cried in that letter, torn it up, and burned it to a crisp. The ashes, evidence, had dissipated in the lake at the meadow. Their meadow. The very meadow she was supposed to meet him at to run away. *I should've gone to the meadow that night. No, I should've beat on her bedroom window and demanded she keep my child!*

He remembered his first year in Paris for college. Seven months later and still in a numb-state-of-mind, he saw a pregnant teen who reminded him of Raven. It gnawed at the anger he'd felt from getting *her letter!* He'd gotten drunk enough to call her about it. Believing she'd already murdered his child, he would still forgive her. Desperately, he needed to speak with the girl he loved. *Come to think of it, she didn't have the decency to return the call!*

Jon's forearms swiped over tens of thousands of dollars worth of scotch. The shattered crystal wasn't nearly as loud as his contemplation. *All these years and Raven had kept the baby!* Eyes closing with uncertainty, he leaned back on his table. The answer was in the tiny town of Bellwood. He groaned.

"Are you all right?" Patricia rushed through the double doors. His secretary glanced at poisonous liquid staining white couches and floor. Shards of glass were all over.

Shoulders tensed, he replied, "Everything will be fine soon. Clear the rest of my week. Have the jet ready; I'm headed to North Carolina."

CHAPTER 22

Jon pulled up the driveway of his parent's French style mansion. He got out and stopped next to the marble lotus-shaped fountain, instantly flashing back to the day he threw up in the turquoise water. The worst day of his life; finding out that the girl he was madly in love with was his half-sister. He walked past it, shaking the memory out of his head.

Jogging up the steps, he rang the doorbell and was surprised to see his dad answer. Jonathan had the same wide-eyed look. His dad had come to his graduation a year ago, but Jon hadn't noticed his hair graying.

Weariness floated off him, making Jon stop in his tracks. Then he felt his father's arms around him. It took awhile to wrap his arms around Jonathan. He let go first, needed to get down to business. There was nothing for him here, no need to dwell on the past. If his father wanted to make a social visit, he could come to Dallas.

"I need to talk to you," Jon gave his dad a hard stare.

"Yes, of course," Jonathan led him in the house like a guest. They walked past the double stair case, marble statues and into an all white living room.

"Are you alone?" Jon took a seat on the heavy plush couch.

"Yes."

"Where is…Lucinda?" He barely recalled the maid that worked for his family when he was in high school.

"She quit."

For a moment his eyebrows bunched together. *Something's missing.* Shrugging it off, he asked about the Dubois Law firm. It was a neutral topic to start with. He didn't want to go hard on the old man, not until he had more information.

"Great," Jonathan said.

That had to be a lie. He wouldn't expect to see his dad home in the middle of the week if the law firm did *great*. Instead of calling him on it,

121

Jon asked "Do you know about a letter that was sent to Raven stating that I *didn't want our child?*"

"A letter? No. I don't know about a letter." Jonathan played with the clasp of his Rolex.

"Are you sure?" *Look me in the eyes!*

Jonathan met his son's eyes for a fragment of a second to repeat himself.

Jon got up. He climbed the stairs and went down the west wing to his bedroom. He walked in, passed the couch and the aquarium that once held exotic fish. Lying back on his bed, he glared at the intricate molding on the ceiling and thought about his mom for the first time in a while. The words he said to Elise the last time he spoke with her were still tangible. His mom had handed him "Raven's letter" with Lucinda standing in the background, eyes flitting about. Mixed emotions draped over him like a wet blanket in the snow. His mom would have the answer. If Elise did, then Lucinda did, too. Pulling his cell phone out of his slacks, Jon blocked all thoughts of his mom.

"Hey, what happened to poker night?" Detective Tyriq Tate said into the phone.

"I had some out-of-town business. I need you to find a woman for me." Jon gave his friend Lucinda's full name and estimated the length of her employment at the Dubois mansion.

~~~

The trip to Brinton was a dead-end. By Saturday, Tyriq still hadn't located any current information on Lucinda, but it only took him seconds to find Raven.

"She is fine. Got a bit of road rage and…" Tyriq paused into the phone.

"And what?" *A felony? That would be this new, irate Raven.*

"Nothing," Tyriq replied nonchalantly, and then he spouted out her address.

Not twenty minutes later did Jon's Ashton Martin pull to a stop behind the Yukon he saw her in a couple of days ago. He got out, noticing a lot of eyes on him. *Wrong neighborhood.* Jon pressed the lock button, and on second thought one more time, then went to knock on the door.

A man with army fatigues, and wife beater opened it. "What's up?"

"Must be the wrong door," Jon stepped back and looked at the number. The guy looked too comfortable. He didn't remember Raven wearing a ring, but then again he had a hard time keeping his eyes on hers.

"Who you lookin' for? We all know each other round here."

"Raven Shaw."

"You're at the right spot. Hold on a sec." A smile appeared at the mention of her name. Dimple guy disappeared in the house.

"Jon?" Raven's eyes widened, staring at his charcoal gray slacks and button up. Sexy, *stuffy*-sexy, on a weekend. Annoyed, she asked, "What you doing here?"

"You assumed I'd send you money without seeing *my* child," his tone was as cold as the hail landing on his pea coat. He hadn't meant to be rude, but she had on "teaser pants" that hugged every curve and a blouse that accentuated caramel covered melons. It was too chilly of a day for her to be walking around like that, but she wasn't outside. She was inside, probably catering to her boyfriends needs. He glanced at her ring finger. *Shacking up!* He let the coldness of the air seep into his bones, let it be his drive.

"*Your* child?" Her bangles jingled as she placed a hand on her hip.

"Yes, are you going to let me in?" Voice still frigid, he couldn't help it.

"I wasn't expecting you, Jon."

"Are you okay, Raven?" Dimples was back at the door, but he didn't have that dimple when he said, "So you *Jon?*"

"Yes, I am. *Who are you?*" He had a feeling that the boyfriend knew too much.

"Stephen!" He stepped out of the house, just a fraction shorter, he glared Jon's eyes. Chest puffed out, he added, "I don't appreciate you coming round here starting nothin'."

"Whoa, nobody is starting *anything* today," Raven stood between them. They stared at each other over her head, neither backing down.

"Stephen, you need to mind your business!" Jon's hands were itching to grab Raven around her tiny waist and place her out of the way when she spoke again.

"Steph, I think you better go home."

Jon hated every moment of their "soft, pawing" exchange. Her hand went to Stephen's chest. As if her touch could pacify an erupting volcano, he backed down.

"We're not going paintballin'?" Stephen looked down at Raven.

"No, but I'll talk with Melody. She won't be afraid if she just tries it." She linked arms with him. Her eyes cut at Jon as they passed and walked down the path.

Jon watched then near the SUV. Her hips swayed like a rose in a summer breeze. Jaw clinched, he waited to see if she would kiss Stephen goodbye, but she didn't. He supposed it had to do with him gawking.

"Hey! Where ya going?" A little voice yelled.

He turned around to see a little girl, zipping by. *Royael.* The anger boiling in his veins subsided. Time slowed. *Gorgeous.* Her pink tutu swished as she ran. A tiara on top her head, long sandy brown ponytails bouncing down her back. Big brown eyes smiled at Stephen as she jumped into his arms. She planted a kiss on his cheek.

Temperature rising again, he watched Royael mope as Stephen spoke into her ear. Stephen tickled her and she laughed–a good laugh. Not the type of laugh that he wanted his child to have with *another* man. Jon's body stiffened. *Does she call him Dad?*

"Sorry, Royael. We can do Pizza Planet later." Stephen put the child down.

"No!" she folder her arms, chubby cheeks puffed. "You promised, so we going today!"

"Not today." Raven placed Royael on her hip as he got in the car.

Stephen gave Jon a last stare, a warning stare. Jon returned his own. When she walked toward the house, Jon asked, "What does he *know* about me, Raven?"

"Enough." She put her hands over Royael's ears and added, "So if you try to kill me just to keep your dirty secret, you're gonna have to kill him, too. Oh, and it gets harder to stay squeaky clean while starting a blood trail."

He glared as she headed inside with Royael and close the door. Touching the cold doorknob, Jon walked in. The living room was tiny, the furniture familiar. He remembered the last kiss they shared on that very sofa back in Bellwood. He followed the sound of Royael's whimpering, up a narrow staircase and into a door. The room was claustrophobic, smaller than his walk-in closet.

Royael sat on her bed. Raven knelt on the floor, rubbing her back. Tears streamed down her face, but she smiled when seeing Jon. Her tone was soft, small, sweet. "Hello, who are you?"

"I'm Jon." He heard himself whisper and seemed to float over, kneeling kneel on the floor next to Raven. Heart melted, he touched her cheek. Warm. Real. Alive. Throat constricted, the words barely came out. "I'm your father."

"No, no. You're not my father." Royael's big eyes expressed sadness for him. She hopped up and rummaged around in her top dresser drawer. "Hold on, okay?"

What did this woman tell my child? Jon looked at Raven. She bit her lip, looking away.

Royael jumped back on her bed. Placed a hand on his shoulder, she handed him a photo of a man in army uniform with Creole similarities. "This is my father. He was a Tuskegee airman."

"Royael, Jon is your father." Raven interjected.

"No, Mommy. You said *this* is my daddy. I told my friends that he died saving America. A hero! So *he* can't be my daddy." Royael looked back at Jon. "Sorry, mister."

"Royael, Jon is your daddy. Remember, we were just playing a game," Raven repeated. When her daughter still didn't look convinced, she added, "He's going to take you Pizza Planet."

"Pizza Planet? Okay!" Royael hopped up, grabbed her toy purse and headed downstairs.

"You told Royael that her father was a Tuskegee airman! You must've been flirting too hard with Chris in history class." Jon blocked her path, forcing himself not to slap that flippant look on her face.

"You've got your nerve bringing up Chris." Full lips pursed, she wagged a finger at him. "I didn't start off telling Royael that, and I'll admit she put me on the spot when asking. Royael's poetic, needed something to fill the void. Should I've told her that you didn't want her?"

"Raven, I…" He wanted to tell her that his mom must've written the letter to her, but Raven kept on ranting.

"*Get over yourself.* Royael is waiting. As far as I'm concerned, she's happy."

He didn't budge as she shouldered him while walking by. It wasn't the time to bring up lies. He took a deep breath before walking out of the room and downstairs. When he got outside, there were three kids waiting at his car.

"Royael went with the neighbors last time." Raven handed him a booster seat. Grinning, she cocked her head toward the other two seats on the grass. "Safety first."

He struggled, placing the seats in the back of the two-door Ashton. She went around checking each one after the kids were seated. He shut the front passenger door and said, "If you were going to assess my ability, then you could've just helped."

"Oh, trust me. I have helped you. Every day I raise your child alone." Eyes in slits, she reopened the door and slid in. "Did you think you were taking my child *alone*? I don't think so."

~~~

Kids zipped around Pizza Planet with pizza sauce on their face, clothes, and hands–touching everything! Jon suffocated on germs.

Parents sat at booths, eating and jabbering, doing everything but watch their kids. After ordering food and tokens, he found Raven sitting at a booth. Glancing at the bright-red, cracked cushion, he made sure there were no "surprises" before taking a seat in his Ralph Lauren slacks. He tried to make small talk as his child and her crew roamed around arcade games and obstacle courses, but the Chihuahua—a secret name he'd gifted Raven—had a sharp reply for everything.

"That's weird. They're usually back by now asking for more tokens and acting like they've been starved to death," Raven said awhile later as she took her last bite of cheese pizza.

"I gave them 10,000 tokens," Jon replied. "I don't think so."

"*You* gave three five-year-olds 10,000 tokens! Ya gotta be kidding me." She giggled and came to sit next to him, scooting close. A mixture of confusion and enticement from her fruity perfume took over him. It beat the smell of dust, tomato sauce, and day-old germs.

"See those boys?" She pointed to a pair of pimple-faces who were following Royael and her friends, picking up tokens that fell out of the girls' pockets. Raven patted his shoulder, chuckling. "Mr. Big Bucks, you're paying for everybody's tokens."

Jon lit up. "Those little bastards!"

"Sit, Mr. Big Bucks!" She smacked his tailored butt. "You can't beat 'em for taking this opportunity. Do you really want to get in a fight with all of these parents on your first visit with Royael?"

"Don't start, Raven." He rubbed at a phantom headache as she continued to laugh. *Call me Mr. Big Bucks again and I swear…*

~~~

A slight ach formed at the pit of Raven's stomach as she watched Jon carry their sleeping child into the house that night. Caressed by the love displayed on his face for Royael and weakened by what he'd written in the letter, Raven took a seat on the couch. Heart split by the need to shield her daughter from his previous views. *But, they connected.*

She grabbed a throw pillow and held it to her chest, letting the day sink in as he took Royael upstairs. Closing her eyes, a vivid image of them on the very same couch in Bellwood took over. *He'd convinced me that he'd never leave.* She'd been hesitant. Lips tingling, she reminisced on his kisses and how, like a dum-dum, she'd caved in. *He made love to me, made me think that he was the only consistency in my life then he abandoned me.*

"I put on her pajamas. She sleeps so hard, didn't wake up."

Jon's voice and the movement of him sitting near, shoved Raven into reality. The scent of amber and woodsy cologne almost had her eyes closing again. Instead of giving into dreamy temptation, she smiled genuinely and replied, "Royael had a good day."

"Do you mind if I stay and look at pictures of Royael? I've missed a lot."

The smile plunged into darkness. *Of course, you did!* A plethora of emotions had her feeling angry and sorry for him all at the same time. Nodding, she rose and went to the bookshelf. She spread photo albums across the coffee table and dug in from the beginning.

A while later, their laughter mingled with the rains patter on the windows. Raven leaned on his shoulder, legs covered by a knitted blanket as she pointed to a picture of a seven month Royael at her first pageant. "She won the highest title in natural and glitz. Now, Royael dominates the pageant world."

Raven told him a story about each photo. She stopped on a picture of Royael in the bathtub with her face and body smeared in chocolate. "She was almost two, stole a candy bar from the checkout stand while I was paying for groceries. It wasn't until I pulled into the driveway and looked through the rearview mirror.... you could just imagine the mess in the dead of summer! Chocolate all over the seats, ugh!"

"She loves chocolate like her daddy."

They sat for hours and he learned about his daughter's life. Looking back on all the pictures had her in a carefree state. She picked up the last book, Royael's fifth year and excitedly told the story behind those photos, too.

"This looks professional," he commented on a recent picture of Royael on the merry-go-round.

"I took it. I'm attending photography school."

"Do you have a portfolio?" he asked.

'Go ahead and answer him. You've been acting as if he's your best friend this evening, same old Jon; right? The boy you've known your entire life...' The voice slithered through her brain.

Raven stiffened, she'd almost gone through the whole day without mockery ringing in her ears. "I'm barely a second year student."

"You shouldn't be shy about it. This picture looks great," he encouraged.

Finally noticing how near they were, she stood hastily. "I think it's time for you to go."

Jon arose. "Okay."

She handed him an old newspaper from the rack next to Grandpa's lazy boy and closed the front door as soon as he stepped out. Peeking through the blinds, she watched him saunter to his car not even using the paper to shield himself from the rain.

"No, he's *not* the same Jon," Raven whispered.

CHAPTER 23

"When are you going to call Raven?" Damien asked for the umpteenth time. "Trinity is starting to sit by herself. Don't you want Trinity to get to know her sister?"

"I don't have time for the drama. I'm almost late," Charlene replied, arms crossed, staring at the vase of lilies in the foyer.

"When's the right time, then?"

"Not now, Damien. The holiday season is over. It's time to get back on track."

"You *are* going to deal with it!" He planted himself in front of the door.

"Raven used *our* child's picture for her next paycheck. She is not my daughter." Her eyelid twitched. She needed to be calm before going to the set. "I need you to be on my side for once."

"Are you serious? We're talking about family. There are no sides when it comes to blood. You can't throw them away. You can't abandon them—"

Charlene's lethal weapon of an index finger jabbed his arm. "Stop being so gullible, Damien! Raven ruined our wedding! She acted all buddy-buddy the night before. The morning of, she was so detached. Then wham!" She banged a fist against the side table and the vase veered an inch from the center. Feeling like a fool, she remembered their regimen of going exercising and to lunch. She remembered belting out Mary J lyrics and Raven singing them perfectly, and it all hurt. Shaking her head, she continued, "The day before I went to complete the midseason, we were supposed to m—"

"Can I get a word in, please?"

"Hello! She acted all secretive that day. Wouldn't meet me and left a vague message, wouldn't call back." *My child could replace me as Meagan. She's just that manipulative!* "B. S., Damien! Of all the days to miss our lunches...I just don't know if it was guilt or-or she'd gotten what she wanted. She had car trouble that day, and instead of borrowing money—"

"It doesn't make sense." He put his hands in the air, flustered.

"She'd planned to screw me from the get-go. I was eight months pregnant, vulnerable, when we bonded over a mutual hatred of her *baby daddy*! The next few months—a split second of a lifetime—we got along, all the while, she plotted." She nodded a pursed lip nod. "Lucky her, in all her scheming and pretending to care, she even got to save me from Marcus! I thanked her. *You* thanked her."

"Charlene." He touched her shoulder as her ranting ceased.

Sighing, animosity failed her. She admitted in a weak whisper, "My eyes saw divine intervention. Raven was my hero, and like any other person whose been saved, my guard was down. I was defenseless... That's when she blindsided me again, Damien. That's all there is to it."

"You honestly believe the crap coming out of your mouth?" His laughter was tense. The tears so easily formed in her eyes and the eloquence of her case had flown over the dramatic-spectrum. "You've been Meagan too long. Your brain doesn't even conceive that you're overanalyzing other's intentions." He waited for her reply of absurdity then added, "Do you think the worst of me?"

"*Yup*. You get to play dual roles. You're here as my confidant, but ever since I got out of rehab and you met Raven, you've been all buddy-buddy with her, too." *If you're going to ask dumb questions, you get dumb answers.* Charlene walked out, slamming the door behind her. She needed to call Teresa her drug and alcohol buddy.

~~~

In a silk robe, Charlene entered the set of Meagan's lavish loft. She passed by nude murals of Meagan that Miguel Sanchez's character had crafted during their *sexcapades*. Her hands caressed a large easel with painting equipment, knowing that the camera zoomed in on that. She glided by picturesque windows of the Upper East Side of New York—a realistically painted backdrop.

Her eyes took on that cat shape she was lusted after as she stopped at the foot of Meagan's bed. An alternate camera zoomed over her shoulder to her desire. Miguel lay tangled in the sheets–from appearances he was naked. Drinking in his bronze, chiseled body and that seductive way he licked his lips, Charlene became Meagan. Heartless-Meagan. She climbed into bed. He cupped the back of her head and gave a hard, maddening kiss. Black demi-bra and matching panties were flooded with light when he tore off her robe.

"You are safe now, Meagan," he said in a melt worthy Latin accent.

Kneeling on the custom round bed, they devoured each other with kisses. Then Meagan straddled her sexy co-star. The camera zoomed in on her tracing her hands over his chest, heart shaped lips in a blood red pout, making promises of love that fans knew she wouldn't keep.

~~~

A piece of fine clay… Charlene felt Miguel's hands roaming over her body. She had to open her eyes and look in the bright mirror of her dressing room to know the scene was over–in unfortunately, one take. *God, help me. Please don't let me think about this man…*

There was a knock at the door–divine intervention? A sign from God? She looked at the large teardrop diamond on her finger and shouted, "Come in."

Barbie strolled in, handing her a folded piece of paper. Grinning, she left.

Inserting her index finger into the slit of the envelope, Charlene wiggled the adhesive free, pulled out a slip of paper and read the few words. *This can't be a sign from God. No, it's temptation with a capital T.*

CHAPTER 24

SHiny bowling balls rolled down the waxed wooden allies, adding to the chaos of flying pins and R&B music. Couples and groups filled each neon-lit lane, slapping high fives or predicting with self-inflated heads–having fun, relaxing on a lively Friday night. Then there was Raven.

"…Jon came into my life–*our* lives. He's tryna take over everything. I mean, just the other day he wanted to go to Royael's kindergarten," Raven ranted as she stood at the bowling machine, waiting for her ball to appear. She hadn't looked at the score in a while. Her head wasn't in the game. She decided to let Bill win. Placing three fingers into place, she braced the orange ball with her opposite hand and got into stance. Then stood up straight and asked, "And do you know what he did?"

"No, I don't know what he did." Bill frowned, seated at the booth next to the computer screen.

"Jon acted all high and mighty when we visited her school. Afterwards, he said he wanted to have her transferred to a *better* kindergarten." Pain zipped the length of her arm; miraculously, she still held the ball. Shoulders tensed, she flung it down the alley. She plopped down on the yellow chair next to Bill and glanced at the score board. *Zero?*

"He even had a damn pamphlet with him like that was his initiative all along. I said 'no.' I barely have time to get to school after working at the coffee shop–that is, if they give me enough hours. He said I should quit my job." She grumbled, imagining her hands wrapped around his muscular neck. Just because he'd given her enough money to pay for the winter term of school, and then some, didn't mean he was scot-free.

"C'mon, Raven, go to your happy place," Bill leaned shoulder to shoulder with her.

F- a happy place! "I didn't tell you what else he said when I laughed at his suggestion that I quit."

"It's still your turn." He pulled away and added a nonchalant, "What did he do?"

"Jon told me that he would have a car take Royael to school." Raven got up and went to the bowling machine. She flung the ball, knocking down one pin. "A car...bull shit!"

"A better school gives her a head start," Bill replied, after getting a turkey–his third X. He was in the triple digits. She was pushing fifty.

"She has a caring teacher and is in class with children from our area." When she couldn't read his expression, she stopped at the machine and continued her venting. "The other day, Jon comes over out of the blue and stays for dinner. How did he know if we'd have enough? Forget that southern hospitality crap. Granny let him stay. She's actin' like he's family." She flung the bowling ball down the shiny alley. "And do you know that he stayed all the way to tuck Royael in. *I* tuck Royael in. This has been going on a week."

"Maybe you can switch up sometimes." Bill put his arms around her, trying to kiss her.

Anger about to explode, she didn't notice. "Do you know what *else* he did?"

"What else?" He asked in a cynical tone.

"I'm sorry, Bill." Raven pouted and kissed him. "No more Jon, okay?"

"Good. No more Jon, at least not for a while."

~~~

Creative energy had Raven itching to take pictures of the glass mansion on the hill. Greenery of trees mirrored off the glass walls. She pulled in front of the six car garage–candy shop–that displayed luxury imports she'd only seen on 007 films. *He still has the Chevelle.* She looked at the black classic with green lime flecks that he used to pick her up in during high school.

'That means nothing and you've forgotten the list.'

I have not! Rolling her neck, tension cracked. She tucked away memories of the good times they had in it. She pulled out a Minnie Mouse overnight luggage as her daughter got out. This would be the first time Royael spent the night with her dad. They walked up a stone fragmented bridge over a Koi pond. Standing in front of a two-story, exotic-wood door, she rang the bell.

Jon opening it and gave Raven a terse greeting then hugged his daughter.

"Daddy, I missed you sooooo much," Royael said when he let her go.

"I missed you, too. We're going to have a good weekend. I have a surprise for you." He patted her head and turned to her mother. "Thanks, have a good day."

"You're welcome. You have a good one too," she nodded curtly at his dismissiveness. He never argued, but she knew their disagreement about Royael's schooling got under his skin.

"I suppose I should take a look around and *inspect* your home for safety." Raven thrust the luggage at his abdomen and walked by. *You're not the only one that can go around making sure things are up to par.* Boots resonated off Macassar Ebony wood walkway she passed a bonsai tree with beautiful twisting branches, surrounded by the Koi pond. A formal living room to her right held rare African art that looked stunning from the natural lighting of the glass walls.

"I suppose Royael can't reach that stick thingy with the pointy arrow," she said nodding her head toward some type of ancient African weapon on the wall.

"No, Raven. Has my home met your approval?" His jaw tensed, but he had to smile when Royael kept tugging his arm about the surprise.

Without responding, Raven walked down a hall. She passed a media room with a large screen and rows of plush seating. A library with stuffy books that she presumed the "new" Jon would read. The "old" one preferred comic books and Goosebumps. She stopped at an indoor pool and turned back to him. "Keep this door closed."

He folded his arms as Royael tugged his Armani button-up still pestering him about a surprise.

She continued down the hall toward a game room with a huge TV. Indigo couches and chairs were placed near blue and silver glass statues. A long fireplace ran half the length in the room dividing a full-scale bar from an arcade. Three old-school games, one of which she knew was Jon's favorite as a child–Pac-Man–lined the opposite gray wall. Instead of continuing the charade of "inspecting" and secretly hating this new-fake Jon, she shrugged. Turning on her heels, she tuned out the happy chatter as Royael showed her father a drawing from class

"I'll be going now," Raven said while Jon overzealously admired a trinket Royael made in class as they sat on a couch. After being ignored, she quickly hugged her child and replied, brusquely to him, "I'll let myself out."

The doorbell rang as she passed by the living room. Feeling in a good mood for having annoyed Jon, she opened the door with a smile. "Hello."

Raven looked up at a very tall, thin woman with beautiful Mali features. The lady's face resembled a clay sculptor of the African art in the living room. Unfortunately, Raven was eye level to her flowing top that exposed, tiny tits and chest bones–*ugh*.

"Who are *you*?" The woman's French accent went well with the curled upper lip.

"I'm Raven. Who are you?" Raven matched the woman's hostile stance.

"I am Camille Laurent. You don't know who I am? You have that tacky camera around your neck. You should know who *I am*."

"Excuse me!" Raven put her hand on her hip.

"Why are *you* in my man's house?" Camille walked past, her pointy stiletto–that any fashionista would die for–pierced into Raven's foot.

"What the heck." She screamed as pain shot through her toes. She turned around and slammed the heavy door–as best as she could. "Excuse you!"

Camille spun around near the bonsai tree—which she was taller than. Placing her hand on her hip and in that French accent Raven hated, she said, "I don't apologize to fashion-tacky *midgets*."

"Don't let the cute face fool you, look at these guns." She flexed her muscles. They were kind of big. She could do one hand pushups, something that bag-of-bones Camille couldn't.

"How dare you—"

Raven repeatedly flashed the camera in her face. The giant's hands went to her eyes, giraffe legs stomping so wildly that she had to move out of the line of fire, so as not to get another toe piercing.

"You're blinding me!" Camille screeched.

"You still haven't said sorry. Do I have to beat your ass?" Raven took off her chandelier earrings, as if that would help the woman answer.

Jon grabbed Raven's arm. "You can't come in my house starting fights!"

Raven opened her mouth to say something. *You're taking up for this asshole?*

'*The answer is obvious, Dumbass. Look at how he's staring at you, but of course, you're beneath him.*'

Instead of defining herself, she huffed. The voice was correct. Shaking her head, she went back to the game room to get her daughter. "Let's go, Royael!"

"No." Chipmunk cheeks puffing out, Royael ran into her dad's arms. "Mommy's being mean."

"Who is she?" Camille looked down at Royael like a bug that needed to be squashed.

"His daughter!" Raven folded her arms. *I guess I'm gonna have to beat this woman in front of my child.* She walked to Camille who rolled her eyes. Turning from the Neanderthal to Jon, she decided the woman wasn't worth it. "You haven't told her about Royael?"

"Can I talk to you without that attitude? It's getting really old—"

Hands on hips, voice a little shaky from anger, she cut him off. "I *said* have you told the Dinosaur about your daughter? Forget this. *My child is not spending the night.*"

Struggling with the luggage, she grabbed Royael's hand and had to drag the child away.

"No, Mommy!" Royael pleaded trying to pry Raven's hands from around her waist.

"Wait," Jon said following her, with Camille behind him, spewing words in French.

"I don't take orders from you. If this woman is going to have you being mean to my child, then Royael is going home." Raven spun back around in her snow boats, but Royael wasn't following her. Retreating, she grabbed her child. "C'mon, you can see your *father* later."

"Raven, please." Jon was at her side in a few short strides as she had her hand on the knob.

"No, Jon. You've never put *our child* first…" *This is a good time for you to apologize, and I'm not going to feel sorry for you anymore so wipe that look off your face.* "When T-Rex leaves, Royael can come back."

~~~

A full moon seeped through the blinds of her bedroom. Raven took out her cell phone, ignored the numerous missed calls from Jon, and dialed Sharon's number. "Hey, girl. I have a gift for you."

"Really! Jon payin' you child support *like* that?"

"I guess he thinks money covers his sins. Not that, though. Do you know Camille Laurent?"

"Yes. She's Queen Diva in modeling—as exotic *and* evil as a black mamba!"

"Good. I have some pictures for you, but I want them to go in the section were fashion experts joke about celebrities." Raven chuckled. If there was anything that came out of the altercation of the day—and having to put ice on her big toe, it was snapping pictures of the giant's collapse.

"All right, girly." Sharon's laughter ended in a sigh. "All joking aside, Jon has been helping you with Royael—without so much of a nudge into the right direction. Now that you've gotten time to feel him out and money is not what you're after, shall we commence the Dubois revenge?"

Raven's lips curled in delight as she agreed. Later that night, she dozed off to Elise's green eyes and replayed the dream of killing Jon's mother. *Raven watched as Elise lay in a heap on the floor of her steam room, slowly dying from the toxic flower-water concoction she'd slipped her.*

"Please Raven, I have to tell you something," Elise forced each word out of parched lips.

"My mother didn't want me because of you. You stole Jonathan away from her! You stole my father from me! Maybe I shoulda been grateful that she was in a coma for such a long time and couldn't safely abort me..."

Raven's eyes popped open. Music was in her dreams. There had never been music before. Yawning, her brain registered the melody from her phone on the nightstand. The tune had permeated her dreams. She answered it, sounding like a toad.

"Finally, Raven." Jon's voice let out pent up air. "You could've at least called and told me that you made it home with our child."

Raven huffed. She hadn't meant to answer the phone. Reflexes. The way he said "our child" made her want to reach through the phone and punch him in the throat.

"Come over in the morning," he said and hung up.

How ironic. I'm dreaming about killing his mom, and he wakes me up.
'Look at the bright side, Dumbass. At least ya didn't finish this time...'

~~~

Bittersweet. Raven stood in the driveway watching the loving father-daughter-moment, feeling somewhat left out as she hugged herself through a cable-knit sweater.

"Is the dinosaur here?" She asked with a half smile. Making light of the situation was better than blowing up. She'd been so angry as of recent; animosity was second nature, even though it wasn't the Christian thing to do. *Forget Dr. Stanton, his advice didn't work.* Sniffling, she thought about her mom.

"No, Camille's not here." He brushed past Raven. With, Royael's head in the crook of his neck, she gave her mom the stink eye as the duo went into the house.

*I can play nice for the sake of my child. Greater is He that is in me than he that is in the world...*she chanted, entering the house with the same Minnie Mouse rollaway. She stood near the pond watching the Koi fish flit in the clear water. Carefree. *No evidence of Camille. I can go.*

A loud screech made her think otherwise. She raced past the stairs and down the long corridor of rooms. Stopping next to an Italian chef statue by an arched doorway, Raven's heart slowed back to normal. Royael was seated on the island with flour in her pigtails, smiling and bossing her dad around. Lighting was bright, since the kitchen was at a corner of the house. It highlighted some sort of creamy batter all over the onyx countertops. Taking a deep breath of nature, since one of the walls were pulled back letting in fresh mountain air, Raven watched the exchange.

"No chocolate chips? How are we going to have pancakes?" Royael commanded jumping off the counter. She marched over to the pantry, where Jon must have been.

He walked out with her on his heels barking orders. A smudge of flour on his cheek that–the old Raven–would've loved to brush off with her thumb. His flannel shirt fit snuggly across biceps bigger than her thighs. There was something sexy about watching a man interact with his child. She couldn't leave as Jon squatted to Royael's level, trying to give his child the world.

"How about strawberries or blueberries in the pancakes?" Jon asked.

Too much for her heart, she willed herself to depart. Her child was safe. Since they were having so much fun, the Neanderthal couldn't be around. Still, she stared as his full lips moved into a mock pout to the uncompromising Royael. *I've never seen my baby so happy...*

Sweet, honey eyes turned to look at her for help with their child.

"Royael doesn't like strawberries," Raven began. "She thought the seeds were ants as a toddler."

"Okay. Maybe we should make a list of the things Royael doesn't like."

"Royael can tell you," Raven backed away. The "we" thing made the hairs on her arms stand. They'd done Pizza Planet and gone to Royael's school, but it was time for him to take over. Time for father and daughter to learn each other.

"How about your pancakes, do you still like them with pecans?"

"I'll be back later," Raven tossed back as she neared the kitchen door.

"You can stay."

She turned around at the large entryway, "I have to get ready for a date." *Before my movie-dinner with Bill, I have a date with Sharon, so we can figure out just what to do with you...*

She walked to the door, wondering if she could still read the expression on his face. *No, he couldn't care? But how does he remember if I like pecans...* Shaking the notion out of her head, she left.

CHAPTER 25

The Malibu pale blue sea mimicked the hazy overcast day. Wearing a pink bikini with ruffles, Trinity sat in front of a seven-month mini cake with hot pink fondant. On a mission, she "army crawled" over the sand toward her yellow bucket and shovel as her parents continually scooped her up and returned her back to the blanket.

"Come back, Trinity. We haven't even sung happy birthday yet." Charlene crawled to her child and picked her up.

"We got company." Damien sighed as she planted the determined baby back on the blanket. They looked to the Scandalous TV camera crew trudging through the sand toward them. •

Charlene rolled her eyes at the paparazzi; particularly at the ringleader. *One, two, three…action.* She plastered on a smile and knew she looked good in a white Gucci bikini. Maybe they just wanted to see her toned body and ask her if she'd gotten post-baby plastic surgery again.

Trinity cried as lights flashed in her face. Damien picked her up.

"Charlene, word on these Scandalous streets is that you and Miguel have been displaying your hot, on-screen chemistry, *off screen?*" The ringleader purred, pursing his glossy lips.

The grin fizzled and her eyes were as big as the O shape of her mouth. No sexy cat eyes, today.

"Excuse me. I don't appreciate you coming over here scaring my child." Damien put the crying baby in Charlene's arms and stood.

"Hellooo," the ringleader indicated for the camera crew to get a full shot of Damien in his trunks. He stuffed his hands in cutoff jeans and stood next to Damien and continued, "How do you feel about your wife's romantic relationship with Loyalties and FamiLIEs co-star, Miguel?"

"No comment," voice dry, Damien stepped out of view.

"I've been hearing otherwise," the man's voice rang out like a mocking song as he rocked back and forth on expensive flip flops. He moved closer to Damien. "Did you see the photos of Charlene at Le'

Fleur–that *fantastic, romantic* restaurant…with Miguel-*Sexy*-Sanchez. *All by themselves.*"

When Damien didn't reply, the commentator thrust the microphone into his face. "Mr. *Shaw*, surely you have an opinion?"

The scene was a blur. Damien planted a hook to the man's nose so swiftly that Charlene didn't have time to react. Oh, but Scandalous TV did. They replayed that scene over and over and over.

~~~

"That A-hole is pressing charges." Charlene gripped a manila envelope and stared at her husband as he chewed on jam and toast. "Why'd you have to go and hit him?"

"He shoved a mic in my face. He disrespected me in front of you and my child. Called me Mr. Shaw." Damien nosily readjusted the L.A. Times and went back to scanning the stock market.

She sat on the stool next to him. Damien couldn't be mad about a useless microphone invading his comfort zone. If she had to guess, he wasn't half mad about being called "Mr. Shaw," everybody knew the A-hole from Scandalous TV. Damien was too much of a calm, collected person to go off. Playing with the knot in her silk robe, in a meek tone said, "I know, but–"

"Did you hear me? No man is going to scare my family."

"Dami–"

"So what is it about Miguel? You want him now or something?" The anger had disappeared from his voice, jealousy seeped through. He put down the newspaper.

Charlene sighed. It was out. His motive. *He's pushing forty and acting like a kid!*

"There's nothing going on." Charlene looked into his eyes. "You've been with me through thick and thin, when I was nothing, and in rehab."

She hugged him. He picked up the newspaper and continued reading.

The next morning, Charlene woke and instinctively reached over to spoon her husband. Jealousy had weaseled its way in their marriage. It hurt to find that his side of the bed was empty. The season had just wrapped up. It had been the best in all six years. They were *supposed* to spend every day of spring together with Trinity. Padding down the hall, she went into Trinity's room. Except for an abundance of stuffed animals in the crib, the room was empty.

Ambling downstairs, she noticed a piece of paper on the table at the entrance, propped up by the milk glass vase of lilies. Her heartbeat quickened as she picked it up. Scanning the words quickly, Damien had taken Trinity on a nature stroll. Her hesitance about Miguel diminished.

She went into the office to check her personal email which she didn't monitor during production. Scrolling down the hoard of unopened mail, she saw a message from Sharon Riley. *The nerve of that woman.* Clicking on Sharon's message, Charlene thought about giving the woman a good, moral talk about her job.

Hello Charlene,

I've been attempting to contact you for some time. I've called and sent a messenger to the studio. Hopefully you check your own email.

Her eyes scanned quickly as she conjured up a terse reply.

Let me get back on subject. First off, I'm not contacting you, for you (if that makes any sense). I'm contacting you for the sake of your daughter. Raven's depressed and spent the whole Christmas season feeling down. I pray next year is better for her.

Charlene stopped reading and scrolled up to the date. Sharon had emailed her almost two months ago, the last week of the year.

Raven and I have become good friends. I've taken it upon myself to investigate the real culprit of the Trinity photos—we admitted to the wedding pictures and nothing more. I've attached the signed document that explains who was privy to that article. Do with it as you will.

—Sharon

Lips pursed, Charlene read and reread the story until her eyes ached. Finally, with a shaky index finger, she clicked on the attachment. A purple magazine insignia taunted her that it was legit. Her heart slowed when she saw the name at the bottom, signed on the dotted line.

While the printer spitted out a copy of the document, she picked up her cell phone and called the perpetrator. "Hey, can you stop by? I have a gift to appreciate all your hard work this season."

Gifts were involved; of course, Barbie was at her house in record timing. The front door opened and Barbie called out, Charlene's spine stiffened as she sat in the computer chair and shouted her location.

At the door in seconds, she twirled a few pink braids. "Hey, Char."

"Barbie," Charlene smiled and held out a gift box with the lavish B' Jori emblem.

"Awe, for moi!" She blew a big gum bubble then popped it.

"You've worked *so hard* to get it." Charlene's smile was stone, but Barbie didn't notice.

Barbie let a little giggle burst over as she pulled at the silk ribbon and took off the shiny red lid. Her face a mixture of confusion as she stuck her hand in, and instead of a purse, pulled out a piece of paper. She bit her greasy/glossy lips. "Char, I…"

"Like I said, you've been *working real hard*." The scar itched, her hands balled into fists.

"I-I…" Barbie backed up.

"Why? I've been good to you. I've missed *months* of my daughter's life!" Charlene bristled, remembering her cruelty. *I disowned Raven.*

"Because you loved me before *she* came around. We always went to movies, lunch, shopping and you were like the momma I never had." Mascara and tears parted caked foundation on her cheeks.

"What if Raven never forgives me?" Her heart shuddered.

"I'm so sorry." Barbie's chest heaved as she cried.

"Put my house keys on the counter when you leave." Charlene watched the girl lumber out the office. She followed, narrow eyeing Barbie as the girl gloomily placed the keys near Damien's note.

"Oh, and Barbie," Charlene began as she couldn't take her gaze off the girl. Barbie turned around, a glimmer of hope in her eyes. Charlene stood close, smiled. Fingers spread, she slapped Barbie so hard that her own body quacked. A thick wad of gum flew out of Barbie's mouth onto the plush white rug. She wanted to slap her again for that, but the front door opened. In basketball shorts and an A-shirt, Damien strolled in with Trinity. Barbie rushed past them and out the door.

"What the hell was that all about?" Damien stopped the stroller inside the door. When she showed him the document, all he could say was, "Ohhh."

That talk of assurance she needed to have with him about Miguel had to wait. Now wasn't the time. She had to go and make amends with her *first child*. Somehow.

Hurrying into the office, she called the airport for the first time since having an assistant. Jazz music flooded her ears. While waiting for customer service, she heard Damien on his cell phone. Tip toeing, she peeked into the kitchen. Daniela's voice rang through on speaker as he fed Trinity a jar of baby food from her high chair.

"We're going back to Dallas," Damien said.

"Oh, I thought Charlene was never going back. You have been talking to Raven, right?" Daniela chattered.

*Great they have a better relationship with my own child...*Charlene grimaced as Daniela talked about "her great grandbaby, Royael." She sighed, leaning against the wall and listened on.

"Yes, I speak with her at least once a week like I have since Charlene was in rehab. I don't know how well she'll take Char's apology, but we're going to try to make it right."

Charlene's heart melted; *I have a good man. He always has my back.*

"...Okay, I'm going with you," Daniela said. "I'll watch Trinity. I think ya'll need some type of vacation. I'm sure it's been hard, ya'll having a baby and...especially with that guy Miguel."

Charlene backed out of the doorway and picked up her cell phone. No jazz tune. The call had ended. She would have to redial and wait in line again.

CHAPTER 26

Jon wrestled with his diamond-encrusted JD cufflinks, praying that Annette would answer the door even though he needed to speak with her granddaughter. With Annette near, Raven's split personality, "Chihuahua," toned it down a notch. Just his luck, Raven came to the door in a leopard mini dress and those sexy, glossy lips in a perpetual smirk.

"Hello, Jon. Thanks for not calling and popping in like usual." Her eyes narrowed. "You're usually so intelligent, but it seems that you've forgotten that *this is not your weekend*."

Her voice was smooth and sweet, yet dripping with venom. Maybe if he closed his eyes, he could imagine when he'd fallen in love with her. They were about eight and she'd joined the choir. Now, he stood on the welcome mat, but never in his life had he been so baffled. Not when Grandfather Pierre's second, Mr. Laurent, found out that Jon was to be Pierre's lead in the American D Hotel acquisitions. Twenty pairs of wise, old-money eyes–from the Devereux board–flitted back and forth as an embarrassed Laurent reclaimed his seat, with deflated self-confidence. Grandfather grinned, nudged him on and Jon had impressed all of the big wigs. This wasn't like that. They'd done the child exchange and kept the talk at a minimum, but they needed to communicate better for Royael's sake.

"I know it's not my week, Raven, but–"

"Royael is at Uncle Oscar's for the weekend. They went camping. You do *remember* my great uncle? He's little brother to Grandpa Otis, the one you left me to mourn all by myself…"

"Move over grumpy!" Annette's voiced in the background, "Come on in, Jon."

Jon walked past Raven into the tiny living room to see Annette seated on the couch, bowl in her lap, snapping peas. Her face lighted when she saw him. *Thank God. Nice to see one Shaw is still happy to see me.* He gave her a hug. "Hey, Granny, how are you?"

"Good, and don't you mind that chile. Raven seems to have lost all her manners these days." Annette rolled her eyes at her grandchild.

"Granny, this is not his weekend." Raven sighed and shut the door. Cutting into their pleasant greeting, she asked, "What is it that you want, Mr. Dubois?"

"I'm going to check on dinner. Jon, you're staying right? I made a chocolate fudge cake, your favorite." Holding her bowl, Annette winked. She passed a glass table with four seats in the small dining room and disappeared into the kitchen.

"Yes, Granny, I'm staying." He smirked at Raven and took a seat on the couch.

"Call her granny one more time. You'll be eating food seasoned with rat poison," she warned curtly, while reclining on the leather chair across from him. "Why are you here? Should you even be rewarded with chocolate, especially since you've taken your girlfriend's side over your daughters?"

"What are you talking about?" He sighed. *Can we have a conversation without anger?*

"You seen the way that dinosaur looked at Royael when finding out about her. How could you fail to mention that?"

I don't know, Raven, maybe because we're not serious. "I spoke with Camille about it. Why did you send those pictures to the gossip magazine?" Her defined shoulders shook as she chuckled. He had to set a frown not to laugh, too.

"The Neanderthal stepped on my foot, not that you care!" Raven looked toward the kitchen to the sound of pots and pans banging, knowing it was a cue from Annette to lower her voice, she did. "My child is not going to be second to one of your little sluts."

"We broke up," he replied, the easiest of lies to his ex-best friend.

"Okay." Raven nodded in satisfaction, then walked toward the door and opened it.

"I'm not leaving. You told me that I'm *usually intelligent*. Thus, I've decided to take advantage of a home cooked meal. It's not every day that I have one. Just so you know, I'm having my chocolate cake, too."

Miss Scandalous

Raven grumbled. Jon smiled. She sat back down across from him, staring him down. They were silently listening to the sound of Annette's content hum and smelling all kinds of deliciousness when her cell vibrated. She answered it. "Hey, babe, I miss you…"

He watched her retreat up the staircase. Legs restless, he thought about Raven with Stephen and went into the green walled kitchen. "Granny, do you need help with anything?"

"Oh, boy, you know I don't need help. It's too tiny anyway." Annette shooed him out.

He backed away slowly as the doorbell rang. *Maybe it's Stephen…that's the only logical reason she wants me gone.* He frowned, just imagining them at the dinner table. Chest out, he opened the door. *It's time to see just how serious Stephen is with Raven–for my child's sake.* A blue sky and a few puffy white clouds were in his line of vision. Eyes glancing downward, he saw a petite woman with a mustard-yellow, long-sleeve dress that fit every curve of her body. When she took off her sunglasses, he instinctively remembered meeting Charlene at the age eighteen. Her hair no longer in Medusa curls; Charlene didn't reek of alcohol, but expensive perfume, Estella's fragrance. Gauging from those beautiful, angry cat-shaped eyes, she realized who *he* was, too.

"Excuse you!" She stormed past him.

He watched her climb the stairs as if she already knew where to go, which was odd because Raven told him that they hadn't spoken since he took her to L.A. to find the woman.

"So you're Royael's father?"

Jon turned back around to see a dark-skinned man, with a goatee and impeccable suit, who stuck his hand out and introduced himself as Damien Wright. As soon as the formalities were complete, Damien sized him up. "Have you been helping with Royael? Financially, I mean?"

"I don't see how that's any of your concern." Jon tried to keep the coldness out of his tone. The man acted like Raven's father.

Damien's mouth set for what Jon knew was a comeback, but the echo of a stampede descended the stairs making them both turn around. Raven had on her I'm-not-listening-face, and it softened for an instant as she hugged Damien.

"Hi, Dad, why didn't you tell me you were coming by? And why'd ya bring *her*," Raven grumbled loudly, with Charlene behind her, trying to apologize for something Jon didn't know. Then her wrath clicked to ON as she frowned at Jon. "Why did *you* open the door?"

Charlene gawked. "Raven, don't refer to me like that. Why are you so buddy-buddy with *him? He* doesn't care about you. I bet *he* hasn't even helped out with Royael!"

Before Jon could retort to the Chihuahua and her equally domineering mother, Annette stood in the dining room, waving her mitted hands. "What's with all this commotion?"

"I came to apologize, but Raven has this thug acting like I shouldn't have been let into the house." Charlene placed her hands on her hips.

I'm far from a thug. Normally he wouldn't have thought about his affluence, multibillion dollar's worth of it. However, the room was too small, making it hard to get a word in while Raven and Charlene threw insults like a sibling rivalry–Serene-versus-Venus-style.

"I could care less about *you*," Raven pointed. "As far as I'm concerned, you are not my mom. Leave now, before I call the police."

"Let's sit and talk about this," Damien interjected, his deep voice momentarily halted the argument. He walked around the coffee table to calm Raven's rattled nerves by rubbing her back. He whispered in her ears and that frown on her face slowly disappeared, but her eyes stayed narrowed and on her target. Turning away from her, Damien said, "Jon, maybe you should go home so we can have a family talk."

"Jon is family." Raven stood in front of him as if shielding him from an unknown horror. He looked over her head at Damien who shrugged.

"*He's not family!* Raven, remember what you told me about the letter. Oh, don't forget the check." Teeth gritted, Charlene sidestepped her daughter and got a few punches in, which, reminded him of a stubborn fly. Jon was stuck in the corner with Raven tugging at her mom and doing a lousy job at stopping the attack.

"Really, asshole." Charlene ranted in between punches. "You tried to get rid of my grandbaby with a check. You can't be family. You're the enemy!"

"Have you lost your mind?" Jon asked. Ready to push Raven–his unnecessary body guard out the way–but Damien pulled Charlene by the waist and told her to chill out.

"Jon was a dumb, rich kid, another teen-father statistic!" Raven's body shook as she spoke to her mom, who stood stunned in her husband's arms. "You were *my mother* and you abandoned me twice!"

Not wanting her mother to get the upper hand in the argument, she grabbed Jon's hand as if they were forming an alliance–saw him as the boy she fell in love with for the sole purpose of rattling Charlene to the core.

"He's a monster, a self-absorbed monster!" Charlene pointed her finger at Jon as Damien held her back. Ranting stopped; her eyes popped out in horror as she looked toward the kitchen and shrieked, "Momma!"

~~~

White light shined down from the hospital ceiling and provided an imaginary thin line, separating them as they sat in a stark white lobby: Charlene and Damien on one side, Raven and Jon on the other. Each man comforted a descendant of Annette Shaw while they waited for an update.

Glaring at her mother while safely snuggled into Jon's chest, Raven felt comforted by the way he held onto her. He'd remembered that all she wanted, *needed*, was his presence. No words, just support. *I'm only playing nice to irritate Charlene. Heck, this might even work in my favor in the greater scheme of things.* That was her mantra. He was her crutch. Contemplating on fulfillment of crossing Jon off the list would keep her pushing forward while her world crumbled before her.

"Damien, this is my fault." Sniffling, Charlene wiped away a stray tear. She hugged him much in the same way that Jon hugged Raven, but Damien didn't hold her back.

He leaned against the chair rest, away from her, and said, "I'm going to call my mom. She's worried about Annette. I need to tell her that Annette had a mild stroke."

Charlene watched him walk around the row of chairs to the sliding glass door, tensing at the sound of Raven's cell phone.

"Stephen...my home?...." Raven hung up the phone, face ashen. She spat the words at her mother, "My house is on fire. It's your fault!"

CHAPTER 27

Orange flames speared the dark sky. Violent flickers highlighted the downstairs windows of the home. As a precautionary measure, the upper half of the home had been drenched as did the townhomes on either side. Mouth agape, Raven watched the destruction from the park sidewalk. Multiple fire trucks and a hoard of men dotted the street aiming water at insatiable flames. It was a sick, hypnotizing scene. If it weren't for glancing at Jon's arm wrap around her shoulder, she wouldn't have known it didn't feel it. Like the fire, she fed on rage.

Charlene was at her side, lips moving. Her face contorted in sadness and guilt. "I'm sorry…"

"No!" Raven moved to the other side of Jon so as not to be touched by her mom.

Royael's baby pictures! The thought struck her like a stray flame. Sprinting across the street with tunnel vision, all she thought of was getting past the firemen to save her daughter's mementos. Then her feet were lifted off the ground as she was grabbed around the waist.

"No, Raven," Stephen pleaded as her legs thrashed in the air.

"Royael's baby pictures!" She tried unwrapping herself from his grip. Overwhelmed with anger, she had to keep reminding herself that he was a friend so as not to pummel him and continue.

"No." He knelt down onto the asphalt, holding her. She allowed his biblical verse to envelop her spirit and pacify her. He continually rubbed her back. Submerged in the darkness of his collarbone, she tuned out the firemen's shouting, the raging fire and the neighbors' empathetic, confused chatter. Concentrating on him, her crying turned into a whimper, finally a sniffle.

When a second voice mimicked Stephen's words, Raven opened her eyes to see Melody as a chubby hand reached out to help her off the ground. Melody hugged her tightly. If only she could stay on the ground, blend in with the asphalt, become nothing… except Melody continued to chant comforting Psalms, and her heart swelled for these two people. They ambled back to the park, sitting Raven down on a swing.

Night blanketed the neighborhood as the last ember went out. The fire chief came over and spoke with her. She nodded her head as he explained that the point-of-fire came from a cup towel on the counter near the stove. Annette's dinner hadn't made it off the stove when they all left for the hospital. She distinctively recalled telling Charlene to turn it off, right after their argument to determine who would ride in the ambulance. Raven didn't even know what she'd said to Charlene, but it was like a slap to the face as Charlene backed out of the ambulance.

Charlene stood at her side listening to the fireman. Raven wanted to push her away, tell her that it was none of her business, yet energy failed her.

Raven rocked back and forth on the swing, watching the crew pack up. She breathed in the lung-abusing smoke, glaring at the yellow tape surrounding the yard as Melody offered to take her home. She shook her head no. When Charlene offered, Raven stood so fast that the swing jerked and went rocking. "I'm not going anywhere with you!"

Charlene sighed, opened her mouth to speak again, but Damien nudged her arm.

"You can't stay here," Stephen said.

"Come home with me," Jon spoke finally.

She'd forgotten he stayed after Stephan came. Finally looking at him, she shook her head. No clear sense of direction, Raven walked to her car. *I'll get a hotel.* The thought of being alone made her shoulder tense as she fumbled with her keys.

Jon leaned against the bent door, looking down at her. "You shouldn't be by yourself tonight."

She didn't relent when he pulled her toward his Range Rover. *He's right.* She couldn't go home with Melody. Right now, she was quite jealous of the woman–her friend. Death, a more inviting notion than being under the same roof with Charlene, made Jon her only choice.

Miss Scandalous

She had no expectations. Settling into the car, she watched Damien corner him right before he opened the driver's door. Even in the dark, there was a glint of concern in her stepdad's eyes as she could just imagine what he told Jon—maybe not, she'd never had a father.

Raven watched dark trees whip by as they ascended into the mountain. *Baby pictures and kindergarten crafts...* Biting her lip to stop a sob, she glanced at Jon from the corner of her eyes. Could he be her rock again—the strength she needed during the storm. Images of his comforting, strong arms holding her up at Brinton Hospital in North Carolina crossed her mind. He'd been the reason she'd coped as a doctor told her that Grandpa Otis had leukemia.

That image was a murmur of hope. Like a white stream of smoke, it floated away.

No. He wasn't her rock. Not anymore, but a means of annoying Charlene.

He also had that aura of certainty about him. She used to love it, now she hated it. But tonight, that seed of self-assurance served a purpose. He'd keep her safe from herself.

~~~

In a daze, Jon pulled in between the Bugatti and the Murcielago. The close connection that he'd seen when Stephen consoled Raven felt tangible. He'd almost gone to her then. Instead, he imagined himself soothing her. He got out of the car, wondering why Stephen hadn't offered to take Raven to his home. Her chunky friend did but not Stephen. *Oh, good Christians don't sleep together.*

In the house, Jon guided her up the stairs to a bridge that led to his master bedroom on the left and guestrooms to the right. Rain drummed down on the skylight as he took her to the first bedroom to the right. He flicked on the light, illuminating a room with olive green walls and potted plants. Not knowing what to say, he told her how to use the system that would darken the glass wall.

When she didn't speak, he went into the adjoining bathroom and turned on the shower. He grabbed a set of towels out of the cabinet and placed them on the glossy white counter. When he walked back into the bedroom, she stood in the center, looking through him.

He rubbed his hand over the waves in his hair. "I'll go find something for you to wear."

Raven nodded, taking a seat on the khaki couch.

Minutes later, she was in the same spot when he came back. He placed a pair of sweats and a T-shirt, from his alma mater next to her. *What to say?* When they were kids, he'd never have a problem turning her frown upside down. Now he, didn't know her.

Since the house would be full of light in the morning, he used the automated switch to close the blinds himself. Steam flowed from the bathroom door. Finally, having nothing constructive to do, he told her good night and was shutting the door when she said his name so faintly.

"Will you lay with me for a while after I shower?"

He had to depend on the movement of her lips as she spoke. *Did she just say that?*

"Please?" Raven looked into his eyes as he hesitated to answer.

"Okay. I'll be back." Jon hurried to his room, pulled off his clothing and kicked off his shoes. Going into the closet, he hastily grabbed a Ralph Lauren pajama set off the shelf. The neatly stacked pile of new pajamas crumpled. Pulling the tag off the pants, he went to take a shower. It wasn't until he'd quickly brushed his teeth that he stopped to laugh at himself. *This is ridiculous! That's my half-sister until I find out otherwise...* He gritted his teeth, cursing Tyriq's inability to find Lucinda.

The melodramatic beat of the rain against the skylight mimicked his heart as he went back to the guestroom. Raven lay in bed, on her side, with her back to him. It was safe to retreat and ignore her plea, but she looked fragile in the large bed. Sighing, he entered and climbed into bed. An inhale of intoxicating mango and papaya perfume sent a flurry of vivid images of their first time together. Inwardly, he cringed. *This is painful. I can't have her. I should've stayed in my room.*

Just before night gave way to day, Jon got up. Off and on

slumbering did nothing for the jitters that consumed him each time he awoke to see if this was real. Back in his room, he got into bed, alone. Warm, heavy eyelids closed only to open wide a while later to the sound of a piercing cry. Hopping out of bed, he rushed back into the guestroom all the while beating himself up for leaving her alone. *Raven had a hectic day. She needs me.*

"Are you okay?" His eyes flitted around her in concern. She sat bolt upright, black hair all over her face, chest heaving.

Shoving her hair back with her fingers, she said, "I'm okay."

"Are you sure?" Uncertainty weighed the pit of his stomach as he sat next to her. Raven lied and that fact was evident when she didn't look at him while replying. He found himself spooning her once again, just until she was okay.

CHAPTER 28

"Hello, Raven. Have a seat." Dr. Stanton nodded toward the grey chaise, her go-to area for serenity. "I'm delighted that I don't have to break out the paper bag today. Am I being premature at assuming that you're progressing?"

"Jon's back," Raven mumbled, recollecting on how he'd stuck to her like glue all weekend. He'd taken her to the townhouse as a fireman guided them around. Nothing was salvageable downstairs. She'd grabbed a singed Mookie off Royael's bed and patted at the soot while feeling Jon's stare. When she'd gone into her room, he'd stood at the door. Back to him, she grabbed the spoon ring and a necklace that Grandpa Otis had given her. Wiping the ash from her hands, she stuffed them into her pocket.

Stanton rubbed the bridge of his nose. "How do you feel about Jon being back?"

"I don't know." Wiping sweaty palms on her jeans, she waited for words of wisdom. When he tipped his chin, a nudge to continue, she sighed. "Jon makes me so angry. Always seeming like a good guy. Now, he thinks he can use money to change everything!" *We were standing in Royael's bleak bedroom, and he said we can go shopping! Really?*

"Take a deep breath, Raven."

"I can't!" Wriggling her fingers, she tried to calm herself. "I saw Elise again. J-just last night!"

"Raven, that's the reason why you need continual counseling." He chimed in as her anxiety wavered.

"I keep seeing Elise! The other night when I was coming from school, I saw the trench coat an-and, I don't know. I think she had on a black wig this time, but, but... to top it off the dreams have come back regularly. I'm so tired of dreaming that I've stabbed Elise with a plastic fork or-or that I pushed her in quick sand, it-it's just too much!"

"The dreams seem to be triggered by the recent stress that you're under."

"But th-the one, the original one, where I dreamed of poisoning her with the toxic flower in her steam room." The hair on the back of her neck prickled. "That one is *always real*. You don't know how many times I've woken up and ran until my lungs almost collapsed! I can't keep dreaming about killing Elise Dubois. I can't keep waking up, scurrying to do an Internet search just to tell me she was alive and sailing on her yacht or doing a *fake-ass*-act-of-kindness for poor kids in Africa."

Stanton put a hand up to pause the crescendo in her argument. "Say this with me…"

She grumbled, but as usual they spoke together: "I did not kill Elise Dubois…" They said over and over again. Each time Raven chanted the words, she felt reality seep into her brain. This was one of the Ten Commandments she had *not* broken.

"Now, close your eyes." Stanton sat back in his seat. Tone a calming breeze, he gave instructions, "Take yourself back to the first time you dreamed of poisoning Elise… Recall how you felt while asleep. Conjure up your first emotion when you awoke… We need to uncover when and why you went from being the victim to feeling so guilty."

Eyes closed, Raven nodded so hard that her ponytail loosened. Her left hand turned the leather wrist-lit on her right wrist until it burned. Stanton had struck the sole reason she didn't seek continuous counseling. She'd hoped he wouldn't get here yet. She opened her mouth to tell the therapist a secret that only two other people knew, and Grandpa Otis wouldn't be admitting it any time soon.

~~~

Jon glanced at the Hello Kitty clock in Royael's new bedroom. An interior decorator had spent the entire day transforming it to suit her HK fetish. From the bed and comforter, dresser, night lamp, even the electronic blinds on the glass wall had been exchanged for a custom Hello Kitty one. He glimpsed at the clock, in two to three minute increments, as Royael jumped on her bed with HK pajamas. She had a clean and fluffed Mookie in one hand and excitedly repeated the words

Jon read from her favorite book.

"You skipped a page." She plopped down next to him.

"I thought you'd rather jump," he replied, turning back a page. Straining, he squeaked the female character's voice. Every time he flipped through the goodnight story, he stared at the clock. *Raven should've been home by now—well, not really home, but back.* Maybe she went to see Stephen after school? As far as Jon knew, she hadn't picked up any—unnecessary—hours at the coffee shop. When he'd stay over to tuck Royael in bed, Monday had always been her free day.

"I'll be right back," he said when the doorbell rang. He walked out of her room, hurried down the steps and to the front door.

"Hi," Raven walked past him and toward the hallway closet.

He watched as she pulled out off a new puffy jacket, rain dropping on the wood floor. She kicked off knee-high boots and tossed them in after the jacket, then closed the door. He opened his mouth to mention the disarray, but thought better of it. "We left you some dinner on the counter."

"I'm not hungry."

"Did you go out?" Not meaning to ask that, he winced while following her up the stairs. His eyes zeroed in on how tightly she clasped her purse with the strap over her shoulder and the leather part tucked under her elbow. *Did she just rob a bank?*

She turned around on the landing and smiled at him. "No, I went to see Granny. I ate icky hospital food."

He didn't believe a single word that past those sexy heart-shaped lips. However, he wasn't in the position to call her out. "I'm going to put Royael to bed. When you get a chance, check out her new room."

~~~

Raven watched Jon slip into Royael's room and closed the door as if brushing her off.

'Maybe because he knows you're a liar?'

Well, I did go see Granny.

'Mind mentioning your visit with Dr Stanton? And that 'guilty bit' of info, eh?'

Disregarding the voice, Raven glanced down the long, shadowy corridor. They'd walked up the stairs in the dark and he'd left her in the dark.

Elise! She couldn't shake the image of green eyes peering at her from the end of the hall. Quick, shaky fingers, she snapped on the light to see a colorful oil painting of Koi fish. *Disturbia?* She searched the picture frantically, reasoning that it had to be the green bubbles in the water.

In the privacy of her room, she rummaged through her purse and pulled out the pills that Dr. Stanton prescribed. He'd only given them to her with a promise of weekly sessions. Her hands shook as she tried to unscrew the top. She jerked at the safety and the pills shot out and onto the bed. Grabbing the closest one, she took it frantically, hearing his words, "Now, tell me, how you went from being the victim to feeling so guilty."

CHAPTER 29

The flowery wall paper was covered by tacked five-year-older drawings. It added comfort to Annette's room at the nursing home. "Sanford and Son" was on the TV while Red Fox exaggerated a heart attack and his son looked on, not amused. With a chuckle, Annette shook her head and grabbed the remote to mute the show as her daughter entered the room.

Charlene grinned back but put her hand to her lips and mouthed, "shhh." She pulled the stroller over to the sliding glass window on the far side of the wall and pulled up the stroller umbrella to shield Trinity from the sunlight. Then gave her mom a hug. "Hey, Momma."

"My baby." Annette patted Charlene's face.

"Momma, I'm so sorry…." Throat constricted, Charlene's voice broke. *If only I hadn't come over, yelling at Raven…if only I had believed my daughter in the first place!* A mixture of anger at Barbie and guilt at her own gullibility gnawed her heart as she plopped down on a seat.

"Child, stop all that apologizing. I'm not mad at you. You're my daughter, I love you."

"I'm the reason you're here," she murmured.

"I'm getting old. You know that. Raven, she doesn't want to know it, but I am." Annette patted her hand. "Don't tell her you're sorry anymore. She's not that type of girl. If you want to work through your issues with Grumpy, you've just got to have a heart to heart. She's stubborn and needs…speaking of the Grump."

Charlene turned from her smile to see Raven at the door.

"Hey, Granny." Raven kissed Annette. Ignoring Charlene, she walked to the stroller and peered at the sleeping baby. Finally, giving her mother the stink-eye, she said, "I missed my little sister."

"Wow, I been here a whole week." Annette smirked. "I was beginning to think ya'll organize a schedule to come at a different time."

Scrapping against the floor broke the silence as Raven scooted the visitor chair away from Charlene's. Annette rubbed at the annoyance in her eardrum, and said, "Both of ya'll need to rest."

"What are you talking about, Momma? I've been on break from the show for a while now."

"*And I* had to take last semester off school." Raven rolled her eyes at Charlene. "Thank God Jon came around. I'm catching up on classes."

It took all Charlene's strength not to suck her teeth.

"I don't mean a *physical* rest. I mean a *spiritual* rest. God don't want ya'll to go through life suffering. Char, you're having trouble with your marriage at home and you," Annette turned her attention to her grandchild, "you're just as angry and unforgiving as you were the day Jon left you pregnant."

Raven huffed.

"How did you know about Damien?" Charlene asked.

"It's all in the gossip mags, but you can't blame me. That Miguel-*Sexy-Ass*-Sanchez is fiooone!" Raven battered her lashes, and then added, "Though, I don't like the way you treating my stepdad."

"Sometimes I wished I would've gone upside yo' head more as a child," Annette chided, she turned to Charlene. "And your head less, Char, because it got you acting all self-loathsome. Put more faith in your marriage. Stop bossing that man around and let him be in charge."

"Preach!" Raven's bangles clanked as she clapped her hands together.

"Raven, I don't know what you talkin' about, because you're just as bossy as she is, if not more. Running around drinking, don't think I didn't hear Stephen carrying you home that one time. And, Jon, you so evil to that boy it's a shame. You can forgive him. Every time I see Royael running around learning something new, dancing and looking so beautiful in pageants or recitals, I just think, he's missed out. That's something he's going to have to forgive himself for. Besides, God doesn't need *no* help judging. Put your faith in God that Jon has come back for a reason."

"He didn't *come back*, I went and got him," Raven spoke under her breath.

"Chile, I'm an inch away from making you go outside to grab a switch off one of them trees. I'm feeling strong enough to swat them legs," she pointed, frowning. "Jon could be signing a check every month and puttin' it in the mail, but he wants to be with you and Royael. Why would he let you move in after the fire?"

"I didn't move in. I've been there for only five days."

"Okay, Grumps, whatever you say. I swear, Otis was the only one that could knock some sense into you. You're as hardheaded as the day is long." With shaky fist, Annette grumbled. Nerves settling, she looked back and forth from her family. "I want both of ya'll to do something for me."

"Yes, Momma," Charlene said.

"Yes, Granny," Raven sighed, stretching each letter.

"Get up and hug one another. Forgive and forget."

They both stood.

Raven wrung her fingers then shook her head, staring at the ceiling. She rushed out of the door, saying, "Sorry, Granny."

Charlene shuttered, watching Raven leave. *God, what do you want me to do! Why must I suffer?*

"She'll come around," Annette assured.

"No, she won't. I thanked God the first time; I've done too much harm. My recent foolishness is just the icing on the cake." She ended with, again, apologizing for coming to her momma's house and acting crazy.

"I understood about the Trinity photos, you just needed to come talk things through, Charlene. You're forgiven." Annette said. When Charlene nodded, she took her daughter's chin in her hand and said, "Look at me, Char. Don't bring it up no more. Don't think about that or the fire. Stop tormenting yourself."

Whimpering, Charlene added, "I know, Momma. I'd just gotten her to forgive me for not helping Otis and for ruining her life with Jon, but, I messed up again."

"Help with Otis?" Annette's eyes clouded with confusion, and then brightened. "Oh, I forgot, she went to L.A. to see if you were a blood cell donor for Otis."

She felt hopeless as if she'd dug her own grave and all she had left to do was let one foot dangle over the edge and poetically step inside. "I left you to raise Raven with…with Otis. He hated me and I left my baby with him."

"Hush. Otis hated himself when he got to drinking. He never hated you."

"Otis hated you for cheating," she blurted. *I was Daddy's Princess and when he got drunk, he hated me.* She could've gotten over Jonathan cheating with Elise or even the day Elise came to show her a big engagement ring. The words Daddy had said shoved her out the door the next day.

"I didn't *cheat* on Otis." Annette's eyebrows furrowed. "I admit it was my fault."

"Then why did Da–Otis want us to leave? Why didn't he love me anymore?"

"Girl, do you know how many times Otis cried over you disappearing?" she asked, head cocked to the side. "As a youngster, Otis was an awful drunk. Hell, me too. Then we moved to Bellwood, got jobs, and joined church. One day, his best friend, Devlin, a man that ran in the crowd we used to, came around needing a place to stay. Devlin acted like he wanted to turn his life around. Being Otis's longest friend, Otis helped him get a job, let him stay with us until he could get on his feet…"

Charlene's eyes widened, knowing where her mother's story was going as she remembered her dad arguing with Annette the day before she ran away. *Daddy was mad about Devlin…he raped Momma!*

"I'd been pregnant time and time before," Annette paused. She couldn't say that she'd waited for Devlin's child to die in her womb like all Otis's children. There had always been that seed of doubt, and some part of her being wanted Charlene.

"That's not your fault, Momma." She wiped at tears forming in her eyes.

"I knew Dev was evil. Heck, when we use to drink, something about him always had my spirit conflicted, but I just didn't take heed. Now listen here, you couldn't help Otis. Raven loved him and I understand you not wanting to tell her that you couldn't help him, but you just have to."

Charlene shook her head no. *It's no use.*

"She's holding you accountable for too many wrongs."

"No. Otis was the only man in her life who never abandoned her..."

~~~

Aisle. B. 3. Aisle B-3... The words rung in her head as Charlene drove home from the nursing home. She glanced through the rearview mirror to see Trinity's big, brown eyes. She drove down a street divided by manicured trees and against her better judgment, pulled into the parking lot of the grocery store. After parking, she reached over to the glove compartment and pulled out the scarf and Fendi Aviators she always wore when going incognito. She adjusted the silk scarf around her head, tying it under her neck.

Her phone rang. Reaching into her purse, she pulled it out. The screen indicated a blocked call. She knew exactly who it was—the only invited costar from Loyalties that did not come to her wedding. *And he should've come, so his imagination could become reality....* Biting her lip, she ignored Miguel and put the phone back. Her insides flushed hot with primal desire. *What was I just doing?* The fuzziness working its way through her brain gradually cleared. She slipped on her shades and glanced in the mirror. *I don't recognize myself...*She got out and closed the door, then opened the backdoor.

Trinity smiled as she unlatched the car seat straps. She held her child on her hip and pressed the lock button before walking into the store. Grabbing a complementary disinfectant napkin next to the carts, she wiped off the handrail and placed Trinity into the seat. She gingerly kissed her daughter's cheek and walked through the store.

Background music played and the air condition sent goose bumps down her arms as she strolled down the meat section. When a butcher started for her direction, Charlene hurried passed. Maybe taking the long route wasn't a good idea. She hastened past Aisle B-3 and stopped abruptly, eyes zipping side to side. A couple walked hand-in-hand down the aisles. In the opposite direction, a woman with gray hair checked the date on a carton of skim milk.

I'm invisible.

Taking three steps back, she turned down Aisle B-3. Breath caught, she was engulfed by endless shelves of alcohol. Her eyes trailed the margarita mix. Weak. Brown liquor. Too manly. She stopped at the vodka. In hesitance, she reached out and felt the cool, sleek glass.

CHAPTER 30

*G*old... Raven's legs flashed before Jon's mind as he flipped the perfect pancake and checked on the sizzling bacon. He thought about their bizarre first week together. Monday night, she'd come home with a vice grip on her purse. Tuesday, she'd slipped in just before dawn. Wednesday, she'd helped him put Royael to bed. Taking the pancake off the griddle, he smiled, remembering their pillow fight with their child. On Thursday, he considered retracting the "Chihuahua" moniker as they sat and watched a Die Hard flick that evening.

Today, Sunday, he'd woken early, needing pancakes to survive her sudden transformation. Placing the crispy bacon on a napkin, he turned off the skillet and poured batter for a new pancake. He walked to the sliding glass wall and leaned on the open apparition. Breathing in fresh air, he wondered if her new mannerisms would last. *I can't take much more of this rollercoaster of emotions.*

"I'm beginning to think that pancakes and bacon are the only things you can cook."

Jon turned toward Raven's soft voice. Arms folded across her PJ shirt, she smiled, appearing well rested, despite her late nights. *Maybe that's it? Raven's trying to adjust to this place.* Smiling back, he hoped she was finally comfortable here. They needed a sense of camaraderie for Royael's sake. He walked to the stove and flipped the pancake, just in time.

"You cooked pancakes the other night for dinner, didn't you?" In fuzzy slippers that matched her pants, she walked over and peered at the thick, creamy batter as he poured another serving.

"Yup." He wanted to ask why she stayed out late. As far as he knew, the photography school didn't have classes that ended well into the night.

"Royael is getting chunky. She might look like you did as a child." She dipped a finger in the batter and smeared it across his cheek. "No more pancakes."

"Raven." He laughed, dipped his hand in the bowl and flicked the batter in her direction.

She ran toward the sink, dodging it. She picked up the sink sprayer and turned back around. "You want to play?"

"No, don't do it." He put his hands up in defeat. She had that teasing glint in her eyes that he remembered so well. "You started it."

"Say you're sorry."

"You're sorry," he replied with a devilish smile.

"All right, sucker." She let the water spray across his T-shirt.

"It's cold!" He grabbed a copper pot from the overhead rack and did a lousy job at blocking her erratic spraying as he walked toward her. Her laughter was contagious as they tussled for the slipper sprayer. Pulling it away, he lifted it behind her and poured it down the neck of her shirt.

Raven's eyes widened in shock, giggling so hard, she could barely get the words out, "Wh-what the hell. That is c-cold."

He reached past her and flicked the faucet off. Water dripped from their clothes and the onyx counters, forming puddles on the wood floor. Knowing how she always played dirty, he warned, "We're even. Okay? No more."

"Truce," she nodded.

"Truce." He gave her a hug, patting the water that ran down her back.

"You're cruel," she whispered in his ear.

Time ceased as he inhaled her. He couldn't take his arms from around her. Her hands glided up his neck and his own scorched the contours of her waist. Gripping her hips, he lifted her. In one fluid motion, her legs wrapped around him and her wet body compressed to his. Needy lips found their match. Years had done nothing to make him forget his obsession's satin tongue as theirs danced in hunger.

"Daddy, Mommy, ya'll burnin' the pancakes!"

The force field that magnetized them separated when they jumped, noticing Royael in the doorway. Jon strode toward the stove to toss the blackened pancake into the wastebasket and Raven headed toward the door. His hand went to his lips, trying to save the feeling. *Damn, Raven's my half-sister until Lucinda, the maid, tells me otherwise*, Jon reminded himself.

~~~

Jon got off the elevator at work with a carafe full of cappuccino that Raven made. She'd said he had a top-of-the-line machine, better than the one at her job. She'd laughed at him when he told her he couldn't use it, and then made him some on the condition that he didn't give any to his secretary.

"Good mornin', Pat."

"Good morn-*ing*, Mr. Dubois." Patricia's silver eyebrows were bunched together. He'd never been late, but then again she'd never heard his North Carolina accent. Or maybe it could be that he chose to wear a polo-shirt and slacks instead of the usual three-piece suit. Either way, her squinted eyes tracked him to his office door. "There's a board meeting in twenty minutes. Your files have been placed on your desk."

He turned on Gucci loafers. *A board meeting?* "Cancel it."

In his office, he took a gulp of the drink and clicked on the calendar icon to see he'd indeed inputted a meeting for today. Exiting the calendar, he clicked on the Internet and searched Raven Shaw, pressed on the link to her university portfolio. There were different pictures from people to nature to objects. He looked at nature pictures with a similar setting from the woods behind his house. Continuing, he saw photos of a man that had tattoos all over his body. Jaw clinched, he clicked out of those, not amused.

His mind went to the solo she did at church just yesterday. He liked the songs–except, for her solo. The chorus went something like, "I wanna be with you." All thought the lyrics meant being with Jesus, he felt a tinge of jealousy when Raven took a seat at the piano next to Stephen and they harmonized.

RING.

Trying to get the scene of them singing to each other out of his mind, Jon answered the phone as cheerfully as possible.

"You *canceled* the board meeting?" Pierre's voice didn't mirror the cheeriness.

"There weren't any new proposals to discuss. The architect is working on the blueprints for the D Hotel in Chicago." Jon sat ramrod straight. "Everything is on track for the Orlando opening."

"I've been told that you took last week off. Did you have a great vacation? Where did you go?" Pierre's tone fluctuated, a world renowned traveler, interest piqued.

"I didn't go anywhere," Jon replied, knowing Grandfather would rather hear him talk about a voyage. Being selective about his words, he told Pierre about Royael and Raven.

"Are they staying with you?"

"Yes." *Is that all you have to say? I said your grandbaby is a great ballet dancer and how beautiful she is and...*

"Hmmm. Don't let them interfere with your work..."

CHAPTER 31

Gobbling the pills that Dr. Stanton prescribed had been heaven for the first couple of nights–a forgetful blur. The premonition of a trench coat Elise was gone for good. Energy high, anger low. Raven lived the best of both worlds, until realizing she hadn't slept a wink. No, she'd been living a nightmare–a fluffy-calming-sleepless-nightmare. She looked at the Hello Kitty clock and forced Royael to go to bed.

"I want Daddy to tuck me in!" She scrambled to the other side of her large bed and away from her mommy's grasp. "Daddy always reads. Daddy always tucks me in!"

"Royael, please," *I can't take this.* Jon had said he wasn't coming home tonight in a text message. *I know we've only been here for a week, but he has to have some type of schedule, for Royael. Or I suffer the consequences.*

"No!" Royael pulled a book from under a feather pillow.

Snatching the book, Raven plopped down and read the words in a quick breath. Stopped every time Royael commented about how Jon read it, she exclaimed, "Enough! It's time for bed, Royael."

Raven chanted the goodnight prayer with her child, still angry that Jon hadn't come home. Maybe he knew that she couldn't sleep and stayed away? The last couple of nights he'd stayed up with her watching Bruce Willis flicks. *I've been trippin'! He's probably confused? This is going to ruin the plan.* Before she could extract revenge, Jon needed to feel comfortable.

Royael was tightlipped as Raven hugged her goodnight. She closed the bedroom door, still remembering that Sunday morning. They'd acted like teenagers. That kiss. *Yeah, he's probably confused.*

Ambling downstairs, she went to the exercise room. The pills had changed her morning five mile run into a nightly run. Running ridded her of the annoying voice. After a lung crushing sprint, arm screaming pushups, and sets of ruthless crunches, she went upstairs still pumped. *These effing pills are a trip!* She'd taken extra care to leave the light in the hallway on. At nighttime, the Koi painting at the end of the hallway reminded her of Elise.

Going into her bedroom, Raven grabbed a pair of pajamas. Noticing her phone vibrating on the nightstand—she'd forgotten to turn the volume up after class—, she answered. "Hey, babe."

"Hi," Bill sounded stressed.

"Are you okay? How was the uh… event in Los Angeles? Did your professor present his findings to the medical board?" She wracked her brain for more information about what Bill told her. She'd been trying to kick Jon out of her house the day Bill left. *That happened the day of the fire. Aw, shit, I forgot to tell Bill about the fire!*

"I went by your house."

"O-oh, I-you were busy at the…the seminar." *Yes, the seminar. That's right!* "I called—"

"You didn't leave a message about your home burning down," his voice raised an octave. "I had to talk with the neighbors. Look, Raven, we need to talk."

"Yes." Eyes wide, she sank onto the cushiony couch.

"I can't do this anymore. You're in love with Jon."

"No, I'm not," the words sputtered out of her mouth. *He's my half-brother!*

"He has that look…like he did when we were in high school. He still wants you. I can't compete with him." Before she could protest, Bill continued with a stutter, "I l-love you, Raven, and you love him. I seen ya'll at church, lo-looking h-happy. Like a *family*."

"Bill, please…" Raven took in her reflection in the dresser mirror. Biting her lip, she recalled yesterday's service. Stephen and Melody had encouraged her to do a solo, to help her through the fire ordeal. *Those pills had me agreeing to everything!* Singing had felt like a boulder was lifted from her shoulders. Using her voice for the Lord had always made her feel good in the past. It wasn't her fault that Jon wanted to go to church and got to benefit from her good spirits! *Effing pill probably made me kiss him too! What's wrong with me?*

'Everybody keeps lovin' and leavin' ya,' the voice quacked. She turned from the mirror in shame.

"I've been busy and will take some blame, but you've loved him even at the worst of times. When we graduated from high school and—" Bill didn't know the full story and his words went from despair to an edge as he concluded, "Jon's always going to be first."

"Bill, come see me." Anxiety rippled through her soul. *I need you.* She paced toward the glass wall, looking at the dark stretch of trees into nothingness.

"Do you know how difficult it was to watch you in church when you sat next to him after service? Ya'll were so close…I have to go."

"Bye, Bill," she whispered and clicked the phone off.

Taking the stairs two at a time, she went down the long corridor into the kitchen, flipping on the lights. Heart pounding and hands clinched in fists, she searched through the drawers. Bingo, she found a wine opener. Going into the pantry, her eyes traced an array of wines on the showcase.

"Eeny, meeny, miny, moe." She grabbed one, used the wine opener and tugged until it popped. White wine splattered all over. She took a swig. *Uh-uh too dry.* Pushing the cork into the nozzle—as best as she could—, she put it back on the rack. She opened bottle after bottle, until finding the best one. *Wow, this wine is older than I am, but it taste so good….*

She grabbed a glass off the top display case and walked out of the kitchen and back up the stairs. At the bridge, she turned left to Jon's bedroom. Feeling for the light, she flicked it on. She stopped to stare at the large bed in the center of the room. There were glossy, colorful paintings on the walls.

She stepped onto clay tile, into a breathtaking Mediterranean-style bathroom, and past double sinks with wooden basins. Turning the knobs for the infinity tub, she wondered how long it would take for it to overflow. With one push of a button, the overlooking fireplace came to life. *I need this.* Her gaze traveled over a duo of French bath bottles. She opened one and poured the citrus and woodsy scented liquid into the bath. It instantly foamed up.

Stripping off her clothes, she got into the hot water. Bubbles soothed and tickled her chin. Instead of using the crystal wine glass, she drank from the bottle. Reaching with her big toe, she turned off the chrome sprout as water started to splash over the sides. It didn't seem logical to keep the thing running and rack up the bill, even if her name wasn't on it. She chugged it. *Should've gotten two…* The bottle clattered when she leaned an arm over and let it drop from her fingertips. A tipsy-grin crossed her lips as she laid back and let steamy suds nurture her wounds.

~~~

Jon tugged off his slacks, letting it drop next to his polo on the floor of his bedroom. His mind kept replaying Pierre's earlier conversation. Deciding not to come home tonight had been ridiculous. Why did he care about Grandfather's view of Raven? Pierre lived all the way in France.

About to slip out of his boxers, Jon heard music. For the first time he noticed light seeping from the bottom of the double doors to the bathroom and opened one to see black hair flowing over the side of the tub. Raven lay in his tub. Steam rose, leaving her face with a glistening glow. Her eyes were closed and heart-shaped lips agape.

"What are you doing?" He asked, stepping closer.

"Wh-what are you doing *here*?" Blue eyes popped open and water sloshed over the sides of the tub as she almost hopped up.

"What do you mean, 'what am I doing here?' I live here." His self-consciousness rose about being in boxers, but she gave an I-don't-give-a-flip glare and nestled back, eyes closed.

"Grab me another bottle of that?" Her hand flickered toward the empty wine bottle.

"That's a twenty *thousand* dollar bottle of wine!"

"So? It didn't do the trick. I prefer the same, please." She peeked at him as if still feeling his presence. He didn't respond. She sighed. "Give me your cheap stuff, but at least try and get one that tastes similar…pah-leez."

"I'm not your connoisseur and no, I *will* not." Jon walked away to the sound of her giggling.

Awhile later, he set up the racks for the pool table, muttering, "I had to take a shower in a guestroom in my own damn house."

Wrestling with the strings on a new pair of pajama pants, he mentally calculated the angle of the striped blue ball. Jon got into position with the pool stick, but a slurred, sultry tune stopped him. Raven's singing rose as she entered the game room. Her bare feet padded against the glossy wood while she sang off key, teetering left and then to the right on a high note. The bottle of wine in her hand tilted, red liquid spilled in each direction that she moved.

She stopped singing and noticed him. "I recorded all the Die Hard films; let's watch 'em."

His eyes cut away from her happy demeanor to the wine. She'd found another expensive bottle.

"This is awe-some! It's the last of the good stuff. We need to go shopping and restock." She took a swig, leaning back with it.

"You can't buy that in America. Besides, it's for special clients."

"Sorry." The tipsy grin fell flat. "Guess I'm not special enough."

"I didn't mean it that way." His thick eyebrows furrowed at her pout.

She giggled then pulled a pool stick off the rack. "Wooow. Okay, um, I'm going to hit the orange ball, like my toe nail polish, hehehe."

"Are you all right?" His tensed shoulders deflated. *Why's she drinking so much, alone?*

Raven aimed, the stick went left and then right of the ball. "Let's make a bet."

"You won't win." He leaned against a chrome bar stool, arms folded, watching the scene.

"How do *you* know?" She pointed at him, about twenty degrees off.

"You've been going at that same ball for about five minutes and it's red." He walked over and tried to take the stick.

"Don't touch me!" Raven waved it around.

"Stop it." Again he went for it as she neared a fire glass figure that cost a poor man's fortune. Seconds later, he cringed when the artwork shattered on the wood floor. "Damn, Raven! Why are you messing with everything?"

"Why are you here? You left that *B to the S* story on my phone earlier," she grumbled.

"This is my house," he reminded her. "I can come and go as I please!"

"Whatever, I'm out." She started to move when he tossed her over his shoulders. Hitting him in the back with her fist, she exclaimed, "Let me go!"

"You're going to step in broken glass." By the time he got into the hallway, she'd clawed at his back so much that he placed her down with a smidge of force. "What the hell is wrong with you?"

"*You.*" She pointed slightly off target again. "You and all you stupid men! You just want me for a minute–a hot minute–then you're off to something…better."

A leaf on a windy day, she climbed up the stairs and he held his arms out ready to make sure she wouldn't fall. He breathed freely when she sank down on the fourth step.

Head in hands, Raven said, "He broke up with me."

Jon huffed, knelling in front of her. *They'd seemed so happy singing together a day ago.*

She added a barely audible, "Nobody wants me."

"I want you," he heard his voice say, though he shouldn't.

"No!" Chin jutted, she pushed his chest and stood. "Not you. I won't ever forgive you."

The tears streaming down her face made his heart ache. He leaned forward to hug her and help her from teetering around. "Raven, you're drunk."

"You walk around acting like you're so good; shoving money in my face, tryna cover up your sins and that letter. I woulda never thunk to kill *our* baby!"

It wasn't the most opportune time to bring up family secrets–there never seemed to be the right time. Mustering courage, he said, "I have to tell you something."

"Save it, Jon. I won't ever forgive you!"

He bit his lip and watched her retreat. *Maybe she won't?*

CHAPTER 32

It was Tuesday again. Tuesdays had once been reserved for hitting the gym and going to lunch with Mom. Now it was the day after Raven had become the ultimate nutcase. Marley's words plagued her all the while she'd lashed out at Jon. She got out and the slammed door. Digging a hand into her purse, she rummaged for loose change and placed it in the meter as a vision of Jon's face coursed through her brain. *Damn those effing pills! They're ruining my plan! How am I going to live with the enemy and entrap him if he steers clear of me?* His guard needed to be down in order for retribution to work, but the pain in his hazel eyes when she'd finished her raving said it was now titanium.

The warm May sun beamed down on the big umbrellas over tables at the bistro in front of her. Chatter crowded her ears as she weaved through the linen-top tables to Damien.

He stood in a cream suit and gave her a hug. Taking a seat, he said, "I ordered your favorite chicken salad as a bribe for you to come to dinner tonight."

"Gosh, I thought we were just enjoying lunch." Raven smirked. "I do not want to see *her*."

"I've talked to you about holding grudges until I'm blue in the face." He took a deep breath as she folded her arms. Then he proceeded with extreme tactics. "Be kind to one another, tender–"

"Yes, Yes!" Raven rushed the rest of the words. "...tenderhearted, forgive one another as Christ forgave you. Ephesians 4:32. Thanks, Dad. *She's* seeing Miguel. Why are you even tryna help?"

"Hmmm, I'm glad you know your Bible. Mind regarding its instruction?" He asked. When that sneer didn't go away, he continued, "After Char went to rehab, I made a promise to get the two of you back together. It's been difficult, you and Char made sure of that, but I won't back down."

Blame it on the pills, her insides ran hot and cold while they ate and Damien made his case. He did a good job at providing witty replies to her terse retorts. He even showed a grin of satisfaction to their playful disagreement as he grubbed on catfish.

"All right." She tossed her cloth on the table as he smiled triumphantly. *What have I got to lose?*

'Certainly not a mother.'

"Where will this shindig take place?"

"We bought the house," Damien replied.

"Bad investment," she smirked.

~~~

Jon wasn't home when she arrived. Usually late for everything, Raven took the time to redo Royael's hair and dress her like a little doll in one of the new dresses in her closet.

'You're stalling…'

I am not. Royael has to wear all these expensive clothes before she can't fit them! Her insides curled as she contemplated what Jon had wanted to tell her.

"Mommy, are we going to a pageant or somethin'?" Royael pulled away from Raven's continuous primping.

Raven didn't have to look outside to know it had gotten dark, as dusk came over Royael's bedroom. Propped up on a plethora of pillows, Mookie had a six o' clock shadow. She flipped on the window thingamajigs for the glass wall. Snail-paced, she packed Royael into the car and drummed her fingers on the steering wheel. Finally, Raven went without him.

~~~

Sitting on the porcelain toilet lid, Charlene rubbed the vodka bottle across her face. Still sealed since she'd bought it, she could almost taste the clear, toxic liquid. *God, have I blown my last chance?*

The sound of footsteps in the master bedroom made Charlene shove the bottle of vodka in the wicker-basket amongst her husband's dirty socks and undershirts.

The bathroom door opened and Damien's head peeped inside. He assessed her silk robe with raised eyebrows. "Raven should be here any minute. Get dressed."

The door closed just as quickly as her heart sunk. *Why won't Damien talk to me?* She knew the uncertainty and worry of seeing Raven and Royael was evident on her face. Oh, Royael, she hadn't seen the child since rattling the girl's pink tutu. *Oh, I may have scarred my granddaughter for life!*

Dragging herself off the toilet, Charlene walked out of the bathroom and headed for the closet. She pressed the switch inside the door and the clothes zipped around. Stopping it, she pulled out tweed trousers. Dressing quickly, her arms prickled when the doorbell chimed. Moving to the windows, she pulled back purple drapes and saw Raven's raggedy car across the street.

"Dear God," she paused at a lack for words. "Please put it in Raven's heart to forgive me for my last outburst. Bring our family together, give us grace…"

Hand on the doorknob, she turned it, taking a deep breath and walked out of the room just as Royael bounded up the stairs with a frown on her face. *Please don't hate me…* "What's wrong?"

"I wanted to show Daddy my baby auntie, *but* Mommy didn't wait for him."

"Sorry about that," Charlene breathed easy. She put an arm around her grandbaby, and they walked to the nursery. The room smelled of baby lotion. Trinity sat in her crib, amongst a throng of stuffed animals and raised her hands when she saw them enter.

"Wow, she's *fat!*" Royael giggled, looking through the wooden bars.

"Yes, Trinity loves to eat," Charlene grabbed the baby under her arms and hoisted her on her hip. They went downstairs as questions from A-Z flew out of Royael's mouth.

"I don't know the answer to that, Royael," Charlene said as they entered the dining room. She stopped short to see her daughter seated at the table and tuned out Royael's inquisitiveness. Gulping, she watched as Raven arose with that unreadable face she'd almost gotten use to seeing.

Raven smiled at Trinity as she held arms out. Kissing Trinity's chubby cheeks, Raven said, "I missed you so much, little sister."

"I'll sit Trinity down." Damien appeared from the kitchen with cartons of upscale take-out food.

Not taking her eyes off Raven, Charlene stood there, arms limp. Inside she prayed hard as time seemed to freeze. A mixture of Roy Timmons and Marcus Webber's voices taunted her. Raven seemed to fade away before Charlene as she pleaded with God to rid her brain of her tormentors. Feeling Raven's arms around her, Charlene cried so hard that her body shook.

"It's okay, Mom," Raven whispered in her ear as she sobbed. "Go ahead and eat without us. Me and Mom are going for a walk."

Raven guided her out the French doors. Marcus's and Roy's words dimmed as they ambled down the patio stairs and around the pool. Rays of sunshine seeped through the trees and enveloped them while they trekked over crunchy leaves through the woods. They stopped at the lake shore.

"Water always brings me peace," Raven said after a moment.

Charlene nodded, throat tight. All she could do was inwardly bless Jesus as she watched her child pick up a pebble from the muddy bank.

"Good." Charlene remarked as a rock skimmed across the peaceful water, creating a rippled effect. "I haven't done this in years. Not since Bellwood, at the meadow past Main Street, but you have to travel the bank a mile or so. That's where it's most private, beautiful."

"Jon and I use to skip rocks there. It was our meadow." Raven used flawless technique. The pebble rippled across the water, sending a few ducks soaring. She giggled at their quacking. "Opps."

"Pretty good, Raven, though you might get a ticket for animal cruelty. I think I can do better."

"I doubt it, but let's see whatcha got." Raven waved for her to proceed.

And she did, starting an all out war—a frenzy of rock skipping. They joked and argued about whose pebble bounced the most and went the farthest. At a truce, they sunk down into the tall, sweet-smelling grass. Wet, warm mud seeped through her designer trousers and ruined her blouse, but Charlene could care less.

CHAPTER 33

She needed this bonding. After astonishment mixed with a smidge of jealousy–the competiveness in Raven– and happiness that her mom had won the skipping rocks, they'd eaten dinner. Finishing the night, they'd chatted for hours. The days following, they talked every day, and Raven dropped her mom off at the airport when she had to go back to L.A.

It took too much out of her to hate more than one person on the list. Her emotions wouldn't be perpetually switched to OFF. Now, Raven had could focus her rage on Jon without becoming overwhelmed. Unfortunately, Jon's leave to supervise the progress of the Orlando D Hotel presented another problem. Wednesday was awful. Raven had stayed up late like normal after having taken the pills. By the crack of dawn, she knew he wouldn't come home. Due to an issue with the opening date of the hotel, so he'd stayed all weekend. After putting a cranky Royael to bed on the following Thursday, she walked through the house, arms around her chest. His scent everywhere, she wondered what to do with him.

The next morning, she sat in the parking lot of the Devereux building, tapping on a tin lunchbox and watching the clock on the dash. Time continued as the voice mentally abused her for this new tactic, this *extreme* change in her plan of revenge.

Finally, she mustered enough courage to go inside. Her stretchy jeans and "drama" tee with a glittery crown didn't fit in with the attire, but she'd been indecisive all morning. Knowing that the voice was probably correct, she squeezed into a crowded elevator before it could shut and had to deftly turn around with the lunchboxes pressed to her abdomen.

All alone at the top floor, she stopped just outside of Jon Dubois's office. Looking through the French doors, she noticed the same secretary. *I've got something for you, old hound.*

"Good morning." Pearly whites on display, Raven strolled into the room. "Please, before you have anything to say. I've come with a piece offering."

"I wondered when you'd be back." A free smirk came with Patricia's sarcasm as she looked at both tin lunch boxes Raven placed on the table. When Raven opened the one with Hello Kitty, she added, "I'm not much for HK memorabilia. There's not a bomb in there or anything of the sort?"

"No." Raven turned the box to her and slid it over.

"If Mr. Dubois is not going to throw you out, then who am I to do so?" Shrugging, she grinned. "Heck, I kinda liked how you put Jon in his place. He's been different since you came around–good different. Thanks."

Raven picked up the second tin box, grasped the door handle and opened it. The sound of typing stopped as Jon looked up at her, huffed and leaned back in the chair. Smile shaky and borderline plastic like Royael's had been all week. Brain fogged, she said, "Uh, I brought a mud pie."

At the glint of anger in his eyes, she bit her lip. *Oh, no!* She instantly remembered the mud pie joke. The last time she'd teased him about it was on her eighteenth birthday, and he'd tossed her into the Atlantic Ocean. They'd been five when she made him a "mud" pie. Annette refused to give him extra fudge cake since Elise had complained about his weight. Raven had used dirt, took out all the twigs, and guaranteed him that it would be just like chocolate, his favorite.

"It's not a… well, it is a…" She opened the box and sat it on the table. If she had to critique her work, this was the best she'd ever made. *Look inside the box!* Biting her lip, Raven went back to a time when she was little, helping Annette with Sunday dinner. She'd asked why they couldn't eat hotdogs like she did with Grandpa Otis and Uncle Oscar when camping. Annette had said, "Soul food brings the family together. Watch when chubby Jon comes over and tell me if you don't see him smiling so bright when he eats." *If he'd just eat a slice of this, maybe we can be friends again.*

He cleared his throat.

"Jon Dubois," Raven started, clearing the memory of a fatter version of him chowing down. She took a seat at the chairs across from him. "I apologize for the way I acted."

"You're forgiven." His gaze went back to the computer, face carved of ice.

Pushing past the hesitancy and the voice that kept ranting about the list, she walked around the desk. Touching his large hands, the typing stopped. "I'm sorry."

"I said it's okay."

Broad shoulders squared, his blasé attitude froze her insides. Bones. Heart. Soul. She whimpered. "It's not okay. I do stupid things when I'm drunk."

"Correction," his angular jaw tensed as he added, "you're *truthful* when you're drink."

"No, I didn't mean it." She felt like her legs were going to run away as she went to a display shelf near the couches and looked at a picture of Royael on the merry-go-round. Picking it up, her thumb caressed her daughter's wide grin. "I'd never imagine Royael's smile could get any bigger than it had that day. At least not until you came into our life."

He didn't say anything. Raven turned back to hazel eyes that seem to be staring through her. She gave her best sad puppy face.

"Raven," Jon stretched her name as if had ten syllables, huffed and turned away.

She walked around his desk and turned his chair back toward her.

"Look at me." She held on to a mask of melancholy with a smidge of hope. It used to work like a charm. "Let me tell you what I mean…I mean let me tell you how I feel about you." *Opps, that's not what I mean!*

~~~

Why must you torture me? He looked away from Raven's blue eyes and the way her lips were parted just slightly as she stood in front of him, apologizing.

His jaw tensed as he remembered the last couple of days coming home during lunchtime to pack an overnight bag to stay at the Dallas

D Hotel. He'd gotten home from Orlando on Monday. The estimated grand-opening setback was a flux. Instead of staying, he'd come by while she was out and sit at the top of the stairs, tormenting himself as he visualized her and heard those drunken words. Then he'd pack another bag. Before leaving, he found himself crossing the bridge to Raven's side of the house–it now belonged to her. His whole house and she had her own side of it. He'd sit on the couch in her room and smell papayas and mangos all throughout his entire lunchtime. He'd even picked up the spoon ring that lay on the dresser, wondering why she'd kept it so long.

Right now, he couldn't hate himself the way he should for leaving her pregnant. Not with her so willing to forgive. Jon tried to swivel his chair around, but her Nike blocked his path. He wanted her to go away, still hadn't contacted Lucinda, still hoped that the maid's reaction when his mother had given him the letter was key to the fact that Raven wasn't his sister. If Lucinda's reaction had just been a female thing…then, what would he do with his addiction?

"Jon, you're not even listening," Raven grumbled, looking him in the eye.

"Uh-huh." He tried to stand up, didn't like being eye level with her. Her soft hand went to his chest, the push wasn't strong, but he relented.

"I said that you've been a very good friend since we moved in."

"I'm supposed to help. You have my child."

"You could've just shoveled out some dough and sent us on our way," Raven said. He rolled his eyes. "… Are you listening?"

"Yes."

"What did I just say?"

He shrugged, "I bought some stuff?"

"*No!* I mentioned that you bought Royael a new wardrobe over two minutes ago. I just *said* you try to cook dinner every night." She let his chin go and stepped back. "I'm trying to tell you how you go the extra mile and you're not even listening!"

Now she looked mad at him, with her arousing puppy dog face

which turned into an enticing pout. He looked just to the left of her, it was safer that way.

"I'm here to make sure you come home tonight. I'm cooking dinner."

"No, thank you."

"Jon, you're so stubborn!" Raven shook her fist at her side. She stepped closer again, reclaiming her I'm-in-charge stance, holding onto the arm handles of his chair. "*You are* coming home tonight and *I am* cooking dinner. I'll make something else chocolate, if you don't want the…mud pie–uh, pie with mud. Now shake my hand."

He knew he shouldn't let her make it so easy to be pardoned, but she shoved her hand in front of his face. He gave it a quick shake. *This reconciliation won't be simple.* Not forgiving her for that night meant that he was safe from his obsession. His obsession wouldn't have to worry about being hurt by him anymore, and that's all that mattered.

"The past has been forgiven and forgotten. Nobody has done anything bad to anybody. We're just two parents trying to raise our daughter, right?" She jutted out her chin, affirmed with a nod.

I guess we've started all over. A grin crept across his lips. He'd like that. He watched the sway of her hips as she neared the doors to leave and said, "See you later, Shorty."

"I'm not that short. Freakishly tall man." she tossed back and walked out.

~~~

Maybe the voice was right about making friends with Jon. No matter how much Raven wanted to make it work for Royael's sake, guilt had a way of pervading her dreams. After a wonderful night of playing Gold Fish with them, she'd dreamed of guilt and Elise. She found herself in the exercise room, pulling back the glass wall and running hard as her anger rose and dimmed in waves.

I told Jon that we're going to let bygones be bygones… She pummeled the punching bag. *We're starting over. I have my best friend back.*

'*Dumbass, what about Elise? What if he finds out–*'

She went hard, giving it all she got. Sweat dribbled into her eyes, mingling with tears of anger. What if Jon found out about Elise before her plan unfolded? The continuous sound of hitting the bag was therapy, pacifying her internal rage. Her hands stopped moving as she felt instantly uncomfortable. Raven turned toward the entrance to see a dark-skinned man, about ten years older than her, lean against the doorframe.

"Impressive." He rubbed a hand over his bald head and the left side of his mouth curved into a smile. "If that punching bag were a person, I might have to frisk you and take you in."

"*Me*, taken by a peeping Tom?" Her eyebrows rose and she squared her shoulders as he walked around the elliptical, toward her. Not as tall or buff as Jon, but Tyriq was lean. And something about him, she wouldn't take her eyes off the guy for a second—not even to blink.

"I'm Detective Tyriq Tate." He held out his hand. Arms folded, she glared at him. After a moment, he wriggled his fingers, realizing she wouldn't shake his hand, and placed them back at his side. Alluring slanted eyes gazed at her workout bra and traveled down her abs to her spandex shorts. "As I was saying, if I get wind of a sexy, short, female assassin in the area, I know where to look."

"Oh-kay, *Detective TT*. I'm sure that won't be necessary," she replied, the narrowness of her eyes slowly diminished. She breathed heavy, even more so than she did while exercising. *I should stop "mad dogging" him…oh, hell, I can't stop staring.* She had to still her tongue from grazing over her lips, and she used all her energy not to gawk at his hypnotizing grin. She glanced over his collarbone in his v-neck shirt and her eyes traveled to stonewashed jeans that snuggled in all the right places. *Maybe this "mad dog" stare isn't working.* Anger simpered as her gaze traveled back up to his ruggedly handsome face, and damn, she reflected his beam.

"Wow," Tyriq began, "she can smile. I guess you're not the Chihuahua Jon pegged you for."

"He said that, did he? Well, you might have to take me in after I wring his neck."

His laughter doused the remaining particles of anger coursing through her veins. When he licked his lips, it was all over for her, that all-consuming rage she felt every morning, the reason why she worked out so hard doused out. Try as she might, she couldn't help laughing, too.

"I suppose I can forget you mentioned that. What would I look like apprehending someone as gorgeous as you? I better get back to the game of pool. I'm sure Jon's going to add my meager salary to his fortune, now that all I can do is think of you."

She giggled and took one last gaze as Tyriq walked out of the room. God, there was something about him. She couldn't put her finger on it, but the feeling was new. Lips just parted, warm butterflies fluttered through her belly as she contemplated, *it usually takes hours to come out of my anger.*

CHAPTER 34

A sea of candles illuminated the bedroom. Charlene's baby-oiled leg was wrapped around the bed pole and Louboutin spiky heels graced her feet. Firelight danced, making it hard to detect Damien's emotions as he leaned against the doorframe. *So much for attempting a special night in his favorite negligee,* she thought. It had taken at least an hour to prim and pamper–only Meagan wore this much make up. *Shouldn't he be rushing to me on his knees?*

Her insides curled when candlelight flickered off a magazine in his hands. He tossed it on the bed as light finally played off the angry contours of his face. He backed out and closed the door.

Leg unwrapped from the sexy-is-me stance; she kicked off her best come-tether heels, while glowering at the paper. One by one, she blew out calming-vanilla candles and the patchouli-romantic candles. *Maybe I shouldn't have mixed them, because Damien wasn't calm nor was he in the mood.*

With fizzles of smoke around her, Charlene sat and snatched up the magazine. Shockingly, it wasn't Scandalous, yet another reputable publication. She read the title "Charlene Shaw's husband brooding over lawsuit? Or Miguel Sanchez?"

The two page spread, featured pictures of Damien Wright–on the left side–looking "brooding-like" while driving around L.A. or taking out the trash. *These were taken right after he'd been subpoena by Scandalous TV.* The other side of the fold showed candid photographs of her and Miguel at lunch. *These pictures were cropped!* Taken at the producer's party for the sixth anniversary for 'Loyalties and FamiLIES', the photos were captured at a nifty angle. It appeared to be just them. (Miguel's fingers had stroked her forearm. She'd replied something witty.) The story had painted a picture of that. Flirtatious and subtle. Then she'd given him a hug. The next photo enhanced his hand on her lower back. Charlene closed the magazine. *How about adding the twenty other cast members that I hugged!*

Tugging into a robe, she went downstairs to explain. She heard the hushed voices of Damien and Daniela traveling from the den. Back against the door, she listened. Daniela tried to pacify the situation. *How can I have a conversation with my husband if he's always running to his momma?*

"A lot of so-called Christian marriages end because one is cheating," came his terse reply.

"You want a divorce?"

"I want the truth!"

"After all the time you've put into this relationship? You searched for her when she first left; then waited for her to go to rehab. Now, you want to just call it quits! What about Trinity?"

"Don't put Trinity into this..."

Eyes wide, she walked away. *He wants a divorce?*

~~~

Weeks dragged by as Charlene went back and forth from L.A. to Dallas. She made sure not to be seen anywhere near Miguel offset. During breaks, she helped Annette move into a retirement residence less supervised than the nursing home, but still had the amenities of on-staff nursing.

They'd just come home from shopping, and Charlene wanted to get rid of the clutter in the middle of the tiny living room. She pulled out a new crystal vase.

Annette sat in her new lazy boy, sipping sweet tea. "You go ahead and decorate my place with all your *fancy shmancy* items you just had to grab. When you leave, I'll stuff it all in the closet."

Charlene rolled her eyes. Placing it in the middle of the table, she attempted to cover a scrape on a secondhand coffee table. Much to her dismay, they'd gone to a Goodwill store, and then finished off the day at the best interior decorator boutique Dallas had to offer. Now, her mom was *pretending* to be pooped, ironically after Charlene decided to unpack and decorate. Instead of giving in to Annette's irritation of her artistic-thumb, she changed the subject, "What if we start having a girls' night out?"

Annette pressed her large calves against the seat, unhinging the leg rest and leaned forward in the chair. "And go where?"

"Oh, Momma, we could go to art galas or a movie or to *eat*... Or we could stay in."

"That's right. We could *stay in*. Then you can tell Raven about the real reason you couldn't save Otis."

~~~

"No, no, no," Annette's fresh press-in-curl rattled as she shook her head, placing homemade crème puffs on her coffee table. "I don't want you to buy me a house. I don't want a mansion, a brand new one, an old Victorian style–like I'd dreamed of as a child–or a little cottage–"

"Oh-kay, Granny," Raven bit down on a carrot and crunched.

"Told ya. Momma's not going for it. In less than three weeks, she's gotten everybody callin' her 'Nettie', not to mention her little entourage and you seen her trying to teach that cooking class when we got here a little while ago." Charlene grabbed a precut brownie.

Just shy of a month at the new retirement home, Annette's popularity had skyrocketed and she had the same pep in her step as she had before the stroke. Noticing the pep in Annette's step as she walked in and out of the kitchen with sweets, Charlene realized that her momma enjoyed their girly-get together, too.

"I know ya'll ain't talking about me like I'm not here. Whatcha mean trying? I'm a *damn* good chef." She reached over and snatched the celery that Raven was dipping into ranch. "I got these veggies for the celebrity. Your skinny behind can eat the sweets."

Charlene stuck out her tongue and picked up another bite size brownie.

"Um-hum, Granny." Raven quipped, "You so good at cooking, that all these old folks can't keep up. I watched one guy in particular that couldn't even write down the recipe."

"Yeah, that's because he was tryna flirt with you!" Charlene tossed a red vine at her daughter. "Momma took over the retirement home with her cooking lessons. Now, the real issue is, are *you* finally moving out of Jon's house?"

"Dang, I've only been there for a month," she said, baffled. "Besides he travels back and forth to Orlando. The opening is at the beginning of summer."

"I'm pretty sure it's been at least two months for you, since Momma's been here a while." Charlene smirked. "I suppose it's… convenient."

"Yes, it is." Her eyes clouded, as if gearing toward an excuse, "When he's there, we spend our time with Royael. He's missed a lot of time with her."

"Um-hum…"

"Sometimes, we even dare each other." She grinned. "Like last week, I dared Jon to purchase something at a dollar store the next time he went on a business trip and…"

"Hmmm…sounds like *fun*," Charlene said. Raven rolled her eyes.

"Quit all that joshin', Char," Annette cut in.

"On a more serious note, Mom, I have something important to tell you. Tyriq, a friend of Jon's, is a detective. I think…" She stopped as Charlene's face registered a chill of fear. "We need to find out who the truck driver is."

"Re-Re is right," Annette nodded as Charlene hugged a faux-silk pillow to her chest.

Biting her bottom lip, now, she tried to make excuses. "Do you trust this detective? I live in the public eye. I can't have people knowing that…"

"Mom, it'll be all right. Tyriq Tate is a nice guy. He's Jon's friend and comes around sometimes. I don't want us to go to a seedy PI who knows your face, if that's your concern."

Tiny insects engulfed Charlene's body. Annette had kept giving her the eye to bring up the Otis-not-being-Raven's-grandfather subject. Raven had to mention Roy. *God, must my life be plagued with reopening my life's worst fears?* She tried not to scratch the scar that was set ablaze

CHAPTER 35

Jon's eyes popped open to a pitch-black night, ears perked to the sound of rummaging downstairs. He pulled on his pajama pants, stepped onto the fur rug and tiptoed to the acrylic painting on the wall. Pressing the latch behind the gold frame, it opened. He tapped the code and the titanium door clacked. Pushing past stacks of crisp bills, he picked up a chrome desert eagle and clicked off the safety. Gun poised, bare feet padding along the floor, he slowly descended the stairs. The moon peeked into the living room, highlighting African artifacts. *Raven didn't even shade the walls!* His house was a burglar's heaven, and she'd left it on display.

To the sound of rustling behind him, Jon did an about-face. Scaling the wall, his eyes scanning as he passed the media room. A burglar could be hiding behind anyone of the theater chairs. He peeked into the indoor pool room and continued. The rustling came from further away. He paced toward the kitchen, cocked back the hammer. "Freeze!"

A high pitch scream shattered his ear drums.

"It's *me*!" Raven stood rigid and edgily mumbled, "If you shoot me, then I guess I won't have to take these pills anymore."

"What you say?" Jon turned on the lights. His gaze softened as she frowned. He put the gun down at his side and took in the beautiful woman in a short pajama set and cowgirl boots. Hair placed in two pigtails–Royael signature style. She reminded him of an innocent girl he once new in Bellwood, a tomb boy and a sexy bombshell all wrapped into one confusing yet enticing package. Upon further assessment, he said, "It's almost two a.m. What are you doing?"

"I'm going night photographing and just wanted a bottle of water. Is that okay with you?" She brushed past him, looking dead ahead.

"It's almost two, I just told you." *You can't go wandering around outside at night.*

"Good thing it's *called* night photography," she reiterated.

He watched her grab a blanket that he hadn't noticed draped over the stairwell. There was also a camera case at the bottom step. Tunnel vision and a peak in hearing had him miss all of these signs. "Where are you going? It's too late for you to be running around town *in the middle of the night."*

"Gosh, Jon, if I wanted a damn daddy, I know to call you. Just outside, dang. You can come and be my—what's the name of that little, fat dog with all the wrinkles—oh, yeah, bulldog."

"Okay." He couldn't help but grin, knowing Tyriq had told her about the Chihuahua-nickname. He placed the gun on the end table in the living room and went to the hall closet for his boots.

"Magnum," Raven said, picking up the gun. She removed the magazine and sat it on the table. "Desert Eagle .50AE—chrome because it must be shiny for you, huh? Oh, and a pearl handle—how cute, how… lame. Has a hard kick, though. The guy at the gun shop did you a good deed."

He rolled his eyes as she swiftly disassembled the barrel. In a matter of seconds, she took out the piston grip and the rest of the items. "Put your gun away. You shouldn't have it in the house with our child, and I'm not putting it back together, either."

She's tryna get me to decline her invitation for night photography. He tried not to crack a smile, pacing up the stairs two at a time. They'd got into the groove of being in each other's company as he traveled to and from Orlando, but she always kept her distance after Royael went to sleep. He placed the gun back in the safe. *Well, at least I can get under her…skin, tonight.*

~~~

Raven rubbed the nape of her neck, watching Jon jog downstairs. He still didn't have on a shirt, and his pants were sagging low, peek-a-boo-ish low. *Keep your eyes on his.* Aggravated at her quick retort when offering him a chance to go with her, she ordered him around. "If you're coming, you gotta do your share of work. Grab that tripod."

"Yes, masta." He mimicked a field slave.

"I can send you away at any time."

"Roger that, ma'am." He held the kitchen glass door open.

Tense lipped, she passed through to a calm spring night. After he closed it, they walked around the pool and stone fireplace. They stopped a couple of yards from the back of the house. Seeing through the vision of a pro, Raven treaded around the open backyard until content with the viewpoint. "I want to get a few shots of the roof's angles. Set up the tripod here." She dropped the folded blanket into the dewy grass, and then as if an afterthought, she mumbled, "Thanks."

Looking through the lens, Raven felt his roaming eyes as she snapped pictures. Holding in her nervousness, she took the camera off the tripod and took a few steps away from him as she took more photos, needing the distance. When complete, she set the SLR camera back on the tripod and fidgeted with her fingers. Mr. Tinker said that this type of photography would be a challenge, with the low light levels. She tapped her lip to her finger and tried to keep her mind *on* photography.

"What are you thinking about?"

By the nearness of his voice, she detected that he was close, too close. Raven stepped back on impulse, looking up at the glass house. She needed him to believe that her mind concentrated on photography. *This is the first time I haven't been able to get lost in taking pictures.* Inhaling deeply, she took in notes of flowers in springtime and tried to put her brain back into the creative mood.

'Maybe you shoulda listened to Charlene and moved. Oh, well, Dumbass is too afraid to live alone and too emotional to go through with our original act or retribution!'

Breathing deeply, she tried not to let the voice ruin the remnants of her creative flow. "I'm trying to consider if I like this, but only time will tell. Let's go. Pick up the tripod. There's a clearing of leveled land about a mile away; unless you want to go to bed?"

"Nope." Jon did as told. "Is this where you took those pictures on your portfolio?"

The space in between them decreased as she stopped to glare at him. *I didn't say you could look at my portfolio!* Though she gave her best "mean mug," she knew he caught her smile when she turned around.

The sound of crickets, and their feet crunching over the land, saturated the silence. In the middle of grassland, Raven unfolded the blanket and tossed it up, letting it float to the pasture.

"What's the difference between those cameras?" he asked, when she exchanged the SLR camera.

"Well, Mr. 21-Questions, this camera is better at taking a photo for a longer period of time. I'm using it for star trails. If I don't F-up, I'll have captured the stars moving, based on the length of exposure. A twenty minute picture, for example, will show the stars in a straight line, but having it open for one shot that last hours, provides a circular star trail. It's beautiful." She plopped down, Indian style.

He sat. "Why don't you turn it toward the moon?"

"The moon washes out the larger stars. The silhouettes of the trees," she pointed to the oak trees that would be at the base of the picture, and then continued, "become stationary black shapes. It's quite poetic. Now, thank me for letting you in on this experience."

"Thank you." He lay back when she did. After a while, he broke the silence again. "This reminds me of home, when we were little."

"Bellwood isn't home anymore."

He took her hand. "We'll always remember star gazing at the meadow when we were younger."

'Oh, yes, the meadow and your dreams of killing Elise. What did Dr. Stanton say about you becoming the guilty party?'

A deep need to be comforted by her old friend took over, but the voice continued to dig its hooks into her spirit. She had to let go of his large, warm hand.

"Are you okay? You felt so tense." Jon propped himself up on his elbow, searching her eyes for the answer.

"I-I'm fine." Though painful, she smiled in an attempt to get his mind off her sudden change in demeanor. A glance at her watch read that they'd been here for almost an hour. "Let's go. Royael doesn't usually wake up, but this would be night, huh?"

She arose. *I'll start searching for apartments tomorrow.*

CHAPTER 36
DEVEREUX HEADQUARTERS, PARIS, FRANCE

Elise sat on a Napoleon armchair in an office designed for a king—a whole lot of them. Pierre had sponsored or lead expeditions across the globe, leading to the discovery of priceless antiques. An Aubusson rug decked the floors. Faberge eggs were incased at focal areas in the large room.

"Papa, please!" Emerald eyes wide, she looked at her reflection in his gold nameplate.

Her jewels-for-eyes always worked like magic, yet his spine was rigid and his expensive veneers were gritted. "I won't listen to you infer that Jonathan is a good man!"

"He's in that house all alone and—" *I've done awful things to my husband.*

"That *mansion* I had built for you? I procured all of his clients and ruined his business reputation. You need to appreciate the fact that he's still breathing. I transferred ten million dollars in an account to get rid of Raven Shaw. The bastard didn't even have the decency to strategize before attempting to take it. Sign the divorce papers. I've more pertinent issues to manage, because now she's back!"

"Raven's back?" Elise's voice quivered. She hadn't kept tabs on her son since he'd left for college. Her brain mentally flashed to the last time she'd seen him. He was eighteen and stubborn.

"Raven wouldn't write this!" Jon held up a letter Lucinda handed him as they stood in the foyer of their home. "She's wouldn't kill our child!"

Elise scampered to keep up as he burst through the double doors and down the marble steps. Her throat was dry and it didn't help that there was no wind in the North Carolina heat. "Raven is... sh she's pr-pregnant?"

"Yes and I'm going to marry her!" Jon turned around near the lotus fountain; cascades of turquoise water reflected off the anger in his eyes. As she stood flustered, he stalked toward his Ducati.

"Raven is trying to trick you!" Elise reached out to him, but he kicked the

motorcycle to the ground.

"No, she wouldn't do that. Manipulation is your calling card!"

Her mouth opened to defend herself, but she noticed the Phantom pulling into the driveway and her papa got out. As far as she knew, Pierre should've been back in Paris and the situation dealt with—Papa said he handled this!

With palms out, Pierre stepped forward. "My son, you should give Raven time—"

"Grandfather, I know she didn't write this!" With gritted teeth, Jon held up the letter.

Hands balled into fist, Elise exclaimed, "Jon, that girl is taking advantage of you!"

"Don't be angry with your mother, Jon." Pierre placed a hand on his shoulder. "Elise means well but doesn't understand. Give Raven time. With the issue of paternity between herself and Jonathan, her grandfather's leukemia has placed her under a great deal of pressure. Time heals all wounds. Come with me. We'll get you squared off for the university. In a few weeks, give her a call. She'll say the letter was a catalyst for venting, and we'll send for her."

Jon nodded, and then turned to his mother. "If Raven never speaks to me again, I'll never speak with you."

"Raven's back…" she mumbled again, still consumed with the pain of that dreadful day.

"Do not reiterate my words!" Chest deflated, he looked her in the eyes and in a calmer tone, said, "I love you more than life."

Understanding how Pierre felt, even with the disappointment in his eyes, she nodded. Before he could continue, Elise stood and sniffled. "I'm sorry, Papa."

"Jonathan is exactly where he's meant to be at the moment—in his own personal hell. My dear daughter, you must always think of Devereux first. The disgrace of this scandal being exposed is irreparable…Jonathan being both of their fathers."

"Yes, Papa." Arms folded around her in self-comfort, she left. Outside of the building, Elise slipped into the back of the Maybach Landaulet. The car lurched forward as she noticed a letter with perfect script, seated next to her. She read it. A sigh wriggled out and her thin

Miss Scandalous

lips formed a line as she crumpled the paper in her fist, knowing exactly where the car headed.

No, not as she suspected. The car turned down the wrong street. Her eyebrows rose as the driver pulled into Devereux's first hotel. It had been the only possession her papa owned before marrying her mama. For decades, the historic hotel was in shambles. Then Pierre got his hands on Estella's money, restoring the hotel to its grand state and striking fortune in other endeavors.

Her phone vibrated in her Prada twill blazer. She grabbed it and her eyes widened and pooled with more tears at the text message. Just then the door opened. *I'll call back soon.* Hands trembling with interest, she placed the phone back in her pocket and slid out of the car. The message would pacify the annoyance of this unscheduled stop.

Strutting inside a marble and gold trimmed lobby, Elise was greeted by name. Pulling on the pearl button of her blouse, she stood in the elevator, going to the top floor. Walking down the hall of exclusive suites, she took in the carved moldings on the walls before knocking at the door. When it opened, Elise stared at a peridot beaded gown that made her mama's twinkling eyes.

"Took you long enough," Estella said. Her popular Stellar perfume seized Elise's lungs.

"Papa just told me that you were staying here." No affectionate greeting needed, she passed over the threshold. Her parents were separated. Usually her mama stayed at the Chateau de Estella in Burgundy, France. *Why is Mama staying here? She hates all things Devereux.*

"I thought that twit kept my name out of his mouth." Estella poured a martini at the crystal mini bar. Eyes narrow, she dropped a green olive in the drink. "I'd assumed out of sight, out of mind, for the both of you."

"Where's your staff? Most surely you don't *serve yourself* or open your own doors?" Elise matched her terseness, and took a sip of the drink that was curtly handed over. They got along in two minute segments. She'd been here for a little over that; it was flight time. "Please refrain from enlightening me. I'm most assured that you don't cleanse your own derrière."

"Sit down!" Estella commanded, taking a seat across from her daughter. The floral bouquet on the coffee table lost the war against the Stellar fragrance. "You can travel all around the world. Nevertheless, I have to send a note to get you to visit your own *Mama*."

"I would have gotten around to visiting…eventually."

"Sure." With a devilish smile, she added, "I've something of the greatest importance to tell you."

"What?" Elise brushed imaginary lent from her twill skirt.

"Raven Shaw and Royael–well, she's a Shaw, but she should be…" Estella's voice trailed off as if in deep thought. Truthfully, she was smarter than most pegged. "Oh, yes, she should be an Anderson. Yes, Royael Anderson. Then again, Jon should too, huh?"

Elise's yacht-tanned skin turned white. "How do you know?"

"Tsk tsk. Your papa got his start in publications. Your posse was always in our enemy's gossip columns; drinking, driving, etcetera. Do you honestly believe that we didn't know?"

Elise rubbed her head. *Royael should be an Anderson…Anderson blood courses through Jon's veins. I should be a Devereux-Anderson! But Zane Anderson was married!*

"As a child, you'd ruined your papa's reputation enough. It took a while for him to concede and have you followed. Just to think, Pierre was *human* when I met him. I was the one making money, and then he invested. He grew my money into what I would never even dream of." Estella went to pour another martini. As if she could read body language–that yearning in Elise's eyes–she handed her daughter a refreshed drink. She gracefully sat, legs crossed. "He's no longer human. All he see's is the elite–the *affluent*. And you my dear," Estella pointed at her, with silk-wrapped-fingernails and said, "were an awful teenager. Nevertheless, he always loved you, always fixed your mistakes, until you met Zane Anderson. You see, he knew when you were pregnant and trying to convince him to do dabble in altruism, by helping his old friend, Jonathan's father, with his law firm. Pierre knew

Jonathan was a dead ringer for Zane. Only, Zane didn't want *you*. He wanted his *wife*. Being the man your papa is, he let you call the shots. You're but a pawn on a chessboard to Pierre. He sat back and watched, delighted in your manipulation. He'd never been more proud of you than the day you convinced Jonathan that you were having his child. Only, you had the audacity to make our Jon a *junior*."

Tears rolled down Elise's cheeks, as she tuned out Estella's laughter. She'd reminisced on Zane for over twenty years. His beautiful brown face would be forever branded in her mind, all because of Jonathan Dubois, the-look-alike. Truth be told, that was the reason she hadn't divorced him.

"Then there was that Charlene girl." Estella winked. "Oh, we know the entire story. She was having Jonathan's child. Then Jonathan's *kids* fell in love…"

Elise opened her eyes and looked around. Mama was gone. Minutes later, Estella returned with an embroidered book, placing it onto her lap. With trepidation, she opened it to see an album with baby photos. She'd never seen Royael before, hadn't wanted to see the child for guilt. Yet one look at the beautiful child's face, and she knew her first and only grandchild.

"You've ruined his life. Jon was in love. All you had to do was tell him that they weren't related! The simplicity of honesty, but no, you had to allow Pious Pierre into the game, when he was just as content observing."

Fingers shaking, she turned pages to a chronology of the child's life. All photos were taken from a distance or side angle. She flipped until there were just empty pockets. Finally, she sat the album on the table as a sob shook her slender body. "I tried."

"I want to see my great-granddaughter. I want Jon to have the love of his life." Estella shoved a picture of Raven and Jon holding hands in her daughter's face. "Look at this! They're in love, but they've denied themselves the choice to love freely because of you."

Elise tried to slap the picture away.

"You always were an evil child."

"Ma, no." Elise scrambled to the floor, putting her head in her mama's lap as she'd done as a child when her mama used to rub her head and sing French lullabies. The look of hatred in Estella's eyes scorched her skin. Her voice shook as she sung and unlike the past, Estella didn't chime in. "Please, Ma. Jon left me a text, forgiving me for the letter. He wants to see me."

"You have until the Orlando grand opening."

"*Mama*, I haven't talked to him in years. Allow me more time to make amends." Looking up from Estella's lap, she entwined her hands. Her mama's tense no clenched at her heart. Throat thick and heavy, she screamed the words, "I'll tell Papa!"

"Good, let the ogre know I'm on his turf, too. Why else would I be at this gaudy hotel. " Estella looked down at her daughter like she didn't deserve to adorn the floor beneath her feet.

CHAPTER 37

"I can't have a guest wash dishes," Raven said to Tyriq as she cleared the dinner table. In basketball shorts and a jersey, she couldn't help but gaze at the definition in his arms.

"That's not how I was raised." He picked up a ceramic bowl with remnants of scalloped potatoes and followed her to the sink. "I stopped by for a game of b-ball and intruded on dinner."

"I can't even get Jon to wash the dishes." Raven rolled her eyes at the giant as he and Royael exited to watch their evening cartoons.

"How about I wash, you dry?" Without waiting for a reply, Tyriq flicked on the stainless-steel sprout. When they'd gotten into the groove of cleaning, he mentioned her and Jon's living situation.

"It's difficult at times. You saw my crazy tactics to get a small kid and a grown one eat broccoli. I'm busy taking extra courses, so it's convenient." Raven hoped he couldn't smell the crap she dished out. *I'm indecisive, so shoot me. No, wait you're a cop.*

When he handed her a cup, their hands touched. He supplied that contagious smile which sent sparks throughout her body.

"If you keep looking at me like that," he began, leaning close enough for his chest to touch the back of her shoulder. His warm breath tickled her neck as he gave a body-warming-warning, "I might forget where we are."

"Exactly how am I looking at you?" She stepped away from his heat.

"Like you might take me down right here in the middle of the kitchen," he licked his lips and grinned. "I'm not as strong as I look, Raven."

"So you can't handle me, Detective?" She laughed, knowing she shouldn't take the bait.

"I might be powerless for a few minutes and let you have your way with me."

"I promise not to–"

"Jump me?"

"Quit that!" She snatched the clean glass he handed and they continued to wash dishes. Guard down, she reminded herself to be on the lookout for his flirtatious ways.

"So I take it, Jon doesn't know about the B&E in Brinton."

She froze, her smile dimmed. How did Tyriq know what she'd done to Elise? Her record had been expunged thanks to Grandpa Otis. Shame crept up her neck, clogging her throat and she became butterfingers as he handed her a saucer.

"Don't worry, Raven," he put his hand on her shoulder, and then apologized for its wetness. He laughed, hers was a forced chuckle. "I won't tell him if you don't."

"Tell him what?" Jon asked.

They both turned to see the man in question picking up Mookie from Royael's chair. Raven opened her mouth to reply, but Tyriq spoke instead. "I wasn't going to mention that I would accompany Raven to the opera that ya'll talked about over dinner. You didn't make any stipulations to the dare and if she has to endure a night of hollering, at least she shouldn't have to do it solo."

Jon nodded slowly and walked out with the bear.

"Thanks," Raven whispered as she went back to wiping dishes.

"It's the least I can do. Besides, it's a date."

She smiled as he winked. Then he went right ahead with those charming jokes. Raven laughed, trying not to take his words seriously. "I have something important to…"

Tyriq's phone went off. He said, "Hold that thought. It's my job."

She took over the washing. When he came back, he apologized but said he had to go.

~~~

Jon ambled down the stairs. He wanted to cringe at Royael and Raven next to the bonsai tree with shorts and matching cheap shirts. He stuffed his hands in jean shorts that had been stuffed in the back of his closet, right along with the crumpled college tee he had on. "Let's get this over with."

When he walked toward the garage door, Raven cleared her throat, "My car."

"Hell, naw." Jon put his hands up in defense. "I'd rather die than be caught in that piece of crap. If I won't let you put it into the driveway, what makes you think I'm getting in it?"

"Are you forfeiting the dare? What are the words that you must say if you forfeit?"

"Not fair. I've been gone all week, giving you too much time to think of an evil master plan—"

"Evil master plan? I had to go to the opera all by myself. Tyriq called from a coroner's office to tell me he couldn't make it. I had a massive migraine all last night."

It was useless, trying to let the note of irritation in her voice role over his shoulders. He smiled so his jaw wouldn't set with jealousy. *She's acting like Ty stood her up for a date.* When he'd heard them in the kitchen, Tyriq had so quickly admitted to escorting Raven to the opera, something felt off. Though he'd known Tyriq for years, he wouldn't put it past him to flirt with her. *Does she like him, too…*

Her voice cut through his self-tormented musing. "Jon, all you have to say is: 'Raven is the *most beautifulest, smartest woman* in the world and—'

"*Beautifulest?*" Hazel eyes rolled as he walked to the front door. The sun scorched his skin and it wasn't even mid-morning. His agitation skyrocketed when the passenger door creaked open.

"Yay, we're gonna have fun!" Royael clapped, getting into the backseat.

"Where? Please not Pizza Planet," he whispered as Raven closed the door. He could still feel the germs, and his shoulders sunk even more when they arrived at Raven's "evil master plan."

The smell of grease, hot dogs, and horse excrement fought the aroma of fire pits claiming to have "Texas's best barbeque." Royael zipped from ride to ride. On the top of the Ferris Wheel Raven whispered in their daughter's ear. Royael giggled, and then they wiggled in their seats.

205

"Stop!" He couldn't stop himself from peering over the side of the cart to a sure enough death.

"Daddy, this is fun." Royael pointed out sky scrapers, continuing to shift. No sooner than she stepped off the ride, did she run across the hay scattered passageway. "Baby horses like Trinity!"

"Maybe the chocolate covered bacon was a bad idea," Raven mentioned as she and Jon meandered behind. Jon paid a vendor in a red and white vest, while Royael hooked her foot into the stirrup of a pony with gunk-idy-goo in its eyes and the attendant hoisted her up.

"I'll be back with the next dare." Raven reached up and patted his shoulder as he leaned against the gate. He grumbled a reply, looked through the lens of her camera, taking pictures of Royael. The pony trotted around and she waved each time.

"Buddy, got something for you." Raven handed him a straw hat with a black-felt strip.

"I can smell the chemicals from here. Not going on my head."

"Uh-uh, this is your dare day. If you can't play the game all you have to say is—"

"This is ridiculous." He shoved it on top of his head. "We're even. No more dares. I guess I forgot how competitive you were."

She grinned. "Remember that time you did a back flip off the swing behind my old house?"

Jon joined in as she laughed. Raven had done it countless times, sometimes doubles. The one time he was courageous—best-friend-peer-pressured—enough, it had been a disaster. "We thought I had a concussion."

"And we hid out in the meadow all night long, while I kept you awake and away from Elise," Raven finished.

~~~

The morning sun played off the flecks of orange candy paint on the Challenger in the driveway. She folded her arms to stave off the spring chill, but mostly the vibes of frustration she got from Jon's happiness. They'd had a good time at the fair until her car died on the way home. Against her wishes, he'd told the tow man to dump it. So what if it wasn't worth much, but it held memories. *Don't you remember the story about Royael stealing chocolate and getting it all over the car? It's just like you to want to replace everything!*

"Do you like it?" Jon searched her eyes for a glimmer of happiness.

"You can't take a person's freedom of choice away." She walked across the stone bridge and back into the house.

"A simple thanks would suffice." His voice rose as he followed.

"You don't understand." Raven crossed her arms as she glared at the Koi fish.

His hands went to the heavens. "No, I *don't*."

"You don't know anything!" She stalked upstairs.

"What is it you want me to know?" With quick strides, Jon caught up with her on the bridge. "You're always busy with school and working at that coffee shop–might I say for no reason! I took the chance to replace your piece-of-junk with a car that's your favorite color and the brand you like. Why are you being so ungrateful? Just hand the keys to the first bum you see walking around and–"

Her eyes welled with tears and he apologized. For the love of all things holy, she didn't know what she wanted from him. *Am I trying to change him?*

'*You want him back. It's infuriating because you can't have him.*'

Warm rays of the sun played off his sandy-brown hair. He stepped closer to her and placed his arms around her. Instinct told her to jump ship, but her heart called out to his. Head snuggled against his chest, she breathed free for the first time in years. She needed to be closer; craved it.

The voice whispered obscenities, causing her to sniffle and stifle the storm of tears that threatened to escape.

Leave me alone. I don't want to cry anymore. Gazing up at Jon, she stood on her tippy toes and placed her hands behind his neck, gently pulling him down. Their lips connected. *Take that!*

A war between good and evil, she imagined the voice as the scarlet caricature with horns and a pitchfork. Tongue savoring her ultimate craving, her broken heart glided back together. She felt an insatiable tidal wave as his hands lifted her and her legs wrapped around his buff waist.

Madness drove him toward the bedroom. He kicked the door closed with his foot, only to slow down, and place her, like a jewel, on the bed. The seconds that it took his hands to leave her body and tug her shirt over her head were pure torture. With him standing in front of her, she leaned forward, snatched the collar of his tank top, ripping it off. Kissing him hard on the chest, her lips continued to his abdomen as his hands roamed through her hair.

'Sunday...'

Raven's eyes widened as she wrenched the cloth of his shirt in her hands. "It's Sunday!"

Shame slammed into her chest. *Aw, shit! My imagination was wrong.* Maybe that annoying voice had a halo with a faint glow?

"Yes, its Sunday," he replied, leaning in to kiss her again.

She turned away and wriggled from beneath him.

I'm on the wrong side of love and war...

CHAPTER 38

Rubbing her hands on her face, Raven stifled a yawn. She gulped down a double shot of espresso and placed the cup into the wastebasket. Going through the swinging doors, she returned from a much needed pick-me-up to see Cassidy shouting out orders in triple. Getting into the barista groove, she helped trim the line.

"Why are you still working here?" Cassidy leaned against the counter and wiped her brow, once the afternoon patrons stopped flooding in. "You're overloading on classes. Not to mention, I've seen you and Royael in magazines for Christ sake—just going to the movies! That Jon Dubois is filthy rich."

"I dunno. The free coffee." She shrugged. *I get to avoid Jon for a couple extra hours. Since yesterday's episode, I can't look him in the face.*

Cassidy opened her mouth, geared toward a serious answer when her eyes bugged out. "God, he's enough incentive for this busy day."

Raven looked toward the door to see the man of the hour, Detective Tyriq Tate. He had an aura about him as most of the female patrons stopped chattering or typing on their laptops to stare at the way his V-neck clung to lean muscle. His lips curved upwards when he noticed her, and she almost didn't perceive the jealous-eyed daggers from the women.

"Hello, Tyriq." She came around the pastry display and gave him a hug. He held on for a nanosecond too long. She wouldn't fight a few extra seconds, though. He smelled divine and kept her mind off Jon.

"Well, well, well…Raven looking as beautiful as ever." He drank her in, stopping on her tube top and brown belt cinched tiny waist.

Keeping composed, she introduced him to a gawking Cassidy and had to clear her throat for Cassidy to respond to his outstretched hand. Raven spoke slowly in an attempt to bring her friend back to life, "Well, Cass, I'll be going now."

"Delicious *and* nutritious, dark chocolate is filled with antioxidants," Cassidy whispered as Raven came back around the stand to grab her purse. They hugged then Raven clocked out.

"You're right on time; I just made this for you." Raven handed him a paper cup of coffee drizzled with chocolate as he held the door open for their exit. A gust of air blew at her floor length dress then she was assaulted by heat. She side stepped a couple strolling hand in hand and bumped into his chest. "Thanks for meeting me. I really need you, uh… need your help."

"Of course, should we go to your place or mine?" As if sexy-slanted eyes weren't enough to have her inwardly feeling like goofy Cassidy, Tyriq shaded those dark eyes and licked his lips.

"Oh, Tyriq." She strolled down the sidewalk, glad he no longer mentally disrobed her. Though, he was acting like they were old friends, lovers even. Her cheeks warmed as he stepped closer to let a jogger with a fluffy dog pass, sending notes of citrus and seawater, with a bit of testosterone her way. Finding her voice, she said, "I need you to find someone for me."

"All right, but you and Jon are making me consider consulting as a PI on the side. He's got me looking for Lucinda, and now, you…" He shrugged taking a notepad out of his jean pocket.

She looked away for a moment and bit her lip as he spoke. *Jon's looking for Lucinda. Why? Does he think there's hope for us…? No, why am I trying to make a connection?*

Tyriq cleared his throat and Raven thought about the task at hand, the imperative mission of helping Charlene. "My mom was raped about 25 years ago at the age of 15 on her way to Hollywood…"

When she finished her story, his head cocked to the side. "Charlene Shaw, the actress?"

"Yes. It was a hard road to fame." She shoved her hair behind her ear, feeling self-conscious under his concerned gaze.

"Look Raven, I don't have enough time to invest the much needed attention to finding Roy." He pulled out his wallet. "I know a guy that can get it done. Stork can get things done." After she had a moment to put the card in her purse, he asked, "Do you have any plans this Friday?"

Jon's looking for Lucinda. Okay, stop it, Raven. Stop it! There might not be a connection, but Tyriq's a busy person and I'm sure he gets a lot of female attention.
"I…"

"Think about it. If you ever need me, I'm a phone call away." He held her gaze as she nodded in a daze, mind perpetually on Jon again. That searing moment between her and the detective was like a candle being blown out. Tyriq gave one last smile before swinging a leg over his silver Harley. She couldn't deny that there'd been a spark between them. A glimmer in her heart wanted to find out how life would transform if she chose the road that would lead to him.

No. She had to let him go. There were certain things she had to do first. If Tyriq stayed around and she'd completed this new, extreme modified mission against Jon…maybe later? Following a hesitant breath, she watched love-at-first-sight ride away.

CHAPTER 39

The second Shaw-girls'-night-*in* didn't come soon enough for Charlene. She sat on the couch in her den, mind fuzzy, thinking about Damien. They hadn't had a meaningful conversation since Scandalous printed pictures of her and Miguel at Le' Fleur. She sighed as Annette walked in and out of the room, toting trays of baked cookies and the likes. Then she almost jumped when a DVD with ashy-skinned, hadn't-slept-in-awhile, zombies were in her face.

"Earth to Mom. I want to watch this." Raven jiggled the movie and sighed. "Damn, I should've got the new Bruce Willis flick–zombies were a *long* shot. All right; we can watch the sappy love story that I *also* rented."

Charlene frowned as her daughter dug in her distressed leather satchel to pick out another film. *Gosh, how long had she been asking to watch the zombie flick?* Endeavoring to be in the moment, she shook herself. Yet, two seconds later, she burst out in tears. "Damien still won't talk to me!"

She hadn't meant to blurt the words, but the pressure in her chest–the draft in her heart was too much. Words rushed out of her mouth; she just hoped it made sense. "I was going to wait until after the movie, because we always get to talking and never watch the movie. But I can't take it! If it's not about Trinity, *he avoids me*. We haven't had sex…in forever! I'm hormonal, one tit is always bigger than the other–" she paused as Raven gave her a sideways glance. "Well, it is! Breastfeeding sucks–no pun intended. I was going to do like one of those supermoms and breastfeed Trinity until she's friggen five! I have to travel back and forth from L.A., that's taken a toll, too. All I want is for Damien to talk to me!"

Raven pressed the remote and the flat-panel TV turned off. She sat next to Charlene and patted her shoulder. "Damien is a good man. He'll come around. And your boobies look perfect."

Charlene burst into laughter, which quickly transformed back into crying. "Yeah, I guess. Enough about me. How's it going living with Jon?" She dabbed the tears from her face with a napkin, hopelessly unconvinced. Her brain teetered from topic to topic. *I need to be more concerned about my daughter and stop acting so high-strung.* "There's more than enough room for you and Royael to live here. Most of the time, you'll have this house to yourself while I'm in L.A. or Damien's traveling."

"I've decided to get my own place." Raven began. "Okay, so I've been lollygagging, with the extra classes, I haven't had time. Maybe I'll pick up an apartment magazine the next time I'm at the grocery store."

Charlene's eyebrow arched as she noticed the determination in her eyes. Instead of addressing the concern she had for her daughter's sudden change of mind, she took out her phone and searched her contacts. "No *lived in* apartments, hon. I'm leaving a message for my realtor," she said, thumbs moving rapidly across the screen. "Voila! I can't wait to go house hunting."

"All right, Mom. Though I've the feeling that this is going to be more fun for you." She shook her head while pulling the business card out of her purse. "I finally spoke with Tyriq about Roy Timmons. He referred me to this guy named Stork."

Charlene took the card, though she'd rather have her toenails pulled off than find Roy.

"I'll go when you decide to talk to Stork." Raven rubbed her back.

"Let's deal with this later." Charlene dropped the card in the pocket of her blouse as Annette walked into the room, placing a tray of Blondie brownies on the table.

"Taste these and let me know what you think." Annette smiled triumphantly.

They both took a piece and praised her work.

"Good. That's the next dessert that I'm trying with the kiddies." She rubbed her hands together.

At the sound of the oven timer going off, Annette began to rise, but Raven popped up. "I'll get it, Granny. You've been doing all this cooking, how*ever*, you've forgotten about your stroke."

Annette pursed her lips and for the umpteenth time said, "I know they don't make grannies like they use to, but I'm old school, chile. We don't break easy."

Charlene watched her daughter exit as Annette gave her the look.

"I don't want to mention it now, Momma," Charlene whispered, knowing Annette wanted her on to bring up the Otis subject. Her body felt like it was being pulled in all sorts of directions as the card burned a hole in her pocket. Damien was mum. Her daughter lived with a half-brother. *Too much is going on to bring that up now.* She dreaded Raven's reaction. Besides it would only take her back to that day her daughter found her.

~~~

I'm married. I shouldn't be so sexually and emotionally frustrated! Charlene picked up a black plate with lilac peonies—her everyday china—and let it slip from her hands. Relishing the sound of broken glass, she continued her symphony of shattered dishes as Damien came rushing into the kitchen.

"What the hell is going on? Trinity is asleep." His eyes bugged out.

"I want to talk!" *I have to call Stork. I need you there for me!*

"Then *talk*. Stop breaking all of our dishes." The nerve on the side of his neck pulsated.

"I didn't do it!"

Damien kept his distance as her screams became sobs.

"I didn't cheat on you with Miguel." Her face a mixture of sadness and disbelief that he was near yet felt miles away.

"Did you want to?" His piercing eyes held onto her every whim.

A deep inhale of cool air traveled through her just parted lips. How could she explain the attraction that happened onset. Acting was a catalyst for cheating on spouses. "A…little. When I'm Meagan I want a lot of things that I know are wrong."

"Meagan wants Miguel, not Charlene." He reiterated then turned to walk out.

She stood in the middle of the kitchen, letting her hands rest on the edge of the granite countertop and her head dropped down. As she considered the words—the half truths—she'd just told her husband.

CHAPTER 40

Is this a consequence from tossing those pills? Darkness so thick Raven had to blink twice to know she wasn't in a dreamless sleep. Eyes adjusting, she grabbed the remote on the side dresser and pressed the button. Sunlight crushed the dimness as the curtains rolled up.

It's almost noon. Jon must've taken Royael to school. The modified extreme act of retribution was up in shambles. On the verge of just letting go, she wanted to avoid him until moving, but, she'd missed her leisure morning taking Royael to school and strolling into photography class in the nick of time. *Great, I've altered my entire day!*

She reflected on the call she'd had with Sharon last night. They'd hashed out this crazy new idea she'd come up with during the week Jon was out-of-town because she'd gone psycho. *I am a flake.* A feeling of confusion surrounded her, and she just couldn't do it. Sharon had said, "We're often afraid to achieve our deepest desires."

She got out of bed to that thought. She was petrified. *Maybe I should do something else? Nothing at all, perhaps?* Lips pursed, she considered letting go of this new tactic.

'Good thing, too. This idea of retribution will only rear around and bite you in the ass! The first idea was best.'

The doorbell rang. Descending the stairs, she rubbed her hand over her rumpled PJ shirt, noticing a big-body cream-colored car through the living room glass, an expensive–old money–car, unlike Jon's flashy rides.

She opened the heavy carved-wood door with both hands to a woman with white-blond hair and green eyes. Her eyebrows rose at the lady's extravagant mauve gown with embellished neckline. *Is this another one of Jon's dares? Do I have to go back to the opera with this lady?*

"Wait a minute." Raven's eyes dimmed in uncertainty, and then widened in shock. "Are you, are you…*you are* DuPont's masterpiece. His muse!"

"Yes, I'm that girl, but most people know *me* by name, Estella

Devereux."

Jaw dropped as Estella pulled her into a hearty hug. Raven was also shocked that floral perfume lingered at her nostrils when the woman pulled away. "I...."

"You're Raven Shaw." Estella patted her back. "And you, my dear, have impeccable taste in photography."

"When you did that pose in the 60s, the one where you bent backwards and..." Raven had to admit she was the first woman with a *French* accent that she didn't automatically dislike. Hand to chest, she tried to calm a swarm of bumble bees. "Jon never told me he was related–"

"I'm his grandmother, but he doesn't like me that much."

"Where are my manners? Come in." Raven moved to the side, noticing a chauffeur take mounds of luggage out of the trunk. He placed them just inside and the canvas luggage stacked almost as tall as the bonsai tree. Estella bid him farewell then turned back to Raven, tapping a finger to her lips.

"You're too petite to be a model. Nonetheless, you know great photography so it's safe to assume that you're of like spirits?" Estella linked arms with Raven as she stared at the luggage in bewilderment. "Let's leave this to Jon. Point me in the direction of the kitchen. We'll have refreshments, and you can tell me all about your photography. How does that sound?"

"I can make an espresso?" Raven offered as they entered the kitchen.

Estella put her bejeweled hands together. "Perfect!"

Raven pulled out the ingredients as Estella went into the pantry and came out with a fresh baguette. They sat down at the table with warm sliced bread and steaming cups.

"Tsk, tsk, we've both overlooked the necessities. I'll get the jam. Go, grab your portfolio." With poise, Estella whisked toward the sub-zero refrigerator.

Raven hurried upstairs. She wanted, no she *needed* this critique. In her room she pulled her leather-bound portfolio out of her backpack and hurried downstairs.

"This is the best espresso I've ever had." Estella set the cup on the table and took the portfolio.

Squirming in her seat, Raven watched her take in each photo.

"Hmmm… there's a development of style growing stronger." She stopped on the photographs of Tattoo Man. "Beautiful specimen." Nodding gingerly, she continued. "Your emotions have transformed over the course of these photos. You've evolved."

~~~

Smiling, Jon pulled into the driveway. There was a pep in his step as he remembered returning Raven's missed call and she'd mentioned that she had a surprise, sounding so giddy—his "old" Raven. And to top it all off, Tyriq found Lucinda.

"Your mother forged the letters that she gave to you and Raven, I'm so sorry…" Lucinda confirmed what he already knew, and he couldn't wait to tell Raven.

"Mommy's home early!" Royael cheered as they walked through the side door.

His eyebrows came together as he noticed mountains of suitcases. *What type of surprise did she have in mind, buying enough Louis Vuitton luggage for a small army?* Then he looked up into Nana's eyes!

Estella drew him into an excited embrace; he half-heartedly returned the favor, patting her back with his hand. Raven stood on the bridge with a Cheshire grin. She jumped, clapping her hands. "Your grandma's here; surprise!"

"What a surprise it is." Sarcasm poisoned his enthusiasm and he couldn't help but notice Estella's cheeriness waver.

"Jon, I need your help with something then we can go to dinner." Raven disappeared down the hall.

Perceiving a Chihuahua-scolding coming on, he started for the stairs as his grandmother told Royael that she had a gift for her. "It's haute couture. Do you know what that means?"

"Nope," Royael replied softly.

"It means that nobody in the world will ever have the same

beautiful dress as you."

"Yay!" Royael clapped her hands.

Everybody is excited about this woman but me! He walked into Raven's room and shut the door. She sat on the couch with her hands folded at her lap. The yellow summer dress she wore made the brown flecks in her blue eyes turn gold. Her glossy, pink lips were pulled into a pout. He decided to look at the top of her head, too angry to let her pretty face control him now.

"Jon, that wasn't nice."

"I didn't know Estella was coming." Stuffing his hands in slate gray Dolce &Gabbana slacks, Jon stopped at the window and stare at the sunset peaking through the trees.

"You barely hugged your Nana. She loves you and talked about you all day."

"You don't get to call her Nana." He turned back to look at her, saw the anger on her tensed shoulders. He didn't care. Today he should've been giving her the news from Lucinda and recommencing their previous festivities. "Why does she have *all* that luggage?"

"Estella's staying here until the grand opening in Orlando."

He rubbed a finger to his brow, staving off a headache. "Who said so? I didn't."

"Be nice. She told me that you and your grandfather bullied her around–well, not you really…your grandfather bullies her around and you let him. Why don't you take up for your Na–grandma?"

He looked into befuddled eyes. "You of all people know how she's treated me as a child. The torment that I went through living in France before high school doesn't jog your memory?" *Don't you care?*

Raven walked to the dresser and plucked a picture from the mirror. "Look at this photo."

He glared at a picture of a shorter, fatter version of himself in front of Cheateu de Estella, holding hands with Nana. They were barefoot, with big grins, carefree, while holding up bunches of grapes. Over ten years ago, the day was a vague memory, but it looked like the time he left at the age of fourteen. *I was overweight and she hated me for it…but we looked like we were having a good time.* The picture didn't make since. He'd remember her calling him fat and forcing him to only speak French until he spoke fluently. And he did recall the feel of aching cheeks after she'd pinched them.

He sat the picture back on the dresser and noticed a realtor listing. His jaw instantly tensed. *You're moving?* That was his cue to leave.

"Pierre seems to have alienated your grandma," Raven said, watching him walk to the door.

"Don't talk about my grandfather. You don't know him, so you have no say."

"I know your *Nana!* In one day, I've learned more about her than I ever knew about anyone else in your family! Elise or Jonathan—all I can say is I know her *and* I like her *and* she's staying!" Raven shouldered him as she headed for the door. Before walking out, she affirmed, "Get ready, we are going to dinner."

~~~

"No, Daddy, I want Grandma to sit next to me." Royael placed her hand on the leather cushion as they made their way around the dark, heavy-wood steakhouse.

"Get over yourself, Jon." Raven patted his shoulder as he slid inside the booth next to her. "You'll live. I did, after our child treated me in much the same way when you came around."

Even with her attitude, the touch almost soothed his brewing irritation. He wriggled his tense jaw; it had been set since he'd learned of her house hunting. He had the attention span of a three-year-old, while he contemplated Raven's realtor listing as Estella told "happy stories" of her childhood visits to France. Drinking cognac, he crunched on ice and tuned out Royael's delight of said "stories."

That night, Royael wanted her great-grandmother to put her to bed. Raven linked arms with him as they ambled into the house, letting the two run ahead. She whispered, "You did well."

"I wasn't trying to," his replied.

She kicked off her sandal wedges and stood on a suede footstool in the living room, a smidge below eyelevel with him. Placing her hands on his shoulders, she said, "I remember what you told me about Estella, but just take this time to love her. Okay, buddy?"

"I *do* love her."

The next move came so natural. His eyes closed as she touched the back of his neck, like she'd done so many times when they were together. Her massage overwhelmed his senses and he almost didn't hear her words.

"…Start over with Nana."

Tensions gone and no longer feeling the delicate caress, Jon opened his eyes as she patted his shoulder. Before he could say anything, she jumped down and hurried up the stairs.

~~~

Raven yawned as she rumpled the towel through her hair. *Those pills were a blessing and a curse…* Swiping her forearm across the fogged bathroom mirror, her body shuddered as she could still feel how she'd kneaded Jon's shoulders earlier this evening. It was a mistake. *I'm supposed to be putting distance between us. I'll feel like a dum-dum if what Tyriq mentioned about searching for Lucinda….* Sighing, she didn't finish that thought.

"There's no future for us," she murmured. Quickening her pace, she pulled on a cream romper and slipped into brown leather boots. Cassidy had called, begging for her to cover the night shift. *Thanks, Cass. I need to get away.*

A gray blur cast over the hallway from the skylight as she walked out of her room. *I'll be glad for long summer nights.* Getting use to the dark, she didn't flip the switch while jogging downstairs.

"Where are you going?"

She turned to see nightfall cast a silhouette on Jon as he leaned on the wood banister at the bridge. Before hurrying out, she quickly replied, "To work. I have to close."

~~~

At the coffee shop, Raven made herself a *triple*-pick-me-up as the night dragged on. She'd helped Cassidy prim for a hot date. After her friend left, customers wandered in from nearby clubs or an occasional diehard bookworm trickled in, taking a corner seat.

"It's ten minutes 'til three. I'm closing soon." She reminded a guy with a mop of frizzy hair that always typed the night away while guzzling mugs of coffee. Standing at the counter, she yawned extra loud. He glanced up from his laptop as acknowledgement then typing engulfed her ears once again.

Frowning, she turned around and went through the swinging door to put away the last load of pastry racks from the dishwasher. A chime sound indicating that the guy left. Locking the backdoors, she cringed when the chime sounded again. *Shoulda locked the front first, but Carrot Top wouldn't leave! I'm so tired.* She gripped the keys tightly, hurrying through the swinging doors. "Can't you read? I'm closing! I'm not making another—"

Voice caught, she stopped within the threshold as the door swung back and pushed her forward. Jon's hands were stuffed into the pockets of his leather jacket and he stared at the black and white photos on the walls. He didn't address her as he moved to another black framed photo of a cup of coffee with cream zigzagged through it. Finally finished, he turned to Raven.

Why are you here? "You like the photos?" Mundane talk.

"Yeah," he replied, eyes still on the pictures.

"I did them."

"Are these the first you've sold?"

"I didn't *sell* them. Sometimes people do things for pleasure and not to turn a profit." Instead of locking herself in the store with him, she placed the keys on the counter and picked up a dishrag. All the tables were clean, but she had to keep moving, no longer sleepy.

"You've given me an idea." He watched as she flitted about in no clear order.

"What?" She asked, squirting disinfectant spray and wiped until the counter was a reflection of her sudden neatness frenzy.

"I may open a hotel that displays artistic flare."

"Good for you." Her eyes brightened, the table was soaked with liquid and sanitizer dripped from the nozzle of the bottle to her knuckles. She stopped spraying and wiped.

"What if I want to use some of your work?"

"Why?" Her eyes riveted up to his broad shoulders. She hadn't notice him standing right before her. Trying to hide her surprise, she moved to another table. Keeping him in the corner of her eye, she wondered when he'd leave. *I've almost re-cleaned all these tables.*

"Why not? What if you become a famous photographer? It's more economical for me to purchase your work now, then later. I loved the photo we did that night…"

She watched his lips move as he referred to them as "we," when she'd done the star trails.

"I didn't come here for that. We'll discuss those dynamics later." He blocked her path as she tried to pass by toward the last table he hadn't seen her clean. "You've been avoiding me. What was that in the hallway when we got home? It seemed you'd let your guard down."

A regret. "A pep talk." Raven backtracked and went polish-psycho on another already clean table. When finished, her heart nearly dropped as he was still here, *still* waiting. She yawned for good measure. "Let me finish so we can go home. I'm sleepy, okay?"

He shrugged and leaned against a table. Hoping the determination in his eyes would wash away, she started on the cash-register counter. The coffee shop was as clean as she'd ever seen it. Cassidy's father might get leery and think she wanted a raise, but she couldn't stop. The coffee-mug clock read that he'd watched her work for over twenty minutes. *"The Sugar and Spice Station!"* She walked to the trolley, rearranging the sugar and cinnamon then moved the brown sugar. Her hands were on the pumpkin spice when he spoke.

"You've been trying to take away my control," Jon said.

She put down the pumpkin spice. *I have not!*

"Taking me out of my element." His deep voice was creamier than the finest caramel. "What you don't know is, I haven't been in control since you walked into my office."

Again, she picked up the pumpkin spice, bit her lip, and considered putting it amid the nutmeg and orange spice. *No wait*, Raven mentally

Miss Scandalous

sang the alphabet and put it after the orange spice.

"You've been in control this whole time. Will you turn around, so we can talk?"

Gulping, she did and leaned against the counter, wringing the cloth in her hands. He sat on a table further away, but his honey eyes were searching hers for a reaction. A reaction that she refused to give. Hope was useless, it was best not to care...

He hopped off the table. In a few strides he stood inches away, looking down at her. "Do you still love me?"

Blue eyes gazing to the floor, her legs had already gone weak and her brain was fried, too. If only she could reach out and steady herself against him. *No.* She leaned back against the trolley, with nowhere else to go.

"Jon, we're half-brother and sister, so just stop." She snapped to keep from crying. Moving past him with a blur of tears in her eyes, her legs were heavy, and her heart was so heavy that it turned traitor to her brain. Sleep deprivation sparked forbidden love. Her insides warmed as he stood behind her, his breath caressing her neck.

"I spoke with Lucinda." He kissed her shoulder. His hand tingled at her nape danced around to her shoulder, and then he pushed her hair to the side.

Jon's arms snaked around her and her body molded, weakening against his. "They falsified the DNA test between you and my father—"

Me and Jonathan...please stop... Breath shallow, she could barely hear for her pounding heart. His kisses teased her skin, making her dizzy. In a last effort to save herself, she took her fingers and pried his from around her waist.

"Stop!" She glared at him, with tears in her eyes. At this moment, she had him exactly where he needed to be. She could extract revenge—

"We can be together." His thick eyebrows came together.

"I have to lock up." Raven swiveled on her heels and went through the swinging doors to do one last inspection. When she returned, he was gone. On the center table lay the spoon ring. *He's been in my room.* She stepped toward it. There was a napkin with the words "your

223

choice" scribbled on it. She balled it up and put it in the trash.

~~~

The sun peeked over the horizon as Raven pulled in front of the glass house. Body, mind, and soul drained from heavy thinking, she walked over the bridge and to the front door. She inserted the key into the slot, wondering if she could fully be happy with Jon's recent revelation. It took all of her strength to push the door open and step inside. The glass walls were shrouded in darkness and all she wanted was the light of the sun to warm her mood.

"What did you choose?" Jon's deep voice broke through the steel gloom.

In fear of losing her mind, she placed out her hand. The spoon ring graced her finger. In one fluid motion he scooped her up. Her arms went around his neck and her lips sought his. Springtime… Love that was once in hibernation sprang to life as every fiber in her being shuttered to his touch, his warmth, his scent.

"Hurry," she commanded in a seductive, primal tone as he carried her up to his room. With ravenous lips, she almost cried out as he placed her down. With a maddening look on his face, he searched her romper to take it off. Before she could assist, his big hands tore at the shoulder straps and it dropped to the floor.

Pulse rising, Raven yanked on Jon's belt as he quickly pulled off his shirt. She pushed at his pectorals-of-steel until he sat back on the bed with a naughty grin. Sultry hands gripped her waist and slid her on top of him. Breast against his, heartbeats on fire. In between sucking and kissing, he whispered in her ear, in English and presumably Italian as her hands trail down his taut muscles. She left a trail of love to his skin as the language of love came out of his just parted lips. Addicted, she couldn't have enough as her lips dawdled over his lower abs.

After minutes of torment, he grabbed a fist of her hair, tugging softly as he declared what he needed. She crawled back up, straddling him. Body ablaze with fire, it was time to commence vengeance, and every fiber of her body would enjoy it.

Before leaving him high and dry, she had to make him love her.

CHAPTER 41

Charlene opened the front door of her Dallas home and looked into Stork's dark eyes. Despite her hesitance, she'd called him. The retired FBI agent wasn't the type that you feed information to over the phone. He had rules and requirements which were written all over his two-button slate-gray suit. His handshake was firm and greeting monotone.

Her heart skipped a beat when Damien came and introduced himself. They weren't on—other than Trinity speaking terms, but his presence sent notes of optimism to her heart. Damien led the way to the upstairs office. Visualizing Marcus Weber laying on the middle of the floor, she almost leaped over the Oriental rug.

Stork sat in the high-back, maroon chair across from them and took out a tape recorder. Smile fleeting, he spoke in an authoritarian tone. "Charlene, I need you to go back to that day. Tell me everything that you remember, everything that you said, everything Roy Timmons said. Describe the places that you went. Even if you believe something is irrelevant, tell me. You're a director, compiling a story for me from the biggest detail down to the most miniscule piece."

She nodded, not really knowing where to begin, yet a vivid reflection of her tormentor crossed her vision. "Roy had a southern accent. He reminded me of Butch Cassidy."

Flapping her hands, she fanned her flushed face. It was suddenly hotter than hell. Having her husband near, even with him rubbing her back, made her fan harder. Part of her didn't want him to know the details. Not to the fullest extent. "The big rig was pale blue…"

Standing up abruptly, she paced the floor. "I keep thinking about the dreams I had, and I don't want to tell you something false."

Stork nodded for her to continue.

Throat clamped shut; the part she dreaded was here. She delved into what she remembered about meeting Roy Timmons's and going in and out of consciousness while in the back of his big-rig. "The trailer had an awful smell…" she thought about Marcus and how he'd reeked of a similar stench. Like the demons that infected him were the same as Roy's. "…and Roy had a gold necklace with a cross of Jesus."

The hairs on her forearms prickled. His necklace had beckoned her to take a ride with him after she'd missed the bus. In a self-comforting hug, she walked to the window, mind on Raven. She peered past the gauzy drapes as a plane zipped through the clouds. Her daughter left for Orlando with Jon this morning. Rubbing her hands through her hair, she wondered if it was a good idea.

"Charlene," Stork's voice seized and forced her into reality, "take your time and think."

"I just don't know." Her hands went in the air in defeat. "What if I tell you something that's not true? Something th-that I dreamed and…" *what if you find him?*

"C'mon, babe," Damien said in her ear as he guided her back to the seat. "Take your time. Just start with the beginning."

"I missed the Greyhound. Instead of going back home, I sat at the bus stop to think. Then I heard industrial noises behind me." She closed her eyes and heard Roy's soothing, country voice console her while she cried.

"He introduced himself as Roy Timmons and offered me a ride…" Eyebrows kneaded together, she remembered them stopping at a gas station in Kentucky that night, right before she'd felt dizzy. Damien wrapped an arm around her as tears streamed down her face and she mentioned waking up in the back of the big rig.

"Mrs. Wright, do you know how long you were there? How many hours? Days?"

"I woke up a couple of times, but I was tied up. There were no windows."

"By a rope? Chains? What material?"

"I-I don't know," she stuttered, fidgeting with her fingers. "It-it was a rope!"

"How was it tied? Sloppy? Boy Scout?–"

"Coiled, like a noose–no, that can't be right…let me think,"

Charlene stammered. Her hand went to her neck. She felt a thick, braided rope laced around it, but wait, *weren't my hands behind my back?* "I don't remember. It had to be days, though. He tried to feed me breakfast a few times and other food throughout the day."

"Did he speak to you when he tried feeding you?"

"No, no–yes! Roy said I was different than the others..."

In her mind, old wounds were whelps again. She continued to tell the story and had to look down at her skin to be sure the stinging sensation was her imagination. No crimson liquid seeped from her soul. Her dark skin was still supple.

"Thank you, Charlene. I'm sure you think this is the hard part." Stork looked her in the eye, and she found herself missing some of his words. As she prayed that he wasn't as serious as he appeared, he said, "Once I find him–and trust me, I will–this is only the beginning."

Charlene nodded, hoping with all her might that Stork would fail.

~~~

In a modest nightgown, Charlene looked at herself in the mirror. Her hand edged upward to the side of her temple and felt around for the scar.

"I didn't know."

Charlene jumped and tensed at Damien's voice behind her. She hadn't noticed his reflection as he stood just inside the bedroom door. Roy Timmons had taken over. She felt him wriggling over her body. She smelt his disgust, mingling with her fear. *Go away, Damien.*

Her shoulders went taut as Damien wrapped his arms around her from behind. He had to pry her hands apart to entwine with his. *I looked into Roy's beautiful blue eyes when we met, but I hadn't been afraid. I should've been afraid.*

"Breathe." Damien applied pressure to her diaphragm.

Taking a sharp mouthful of air, she remembered when Damien had forced her to ride on the freeway. She'd had a phobia for years and her husband had broken that trepidation. Could he break the fear that coursed through her veins just now?

"Don't let Roy take control," he whispered. His hand slid up her arm, trailed her shoulder, and up her neck. He reached around her iron-straight hair until he felt the lump on her forehead.

Charlene's head dipped in shame. She wanted to be alone. She tried to pull away, but he turned her around. Then she saw something she'd never seen before... tears in her husband's eyes.

"Please..." she tried again to move out of his searing gaze. *What must you think of me?*

"I'm sorry." He held her tight. "I won't ever let you go."

The shame she clung to chiseled away. Her laden arms went around his waist, letting his words–strong, powerful words–stroke her spirit. Kissing Damien was the only way to rid her conscious of Roy. Her mouth frantically hungered for his, and he stopped her with a thumb to her plush lips.

His thumb traced her pouty mouth. He reached over and kissed her breath away.

Slowly. A time-stopping desire that intensified as he gave her the best love she'd ever had.

CHAPTER 42

Water rushed along the shores of the Orlando Devereux Hotel. Employees hoisted canopies, with the gold "D" crest, around a stage for the night's grand opening. Arms resting on the balcony of the penthouse suite, Raven prayed for her mom's talk with Stork as salty wind flowed through her hair. The first day of summer and the elements were being particularly difficult as she opened her eyes to see a set of workers below scurrying toward a runaway tent.

She grabbed the towel next to the Jacuzzi, wrapping it around herself then walked back into the living room of the suite to dress for the night. She sighed, thinking about meeting Pierre Devereux, and she hadn't seen Jonathan Dubois in years–and years wasn't enough time to still her anger from the way he'd tried to toss money in her face and discard her. *At least now when I finish with Jon, and target him, well, at the very least, I'm not his child…*

It had been a busy morning. She hadn't seen Jon since their arrival last night, and even on the Learjet his blue tooth was glued to his ear. Ascending the spiral staircase, she went down a long crystal and gold decorated hallway.

"Not like that!" Royael's snappy voice stopped Raven just outside the door. If it weren't for the chipmunk tone, Raven would've bet money that the rudeness didn't come from her child. She peeked inside to see her daughter in a royal purple bubble dress and Amethyst earrings, while a stylist curled her hair.

Making a mental note to reprimand to the girl later, Raven walked down the hall to the lilac textured room she shared with Jon. He stood at the vanity, adjusting a satin bowtie. She licked her lips at scrumptiousness-in-a-tuxedo and prepared to sneak up behind him when he turned around.

"Do you like the dress?" His mischievous smile faded. "C'mon, Raven. You're not ready."

"I thought we had an hour or so." That's what the ultra-glossy invitations read. Besides, she planned to be prompt.

"You have thirty minutes." He looked at her in the mirror while brushing the waves in his hair.

She sat down at the edge of the bed. "Why didn't you tell me you got me a dress? I could have saved hours of shopping with my mom."

"You can wear yours to the next event." He sprayed intoxicating cologne and gave one last look in the mirror. Pecking her cheek, he left the room.

This doesn't feel like control. She waited for her conscience to give a sharp retort. Eyebrows knitted together, she recollected to the last time the voice spoke. *It's been a while. Woohoo!*

After a rushed shower, she stepped onto the cold marble just as someone knocked on the door. Putting on a thick robe, and quickly wrapping a towel around her hair, she stepped past the vanity into the bedroom and opened it. A woman with a curly afro walked in, toting a large rollaway.

"Sorry, I'm late. I'll set up while you get dressed. Let me know if you need any help." The stylist stopped at the vanity that separated the bathroom and the bedroom.

"Thanks." Raven hurried to get ready. Dressed, she rubbed her hands down a buttery-soft gown that fit like a glove, falling to the floor with a short train. Her heart drummed wildly as she turned and examined herself in the full-length mirror. The plunging neckline stopped just above her belly button, one false move and the guests would get a free view of her goodies. Looking over her shoulder, her eyes bugged out. *My whole back is exposed.* She could imagine Granny shaking her head and warning, "You gonna catch a cold, just to get a man to look at you."

"You look gorg'," the stylist said as Raven sat on the cushiony white chair. The bright lights shined down on an arsenal of hair products. "Since your dress is so exotic, I wanted to put your hair up. Trust me, you gotta show off these earrings Jon bought." She ran her hands through Raven's hair. "You should take off that ring. It doesn't go with the sleek style or the gold dress."

"No, I'm wearing it." Raven turned the ring with her thumbs.

"Okay, what about the bangles? They don't go either."

"I'm wearing those too. Look, I really didn't need help getting dressed. I'm not a celebrity." *I know just how I want to look.*

"Hey, I get it." The stylist finished a ringlet of hair with the curling iron and patted her shoulder. "You're not use to the limelight and being in all of those magazines. Tonight is a big event. God forbid you go out with one strand of hair unkempt, the world will know."

Digging through the side compartment of the leather case, the stylist pulled out a couple of magazines and placed them into Raven's hands. As her hair was being curled, she scanned over the papers. Though the articles hadn't bashed her physical appearance, she'd been resorted to the title of Jon's "baby mama" and was as important enough for an "on-and-off again fling over the years." One magazine suggested that she'd gotten her claws back into him when he moved to Dallas.

"Playboy settles," she said under her breath. Having enough of the awful untruths, she pushed them onto the counter with the rest of the junk. A stretched string of breath escaped her lips as she tried to settle the knots that were playing twister within her abdomen.

The stylist finished by placing a long chain around her neck. The gold, infinity pendant dropped the eyes to her chest. She blinked her eyelids, a beautiful peacock of art. By celebrity standards, she was ready. *Now, how am I going to wear these Versace stilettos all night? This is not me.*

~~~

Aliens. Raven felt like she and her child were extraterrestrial beings–the little creepy ones with small bodies and balloon-sized heads–as Pierre Devereux sat across from them at a round banquet table. Too bad the bouquet of orchids in the center wasn't taller. He sat next to Elise. Raven tried not to gawk, thankful that Elise kept averting her eyes. Only one of her enemies hadn't showed. *Why wouldn't Jonathan be here for his son?* She tuned in every time a round of claps commenced, while a few of the board members of Devereux Corp gave speeches.

When Jon stood up, Raven whispered "Good luck" as he kissed her cheek. Stomach full of imaginary pop rocks, a few bites of house salad, and filet mignon, she watched him venture to the stage. His confident stride turned the heads of D Hotel's most exclusive investors and guests, the super wealthy that could buy her a gazillion times over. *This is not me...*

"Don't worry," Estella said into her ear. "He's an old dog! They're more bark than bite."

Raven's eyebrows scrunched, until realizing that Estella attempted to comfort her after the introductions with Pierre. He appeared polite enough, but something about him just didn't sit right with her. Maybe he was a posh vessel–an empty body. No organs. No heart. She gave Estella a weak smile and listened as Jon began his speech, making sure her spine was straight. She hadn't sat back since arriving. His ambitiousness enticed her, along with half of the other female-dummies batting their lashes. Raven's eyes narrowed as she looked around, trapping Elise's green ones for a splinter of a second and was caught off guard when she heard Jon mention her name. Instantly, she felt guilty for not being focused. Once again, she averted all her attention to his speech, trying not to think about how out-of-sorts she felt. When the attendants came around with silver carts of dessert, Elise excused herself. Raven braced herself to stand as Royael spoke.

"Daddy, I want to go to Disneyworld. This is boring!"

"We'll go later," Jon replied.

"Yes," Raven added, arising. She hastened toward the double doors and had to slow herself down while pushing through them. She peered down a hallway with mermaid and sea-creature gold-marble statues and gazed around guests in ball gowns and tuxedos. Just like her, *but not* just like her. She looked toward the restroom; maybe Elise had gone in there. Slipping into the powder room, with gold-textured walls, she sighed. *Aw shit!*

Towering almost as high as the chandelier, Camille threw daggers of hate. "Hello, little *girl*."

"Good evenin', Godzilla." Raven tried to pass her, toward the stalls.

"Sit with me." Camille grabbed her arm and plunked them both down on a silk chaise.

Jesus, help me out here. This is Jon's event.

"I love that tacky ring of yours, it's so...*you*."

"How cute, you're still stuck on me. My bad, though. I assumed it would be easy for Miss Camille Laurent to nab a new sugar daddy." Her heart started booming again and anger rose like waves. Light gray. She saw Camille as the punching bag in Jon's house, could feel the euphoria of pummeling her face. Dark gray. *Not now, I can't feel this anger now.* Breathing in and out, like Stanton had taught, she calmed herself back to light gray.

"No sugar daddies tonight. Where would my manners be since Jon invited me, you silly goose," Camille giggled, leaning over to pat her shoulder.

"That's bull. He wouldn't invite your T-Rex looking ass!" Raven stood as dark gray descended.

"Yes, he did. Look at me, little girl!" Camille arose gracefully and pushed her index finger in Raven's face, and it was slapped back down. "I'll get him back."

"Camille Laurent, you will *not* behave this way in my hotel." In a lace gown, Elise embellished the doorway of the restroom and the sitting area. "Jon doesn't want a vain puppet like you!"

The dinosaur scampered out of the room, thoroughly insulted.

Raven looked at Jon's mother. Bristling, she was unsure if the woman took up for her or just saved Jon from Camille. Mood still dark, a devilish grin took over. "Glad to see your hair has grown back, Mrs. Dubois." *Opps, I'm supposed to talk to her about all those wasted years Royael didn't get to see her daddy...first.*

"Actually," Elise began, twirling her finger through a string of pearls. "This is a wig. Though my hair *has* grown back, I've taken a liking to them, since you broke into my house and put hair removal into my shampoo. I'm still appalled that the wrinkle, old man sweet talked—"

"Actually, that *wrinkled, old man*, Grandpa Otis, had a nice talk with my father." Raven smirked. Black overwhelmed gray as her eyes narrowed. "Wait, wait, Jonathan isn't my father, now, is he?"

Elise shrugged as her lips curled in contentment, then she pivoted on her heels to walk away, but Raven stepped in her path.

"I suggest you move. *Otis* can't save you anymore." Elise stepped closer and pearly-white teeth came out to play. "Aw, he's dead. This is not the little town of Bellwood. You've fooled a few with that designer gown, but I know trash when I see it." Her nose crinkled as she stepped closer, "When I smell it. There will be no more of your shenanigans, Miss Shaw."

"Thank you, Elise. I love you so much," she began and almost laughed when Elise's face paled in shock. "You've always been good at stooping to the gutter and your mannerisms smell like–your true colors… *shit*. It's a good thing you weren't born poor, because wealth is all you have."

"It's too bad. Well, you reaped some of the benefit of my wealth, being connected with Jon."

"Um-hum. Do you remember when I'd get into fights as a child? I'm sure you do. That's one of the reasons you wanted Jon to stay away from me, right? Except you don't know that besides fighting my battles–the name callers and gossipers about my mom– I fought Jon's battles, too. The people that called him fat," Raven paused as Elise placed her hands on narrowed hips. "What you also don't know is that I'd feel a since of exhilaration. It felt *oh, so good* and then I'd blackout. Beat the shit out 'em, until Jon or someone else could pull me off. Now, I haven't fought in a while. As a mother, I let it ride. I hold it in– my anger. Remember that the next time you cross me. You'll see *just how much* I've been holding in."

"Hmmm, is that so?" Elise beamed brighter than the sun. "I'm thoroughly insulted. I've known you since you were a wee baby. It hurts my heart that you would resort to threats."

Raven gave her a sideways glance at her mockery. "No. Not threats. Promises. *I promise* the next time you mess with me, I'm going to beat you until my heart overflows with joy."

"Sounds barbarically delightful." Elise's green eyes twinkled as she made her exit.

"Yes, it may very well be…" Raven sat, closed her eyes and rubbed her face. She screamed obscenities into her hands and a blonde walked past, with a turned up nose. *I can't be that person, not for Royael, not for myself! Oh, but I want to.* She hurried out the door. To her misfortune, she ran into Pierre.

"My dear, accompany me to the terrace." Before she could reply his chilly hand guided the small of her back.

A warm oceanic breeze forced air into Raven's lungs, reminding her to breathe. An attendant offered them champagne from a silver tray. She hadn't had a drink all day but took the one that Pierre handed to her. She watched the less wealthy—but rich—celebrating the grand opening of the hotel on the oceanfront. Board members and other Devereux employees slowly trickled outside to mingle for PR purposes. Live jazz floated on the salty wind in their direction.

"You're wearing one of my rings."

Raven looked down at her hands on the marble slab. "I didn't know…"

"I gave a case of those very spoon rings to Elise. Between you and I, she doesn't know the value of antiques. I'd love to see her wearing something from a different era, of course."

He smiled down at her, causing the madness to waft away. She noticed that he had Jon's gold eyes—that softened his appearance. Well over six feet, with a full head of wavy, dark-blond hair, Pierre also had definition of muscle beneath his tailored tux, exemplifying that he was in the prime of his life.

"If she only knew how much it was worth," Pierre shrugged and took a sip.

She found herself saying, "It's magnificent, no matter the worth."

"You're absolutely correct."

They stood in a silence of contentment for a while. Maybe he wasn't half as intimidating as he appeared? He seemed genuinely interested in her, asking about her being a photographer.

"I just finished my second year in the program." She remembered when she and Jon were young and they'd burn insects under magnifying classes. This was her moment to be scrutinized but under a magnifying glass with 'smiley faces.'

"So you *don't* have any experience?" Pierre asked.

"I'm learning. I would be happy to show you my portfolio."

"I've already seen it, my dear." He stepped close and whispered in her ear, "You assume a man of my stature doesn't know all about a girl like you?"

Yup, this is the worst day ever. His iron wing had her pinned to the spot. Faster than the snap of a finger, he'd gone from sexy-seventy to devious-dog.

"I know you more than you know yourself. You didn't want Jon in middle school."

"How did you arrive at that conclusion?" She scoffed. *Whatever, you won't be getting the best of me.*

"Jon was depressed and in love when he moved to Paris at the age of fourteen. A series of unfortunate events occurred when you noticed him as a senior. He wasn't so *short* and *fat* then. You used him, got yourself pregnant for a paycheck. I'm aware of what he sees in you. You're an exotic beauty." His warm breath singed the side of her cheek. "You filthy little vixen. Give it a couple of months and you'll be back in the gutter where you belong. And my Legacy will be over you."

"Pierre, this is a grand opening, I must say."

They both turned to see Tyriq sauntering onto the terrace.

"All the credit goes to my Legacy." Pierre patted Tyriq's back, took a sip of champagne and walked back into the hotel.

This is not me... Raven turned back to watch the festivities. Fireworks played off her glossy eyes, but she wouldn't dare let a tear fall. She downed the gold-trimmed flute of champagne.

"So did I save you?" Tyriq folded his hands on the banister.

"You don't know the half of it. I was getting ready to–" Raven flexed her fingers, making a "wring the neck" symbol then said, "On second thought, I shouldn't be telling you *the law*."

He mirrored her smile. "No, you probably shouldn't inform me of your plans to commit premeditated murder."

"Well, thank you for the advice." She felt as self-conscious as she did when first putting on the revealing gown as his eyes roamed over her body. When his gaze stopped at her breasts, her breath caught. *Did he have x-ray vision?* She folded her arms across her chest.

"I think I've got you pegged." She winked at the man in the Armani suit, loving their carefree game. "You're the bad cop. You get your kicks off taunting criminals?"

"That's me. If you want an example, I'll pull all the stops, tie you *up*, pat you *down*." He licked his lips. "That's only the beginning."

Laughter came from deep down in her belly, trying to take the nervousness out of his obvious flirting. *It isn't our time, yet.* Head tilting slightly, she became serious, "How do you do it? I noticed that your mother, a Tate, is on the Devereux board. So how do you get away with wearing jeans and riding a motorcycle and…roughing it? —taking bad guys down with guns and stuff. These people are stuffy; they don't look like they would like—"

She paused when his eyebrows rose. "I'm sorry, Tyriq. Am I insulting you? You clean up very well. I'm just saying, that most of these people have advanced degrees and…"

"I'm a handsome, uneducated, hothead?" He asked, face blank.

"No, no," she patted his shoulder, "I'm sorry."

He erupted in laughter. All of the air expelled from her lungs. Frowning, she folded her arms. "Go ahead, Detective TT, get your kicks at my expense. I'll have you know, I've had a hard day."

"Hey, you called me the bad cop." He gave one last chuckle, "I know what you mean. Jon is the guy that speaks five different languages. Pierre uses that creepy voice to refer to him as a Legacy. Jon's gone to school in France and wears suits every day. I'm born and bred in it, but I'm supposed to be part of this crew?"

"Yeah, and they look at me like I don't belong. Even in Versace. These are killing me by the way." She took off the heels and wriggled her toes then slipped them back on.

He lifted her chin. "Don't belong. That's why Jon loves you, because you don't belong."

Raven bit her lip. His callused hand traced her shoulder and grazed her arm as it went down to his side. Tension mounted between them. He liked to joke, maybe even with every woman he met, but he'd never intentionally touched her in all of the time that they'd known each other.

"We better get back to the party. That gorgeous date of yours might be getting lonely," Raven said. *Yes, we're right where we should be.*

"What's going on out here?" She jumped when she heard Jon's exaggerated tone. Instinctively, she moved away from Tyriq and noticed Pierre just inside of the doorway. Mr. Devereux had a sneaky twinkle in his eyes. *Did he just send Jon out here?*

Jon walked over with a smile.

"I was saving Raven from the 'legacy talk.'" Tyriq backed away.

Jon's arms wrapped around her, his lips brushed her neck with a soft kiss. An image of Tyriq winking at her before disappearing into the hotel, embedded in her mind as her eyes closed. She allowed Jon's kisses and Italian sexy words to tease and sooth her heart.

After a moment she opened her eyes. "Legacy?"

"Don't mind Grandfather. He always calls me that."

Raven turned to look at the roaring dark sea. With so much love in him as he spoke about Pierre, her heart sank. She didn't want anything to do with a stupid legacy. The old man had talked as if he were worshipping Jon. *That sick bastard needs Jesus!*

~~~

The next morning while Royael ate breakfast and everyone got ready to go to Disneyworld, Raven slipped upstairs to call Charlene about the meeting with Stork.

Jon's phone was on the dresser besides hers. Instincts had her fingers glued to it. *He loves me.* Trust made her put it back down. Grumbling, she picked the sleek phone up again and scrolled down the numbers. There were missed calls from Camille, from last night and yesterday morning–*before* and *after* the opening. Channeling her inner-PI, she clicked on Camille's contact number to see the call history. They'd talked on a few occasions even after the night at the coffee shop. *Okay. There has to be a good explanation for this. How to go about it?* She waited for a quick reply, but the voice was really gone.

She decided to ask Jon about Camille after they'd taken Royael to the theme park. But the next day he surprised her with a day on *The Stellar*, Estella's super yacht. Estella and Royael played on the boat, and after lunch, yet another surprise. He'd had all the equipment necessary for underwater photography. Camille Laurent was far from her mind as was the voice.

CHAPTER 43

Charlene bit her nails down to the white meat, thinking about the new season. Miguel had become Meagan's ally on season seven, meaning lots of manipulation and intimacy between the characters. Off set, he'd reluctantly caved to her wishes to keep their distance. From yards away in the shadows of the filming area–if they weren't doing a scene together–she'd perceive his eyes devouring her...

"Char, grab that pot off the stove," Annette ordered. She'd had a busy day yesterday teaching her cooking class and was content sitting at the kitchen nook, commanding Charlene around as she bounced Trinity in her arms.

Charlene did so gladly; being in the kitchen kept her mind off the impending show and Stork's relentless search. She turned off the greens. Watching her husband through the French door, Charlene's eyes bugged as he stood at a brand-new grill, big enough to sustain a football team. The fire was eyebrow level. *To tell or not to tell?* But that would spoil his fun.

"I spoke with Raven the day after the hotel opening in Florida," Charlene said as she moved around doing everything Annette instructed–even though she already knew how. "She sounds like she's in love."

"Is that so?" Annette stopped bouncing her grandbaby. "Now, don't you go getting any bright ideas when they arrive. Raven has forgiven him his faults."

"But Momma–"

"I know you hear me!" Annette wagged a finger at her daughter as Trinity pulled up on the chair and bounced on chubby, shaky legs.

"Their related!"

"You don't know everything, Char."

Charlene pursed her lips and nodded as the doorbell rang. Rubbing her hands on the "I love the chef" apron, she walked down the hall, opening the door to the trio, the catalog family. Then there was Estella.

Charlene knew the model from magical cosmetic bottles cluttering her bathroom counter. The older woman looked like an expensive, eclectic mess in a floor length skirt, bedazzled shirt–which had Royael's name written all over it–, and an abundance of jewelry.

"Hello," Charlene said greeting all of her visitors with a hug, even Jon. She gave him a wide smile. *Quiz time's later, sucker!*

"Jon, you should go outside and help Damien. He's awful at barbequing," Charlene said, guiding her daughter into the kitchen. Royael and Estella followed.

After Raven made introductions, Estella exclaimed, "Smells divine. I wish I knew how to cook."

"We didn't make the biscuits," Annette said. "How about I teach you how to do that?"

"Momma, we weren't making biscuits." Charlene sighed. They'd been in the kitchen all morning. *I should've picked you up from the old folks home when the food was ready!*

"Hush, chile. Do you see that fire out there? Damien will be forever, and I know Jon can't cook."

Raven laughed. "Jon might know how to barbeque a bacon-wrapped pancake."

"We gotta give them time to test out that new grill and burn a lot of meat." Annette stood slowly. Raven tried to lift her from under the arms, but she swatted at her. "I was just on my feet too long yesterday. Re-Re, get out the way. Char, get out the ingredients. Estella and I are making a 7up cake."

Leave it to Momma to use food as a means for bonding time. Charlene went to the cupboard and took out a large bowl. Estella stood at the island ready to do as told.

Chatter and laughter infused around the informal dining. Acrid blackened meat and an abundance of aromatic side dishes donned the table. Charlene waited patiently, half expecting Damien to commence with the interrogation. They were against Ravens living with Jon and despite Annette's warning, she would gather the truth. With her elbow, she nudged her husband's ribs.

"Not right now, Char," he said under his breath.

Awhile later, she rubbed her hands together as she watched Estella playing on the floor in the family room with Royael and Trinity. When Annette arose from the table, Damien patted her shoulder.

"It's about time," she asserted from the side of her mouth. She'd been forced to watch Raven and Jon fed each other in much the same way she'd fed Trinity—minus the "more, more" and fat-fisted ruckus the nine-month-old made.

"So Jon what are your plans, with regard to Raven living in your home?" Damien asked.

Finally, they weren't goggling at each other. Jon turned away from Raven. "She can stay as long as she would like."

"Are you concerned about shacking up in the eyes of the Lord?"

Charlene watched for any signs of nervousness as he answered the questions with ease.

"I'm sure your business doesn't set its roots in Dallas. How'll Raven and Royael feel when you move back to France or another country?"

"They're welcome to come with me," Jon said.

"You can't take my grandbaby out of the country. We don't really know you like that," Charlene exclaimed. *Oops.* So far she'd been the good guy, just sitting back, letting Damien ask his fiddle-stick questions. *All right, game time!* "What if you take them somewhere and they want to come back home? What if Royael gets lost or…or…"

"Calm down, Mom. We'll watch Royael as we do here in Timbuktu, if that's where Jon has to visit to open a hotel." Raven interjected and gave a stiff have-you-gone-mad chuckle.

"How was your lifestyle before settling down with Raven? Were you a hoe?" Charlene asked. *I can't let up now. I got to find a loophole.*

Jon sputtered on his lemonade and started laughing.

"Mom, you can't just call him a hoe." Raven frowned.

Jon wiped his face with a napkin, and then wrapped his arm around her before proceeding. "I'll admit that my lifestyle hadn't called for monogamy in the past. I did date."

Charlene sipped her drink. *So you* were *a male slut!*

"Raven, let's go clean the kitchen," she said, when the tension expired, knowing her daughter was a bit annoyed after all her questions.

"All right, Mom." Raven arose from the dining chair, and they walked into the kitchen.

"Raven, you do recall that Jonathan is father to both of you?" She asked, turning on the hot water and pouring soap into the sink. She wanted to shake her daughter's shoulders and slap the girl.

"Don't worry about that, Mom."

"What do you mean, don't worry?" She turned away from the sudsy flurry.

"Elise lied, okay!" Raven's hands were raised fists.

"But that means…" Charlene's voice constricted and broke.

Raven reached around her and turned off the water as it had pooled dangerously close to overflowing. Standing less than an inch away, she put her hands on Charlene's shoulders and stared her deep into the eyes. Speaking slow and clear, she asked, "All I want to know from you is, beside Roy Timmons, was there anyone else?"

Charlene gulped at the flicker of terror that momentarily reared itself in her daughter's pupils. Then her child took on that emotionless façade, Charlene knew her for. And now, as she stared her child, she didn't know how to react. How to console her?

How is she handling this so well? Charlene bite her bottom lip, looking at a mask of marble. *Oh…she's in love…*

CHAPTER 44

Blindfolded, Jon led Raven by the forearm. They were downstairs, but that could mean anywhere in the huge house. "C'mon, Jon, I don't like surprises."

"You love surprises but hate the anticipation," Jon corrected. "Now, turn left."

About to agree, her nose crinkled. The smile on her face wavered. "Uh, what's that burnt odor?"

"Are you ready?"

"*Yeah*." Raven clapped her hands together. He tugged at the string of the blindfold and it floated to the floor. All she could say was "Oh..." as she looked at the kitchen table to see a chilled bottle of wine–the really good, expensive stuff that he'd harped about before–, lit tapered candles, and burnt...well, it looked like some type of noodle and black chunks of disgustingness.

"This is what you're not going to eat," Jon replied. Her arched eyebrow rose in that sexy way he loved. "Remember you wanted chicken Alfredo for dinner tonight."

"Oh-kay...so why didn't you just take me to Olive Garden?" She didn't know whether to laugh or frown at food. Diamonds in her eyes, she was in love. Romantic times like this turned her brain into a warm, healthy serving of oatmeal. And, like the flake she was, she'd all but forgotten her plan to break his heart.

"I just wanted you to see all the energy that I put into cooking for you."

"I appreciate it, but I'm still hungry," she replied in a melodramatic tone.

"Let me finish." He put his finger over her plump lips. "I'm taking you to Sicily."

"Aw, Jon! I've already been there," she said as her bottom lip protruded, "that place off Canter Street has nothing *on* Olive Garden and the bread sticks, *delish*."

"Sicily, Italy!" he laughed at her, shaking his head.

~~~

"That was gooood." Raven patted her belly as her wedges clopped over the stone pathway, leaving a quaint family-style restaurant–a gem in a maze of meandering streets with tiny foreign cars and mopeds. Upon arrival, Jon had surprised her with breakfast on a private beach. A perfect day, filled with sightseeing. She'd photographed ancient structures with weathered stonework that would grace her graduate portfolio. A sea breeze, with a hint of fragrant soaps from a specialty shop about two doors ahead, chilled her bare shoulders and ruffled her maxi dress.

They strolled under sprays of stars and a bright moon and stopped next to a small gathering on a street corner; all spellbound by a crooner whose belly protruded between suspenders as he sang. She didn't know what the brawny man sang, but his melodic-bass voice laced the perfect serenade.

Jon tossed a few Euros in a hat near the singer's feet. He wrapped his arms around her from behind. He brushed her hair over her shoulder and nuzzled her neck.

"How do you say, 'I love you' in Italian?" She whispered.

"Tu sei la miaragione di vitae perchésorridoogni giorno. Tu seitutto ciò che èperfettoper il futuro," Jon said, in between kissing and sucking.

"I don't believe you." She smirked at the mischievous grin on his face. "Oh, well, it'll take me years to learn that so, I won't be able to say I love you until I figure it out."

He bit her neck, saying more words that frazzled her heart and made her body go weak. Voice breathy, she chided him, "You better stop, or we might not make it back."

"Right here, right now is fine with me."

Perceiving hunger in his eyes, she hid a smile and ran toward the D Hotel, well, in what she thought to be the right direction. It was hard thinking with him keeping up behind her. She weaved through vacationers and locals out for a night stroll. Before she could make a choice at an upcoming T in the road, he took her hand and guided her past old structures and a historical church she'd photographed earlier. Veering toward the U-shaped driveway at the D Hotel, they dodged a Bentley pulling in and glided in front of a valet boy attempting to take off in a blue Alfa Romeo. Slowing to a fast pace–mimicking the opera background music–in the hotel lobby, they were blinded by tourist taking their pictures.

She waved as the gold elevator doors closed, and Jon whipped her around. A graceful ragdoll, he lifted her up against the side wall with ease and jammed the red STOP button. Before his greedy lips found hers, a protest escaped her lips, "Jon, wait…" When his mouths trailed down her neck, she started another round of "not yet" and "not here." Trepidation of being seen through secret elevator cameras waned as his hand massaged her breast. Brain fuzzy, she heard the sound of cloth tearing but didn't know what was going on until she looked at her halter fabric in his hands.

"Do you want me to stop?" He finally said in English.

"No," *please, don't.* She moaned, needing this greedy love.

Later, she shrugged into Jon's blazer as he pushed the elevator back into drive. She picked up her dress from the floor, with stitching beyond repair. "Will you ever quit ruining my clothes?"

"Probably not." Jon grabbed her hand and they hurried down the hall, laughing.

~~~

The balcony's sheer curtains danced to a gentle wind around light-blue textured walls. The sound of seagulls awoke Raven. She turned over to see Jon's side of the bed was empty. Pushing back the feathery comforter, she sat up, and grabbed her cell phone off the nightstand. Smiling, she listened to a vibrant voicemail from Estella and Royael. Excited about the fun time that the two were having, she grabbed a cotton robe, with the Devereux insignia and put it on. Going into the living room of the suite, she said, "Royael won Grand Supreme at the pageant Estella took–"

Raven stopped mid-sentence, lips taut. Jon sat on a gold paisley chaise, speaking on his cell phone in a hushed tone. Something about his demeanor had her on alert-mode and all she could think–or see– was the magazine that read "Playboy Settles." *Or had he?*

Jon pressed the end button and slid it into his pocket. "Good morning."

"You didn't even say goodbye." She took in his every move as he stood and walked around the coffee table with a fresh crystal vase of cymbidium–yellow orchids. When he reached over for a kiss, she turned her head. In a weak voice, she asked, "Who was that?"

"Nobody important."

"Don't *lie* to me." She sighed, feeling foolish for forgetting to ask about Camille. Woman's intuition. An image of Camille's long legs wrapped around him burned in her brain. Maybe he'd pulled that elevator stunt with her, too. Maybe he'd brought her to one of the D Hotels around the globe? Maybe.

This.

One.

"I said it was nobody that mattered, Raven."

She swiveled on Italian marble and stalked to the bedroom. At the dresser, she pulled out her clothes–the ones that hadn't been torn off. *Great, I'm stuck in a foreign country–*

"Re-Re, look at me." He yanked her around and she whacked him with a pair of *off-brand*-skinny-jeans. "She's not important. Remember the day in my office when you apologized for being…"

Her eyes narrowed, testing him to insult her.

"You're the one that said we're not going to dwell on the past. She's from my past."

"I'm from your past, too. Remember?" She looked away from his pleading and didn't want to make it easier for herself to become his little dum-dum.

"You're my future and that's what I told you last night. I said you are my reason for living." He pulled her into his arms. "Now, will you let me love you?"

Teeth gnawing on her bottom lip, she glanced at the man that had her heart. Sighing, Raven decided that she needed to believe in his love. It meant not thinking about the night he told her of his talk with Lucinda. Love covered up the fact that she was Roy Timmons's daughter.

~~~

Back at home, gripping a plastic red gun, Raven aimed it at the screen of a classic arcade game. She shot bandits that popped from behind boxes and barrels of a Wild West simulation. Smacking Jon with her hip, she took the kills on his side, too. The game ended. A gruff, cowboy with a red bandana and a dusty hat appeared, pointing a celebratory bottle of whiskey at her side of the screen. She put the gun in the case and danced a jig around the loser. "I'm number one, sucker!"

"Remind me not to play with you anymore." Jon placed his gun in the hoister. "Even though I just beat your ass at Pacman and didn't gloat."

She began to robot dance. "You shoulda. It sucks to be you."

"I have a confession to make," Estella said from the archway of the room.

From the worry etched on Estella's face, Raven straightened up. They took a seat on the couch. Gone was the rosiness in Estella's cheeks as she'd shown them photos of her and Royael at a pageant the past weekend. Raven gave her a smile, hoping to take away some of her tension.

"It's not my story to tell, really…" Estella twisted the diamond ring on her index finger.

"It's okay, Nana, go ahead." Jon encouraged with a head nod.

"I came before the Orlando hotel opening because I wanted to spend time with my grandchild. Then I got here and really enjoyed myself; hence, forgetting my situation. I've enjoyed getting to know Royael and I love her—and you all, so much." Estella looked back at forth, eyes glistening.

"We love you, too," they replied in unison.

"I must admit that I also had an agenda. I wanted Elise to come clean with a secret that would surely bring you'll together which doesn't matter now." Her mouth quavered as she smiled. "Anyhow, both of you deserve the truth. Elise didn't deceive you, Raven, because you were poor. That most certainly wouldn't be a reason to keep you apart. As a matter of fact, Pierre was a toe from living off the streets when we met. His family had the one dilapidated hotel in Paris and–"

"Yes, Nana" Jon sighed. Raven nodded, knowingly. She'd mentioned it many times.

"Well, the two of you being together would ruin the Devereux-*gaudy*–image. Elise wanted to make sure nobody knew that Jon was not Jonathan's son…" Estella told the story of her daughter and Zane Anderson.

"Wow!" Raven said.

Jon's lips were set in a line.

Raven wondered how he felt learning that Zane Anderson was his father. The uncertainty of not having a father was second nature to her. It seemed just yesterday that they were asking Alvin–Charlene's childhood friend–if he was her father. But, Jonathan had always been Jon's "father." *Elise sure did tangle a web of lies, using Jonathan as my father and Jon's…*

"Estella, tomorrow morning have your bags ready. The jet will be taking you back to France or wherever it is you want to go." His emotions turned off as readily as the flick of a light switch.

Mouth agape, Estella watched as he walked out.

"Let me talk to him." Raven patted her shoulder, feeling that pain that radiated from her eyes. She hurried down the hall and out the front door.

Crickets chirped on a warm summer night. Stopping dead in her tracks, she watched him straddle a blue Ducati. In an instant, she became a teen again. He held out an extra helmet. She took it and got on the back of the bike with him, embraced his muscular waist and considered postponing the talk until after the ride. He wouldn't discard Estella if she could help it. *Elise had instilled awful values in him as a child, always making it easy to run away from pain.* Except, he couldn't hide from the truth. The secret hadn't been his grandmother's fault, but it sucked to be the messenger sometimes.

~~~

The next morning, Jon crept out of bed to have a heart to heart with Nana. The Ducati ride had cleared his mind. Having his love near, helped him see life through a new lens.

He needed to have a chat with Raven when she awoke. In his joy to find out that she wasn't his sister, he didn't consider what that meant for her. Nana's confession had brought that to his attention. He remembered the day Charlene said that a truck driver had raped her. Now, he needed to comfort her.

He brushed his teeth and washed his face. With one last look of raven hair and a petite, sleek frame, he walked out of the room and across the bridge. A sunbeam lit the glossy, wood floors from the cracked door. He knocked lightly. When she said "come in," he did, allowing his eyes to adjust. At the corner of the house, sunlight came from two glass walls. The linen was in a neat pile on the floor and her knickknacks had already been stored. She repositioned piles of luggage.

"Nana, you can stay the rest of summer until Royael starts school."

Putting a diamond necklace into her jewelry armory, she didn't look up. "No, thank you."

"Nana," Jon sighed as she padded into the walk-in closet. He heard sniffling and rustling.

"You don't have to call me 'Nana,' not anymore."

"I'm sorry. I was angry last night. I'm a Junior to a man that's not my father!" He beat at his chest, almost ready to cry as she came out of the closet with tear filled eyes. "I should change my name to Zane Junior. Damn, that doesn't even sound right."

"No, you're Jon." Estella patted her eyes with a silk hankie and moved closer to him. "You're not just a Junior and you're not just Elise's child. You're a successful man, a father, a bit controlling when you want to be, a tad superficial when it comes to those sports cars, but all things considered, you're a darn good man!"

They hugged. When she pulled away, she said, "I guess I'll let you still call me Nana."

"Thanks. I'll help you put this village worth of luggage back into the closet."

"No, I've thoroughly enjoyed my petit protégé. I'll return next summer and maybe, Royael will visit me in Paris. You and Raven are always welcome."

Jon nodded, taking in her words. For the first time in his life, he would miss her–all due to Raven. He remembered their conversation a year ago. Estella had attempted to profess the truth, even then. That would have been an extra year with his child and his Raven. Ever since he moved back to North Carolina to attend Brinton Prep for high school, he'd harbored negative feelings toward her. *What would I've done if Raven wasn't home when Estella came a few months ago? Would I have let her stay or spent time with her?* He knew the answer was no.

"Now, I do have one last question for you?" Estella folded her arms.

"Yes," Jon replied, taking a seat at the edge of the bed.

"Why in the world was Camille at the grand opening. She never comes to events not even when her father received a Pierre's prestige award. You don't still have feelings for her, do you?"

To him, it was funny how affluent people settled for others in their class even though they hated each other. He'd given her a promotional invitation because she was at his office when he received the final prints. He hadn't thought she would come or blow up his phone so much.

"I don't know why she won't get the picture. She's nothing like Raven; I have no feelings for her. We were always about just having fun."

Back in the master bedroom, Raven rolled over and pouted. *Aw, man, did Jon go to work?* He'd taken off a lot this summer—a trait that a Legacy need not possess.

"Legacy." Raven chuckled and swung her legs over the side of the high bed. She walked down the hallway, wanting to apologize to

Estella, since she hadn't talked with Jon last night. Placing a hand on the knob, she stopped when hearing her name. Was Jon declaring to Estella just how much he loved her? The way he did when her parents gave him the twenty-*thousand* questions?

"...Raven. I have no feelings for her. We're always about having fun."

No feelings…just fun…Playboy did not settle!

Veins flamed. A zombie with no brain, she ended up in her old room, with its calming green walls. She sank into the cushiony sofa. He owned her. A piece of her soul would always be connected to him. Her revenge…she'd intended to make him fall in love with her again then leave him. *The Jon, the old one, would have been heartbroken. Sharon said we fear what we most desire. I desired to love him! And I plunged into it. He signed his name upon my heart. I've given him my everything!* Trembling fingers went to streams flowing down her cheeks. Arising slowly, she went into the bathroom. She placed her hands together allowing cold water to pool into them and splashed it on her hot face.

Prime time for verbal, mental abuse, she needed to be put in her place. Of course, the voice had been right about her excessive adjustment in her plan as she sat in front of Devereux Corp, trying to determine what she'd do. It was right; she couldn't make him love her without loving him. Instead of the voice, someone knocked on the door. Raven gave one last look in the mirror; outwardly normal, but inside…dying. She opened it. Jon stood in a grey suit and striped tie. Debonair.

He smiled and kissed her softly on the lips. "Why are you in here? I thought you moved all of your stuff to our room."

Once again, her body became a traitor to her mind as his lips lingered. It took all of her might to step back on the shag rug. *I am not your dum-dum.* "I'm moving out."

Face grimacing as if he'd been slapped, he asked, "Why?"

"I can't do this."

"Do what?"

She closed the bathroom door in his face and locked it.

"Raven, open the door. Tell me what's wrong."

She listened as he pled, and waited for the voice to remind her of all the bad things he'd done to her over a lifetime—needed the motivation like she needed air.

Guess I have to motivate myself! Trust and believe, Jon, you're not going to like this.

The rollercoaster-of-fun, Jon mentioned to Estella had run its course. They'd reached their climax only for Raven to realize that it was solely for his enjoyment. She'd been banking on forever. He'd been splurging on a short ride. The magazines were right. Pierre was right. Those zigs and the zags had thrown her for a loop. Not love.

Placing her hand over her ears, she waited for him to leave.

Now came the hard part. She had to get over him, *again*.

CHAPTER 45

The day after Raven moved into a condominium down the hill, Jon ended up at Bella Jeweler in Beverly Hills. He'd felt like his heart had been crushed. Once again, he was that shy fourteen year older in love with her and couldn't tell her how he felt. It had been so easy at her parents' home and it came natural with Nana. Except, looking into Raven's eyes, he felt something *different*. Maybe she wanted something better than that tacky spoon ring? Commitment.

"Hello, Mr. Dubois, how can I help you?" The redhead's voice was as soft as the strumming of the harp player in the center of the store.

If Raven hadn't shutdown so coldly, he would've laid on the asphalt, in a tailored suit made of the finest South American Vicuna fabric. *I shouldn't have let her leave.* Instead of dwelling on the past, he returned the smile. "Giselda, just the lady I was looking for."

She opened the sleek, white apparition separating the displays and went to the men's jewelry.

"I'm not here for me." Jon stepped toward the engagement rings.

Giselda followed on the other side of the display. "Congratulations! Do you have any particular cut in mind? We also have the loose diamonds and design options available."

Jon glanced at the flawless diamonds, nothing popped out. "I want to design the ring."

"Very well." She motioned for a junior associate in a tan department store suit. "Get the jeweler and a glass of champagne–actually, bring the bottle. The best of the best." She whispered the last part. Grinning, she turned back to Jon.

~~~

Charlene snatched her shades from over narrowed eyes as she watched Jon stroll into Bella Jeweler. She itched to walk over and backhand that smile off his face but didn't want to draw attention to herself. Paparazzi could smell celebrity emotions in much the same way sharks could smell a smidgen of blood in a thousand mile radius.

Momentary madness manageable, she gingerly placed the aviators back into position.

"Char, I'm assuming this shop therapy isn't working." Teresa dangled a purple B' Jori gift bag with tissue paper in her face.

"I, uh," she adjusted her many shopping bags into one hand and grabbed Teresa's hand and pulled her forward. "I just saw Raven's ex. We're going to see what he's up to."

They passed a group of trust-fund-prepsters coming out of a young men's boutique that stylishly displayed pricey polo shirts and stopped just outside of Bella, backs against the cement wall.

"Look inside, T."

"All right." Teresa craned her turkey neck to glance just inside of Bella's wide windows. "He's looking at jewelry... that cost more than all the homes on my block."

"Dang it, T! I've only gone into Bella's *once*. When I first started Loyalties and could only afford microscopic-diamond earrings. What type of jewelry?"

"Girl, I don't know. But he's *fine*, I sure would like to climb that—"

"Don't tell me." Cringing, she moved around Teresa and peeped into the window. "He's flirting with that lady! You didn't tell me that."

"From the looks of it, she's flirting with him and for good reason, too."

"C'mon." Charlene pulled her along as the attendant's head cocked to the side, peering at them. "I could just wring his neck!"

"I'm banking that you can wring just about everybody's necks today." Teresa giggled, thighs wiggling as they hurried along.

"Probably," Charlene said.

"Is it that time of the month?"

"Naw. Stork called, saying he's gotten closer to Roy." She fumbled with the alarm to her silver Benz, tossed her bags into the back seat of the two-door and got in.

"And that's not a good thing?" Teresa nestled into the passenger side.

Finger ready to press the push-to-start, Charlene leaned back.

Voice shaky, she said, "I guess."

"Talk to me, Char, that's what I'm here for." Teresa shifted her full-figured frame.

"I don't want Stork to find Roy. A part of me hopes that if Stork finds him, he's either dead or a Priest that's been living the holy life and I'd feel too guilty to react. Heck, I just hope Stork fails." Charlene ended, shaking her fists.

"Avoidance," Teresa started and they both chanted the Drug and Alcohol rehab definition and motto.

"Yada, yada, yada, T. You know there are times when you just wish you can let *it* be. Besides, I have to worry about Raven. She wants to go with me if we find Roy. Damien refuses, saying he might try to kill the man."

"And rightly so. What's wrong with letting Raven come with you? I think it'll strengthen your relationship. Besides, we all need support sometimes."

"I want to shield her from that part of my life…"

CHAPTER 46

One month, two weeks, four days, three hours, and five minutes and counting...was the last time Jon's lips touched hers. Raven felt like her insides were going to explode. He'd tried to weasel his way back into her heart during the child exchange. He couldn't love her. *I'm just a game to him–a trophy.* And now, she was tempted to force him into meeting at a gas station so they could pass Royael like a sack of potatoes. Each time he'd drop off their daughter, he'd stand in the doorway and give her the puppy face–making her two snaps away from forgetting his "puppy" mask was a *dog* in disguise. He even tried to put on the charm when they took Royael to her first day of school.

Raven sat in the choir section as the preacher droned on and nodded when everyone else did, but she couldn't stop thinking about him! After a night at the D Hotel in Sicily, he'd taken her to his home in Abruzzo, Italy–saying he'd bought it years ago because she'd love the wild orchids. *And I did...* She sniffled back a tear and shouted "Amen" as the congregation did.

Then they'd traveled all around Europe to fill up her passport. *Stop it, Raven! Stop thinking about him.* She concentrated on what she'd buy Trinity for her the baby's upcoming first birthday. Seconds later her mind went back to Jon. Scanning the church members, Raven saw exactly how to get her mind off Jon. After church, she planted herself in the path of distraction.

"Hello, Bill." Raven attempted to psych herself into believing that he was on Jon's level, with ankle length green corduroys and a matching plaid shirt. She noticed how his breathing decreased as they hugged, just what she needed to know. Her body sunk slightly as she inhaled him. Bill didn't smell as good as Jon, didn't give her the same bear hug. His arms weren't as strong. He *was not* Jon.

Forcing herself to listen to his chatter, they walked through the parking lot. *Concentrate on his words.* Before they reached the parking structure, Bill took her hand and she decided that they should start over.

~~~

After their first–forgettable–reconciliation date, they stood under the porch light. She thought about the greasy food at the buffet they'd gone to as Bill kissed, rubbed, poked and prodded. She opened the door and stood in the frame, blocking the entrance. "I had fun tonight."

"I did, too," he replied, his breath steaming in the cold night. Fall had claimed the late, warm evenings, and she almost wished she'd gone out to dinner with more than a cardigan.

"Okay, goodnight." The words were a lengthy melody–a hint–as she stepped backwards into the entryway. He followed as she flicked a bright orange lamp on the side table of the couch.

"I know we just got back together, but I love you, Raven." Bill knelt on runner rug at the entry that separated the dining room/kitchen from the living room.

"Get up, Bill, get up!" She gasped. *Oh, my gosh! What am I doing to this man? To myself?* Her eyes widened at a two carat round diamond. She looked at the clock on the cable box. Her only thought was about Jon dropping Royael off.

"Marry me!" On his knees, holding up the box, he scooted forward.

"I…" She stepped in reverse, hand holding herself up on the back of the headrest of the burnt orange, suede couch. Her eyes mirrored his. Only hers were wide with horror, his with desperation.

"I'm leaving it here, Raven." Bill stood, snapped the box shut and placed it on the end table. He moved to the front door, put his hands in his pockets and stared at the box as if to make sure the ring wouldn't fly away. "I thought it might be too soon."

"Bill, I…" She started as he looked at the carpet for a second, then back into her eyes.

"I didn't know when I'd get the courage again." He shrugged, transforming into the geek from Bellwood. "Just think about it."

"Good night, Bill." With a peck on the lips, Raven ushered him out

Miss Scandalous

the door. Sighing, she picked up the box and gingerly walked to her bedroom. She placed the ring on the dresser and sat on the edge of the bed, thinking about calling Charlene. While the soap opera filmed, they didn't talk much. She thought about calling Melody or Cassidy. They'd gone out more often since her mom went to L.A.

Instead of picking up the phone, she took a shower. *Why is it so hard to let Bill in?* She imagined the love that shown in his eyes as she scrubbed with a loofa. The flurry of brown-sugar suds soothed her as she considered him the perfect man–smart, sweet, kinda cute. She sighed, turned off the water and got out.

Back in her bedroom, she put on cozy pajamas and was pulling her feet into fuzzy socks when the doorbell rang. She walked to the living room and opened the door, standing behind it so Jon could carry their sleeping child to bed. With arms folded, she waited.

"Raven, can we talk?"

"It's late." She shooed him out and quickly jammed the deadbolt. Leaning with her back against the door, she laughed at herself. "I was a fool…No more fun for you."

Reclaiming her comfortable position on the couch, her hand had just grazed the remote when the doorbell rang again. Mumbling cuss words, she scurried over and looked through the peephole to see Royael's favorite bear. *Sneaky bastard.* Cringing inwardly, she opened it. She watched as he and Mookie disappeared down the corridor. In a flash, he was back.

"Tell me what's wrong?"

"Go home." *I've been a dum-dum!* Raven opened the door.

Hand above her head, he slammed it shut. His other hand took hold of the doorframe, leaving her imprisoned between it and him.

"Talk to me, Raven." His hazel eyes searched her non-complying face.

When her lips clamped shut, Jon picked her up, eye level and tried to kiss her. She turned her head. *Where's the voice when I need it?* A bobble head, she shunned her desire. He grabbed her chin and bit the flesh of her bottom lip, just enough pressure to make her miraculously transform into his little dum-dum. *I'm so stupid…* Surrendering to his touch, she let him carry her to the bedroom.

Jon kissed her collarbone, his lips and hands roamed around leaving a trail of fire. He dropped to his knees, bunched up her shirt and nibbled on her abdomen. "You want me still, don't you?"

"I want you…I neeeed you…" Powerless, she let his tongue glaze over her belly button. Leaning against the brass pole of the canopy bed, her whole body went limp as he hoisted her legs around his shoulders.

~~~

Dreams were sweet, but reality was ripe and for the taking. Opening her eyes, Raven let her hands slip under the sheets, trail down his six pack and wiggled under the elastic of his boxers. His eyelids fluttered open. And his mouth curved upward.

"Damn… I have an early meeting," his voice was thick. He slipped one leg over the side of the bed, and then the other. He shrugged into his button up, eyeing her, "I expect you home tonight."

Raven nodded. She'd have to tell Bill it was over *again*–plead for forgiveness for her foolishness, but tonight she would be warming Jon's bed and hopefully for the rest of her life.

Jon pulled up his jeans. Sitting at the edge of bed, he laced his Gucci sneakers and his eyelids slowly narrowed. Holding his breath, he arose, glaring at her dresser. He picked up a black, velvety box. "What's this?" He sucked air through his teeth as Raven bit her lip. Opening the box, he brought it to the bed, attempting to jog her memory. "Is this from Stephen?"

"From Stephen? No." Her eyebrows kneaded together.

A vision of them singing together at church left a taste of disgust in Jon's mouth, but she'd denied it was from him. His memory became a slideshow of her washing dishes and flirting with Tyriq and how they'd been alone on the balcony at the D Hotel opening. *How many men are you messing with?* "Who is it from?"

"Bill Mack."

"Bill, *Alligator Bill?*" He flung the box, it bounced off the door and her shoulders jumped. "You're dating nerdy-ass Bill Mack. Are you sleeping with him?"

"Hey, he's not that much of a nerd anymore. And that's none of your business." *I'd be dumb as a skunk to admit that I've been making him wait, the way I shoulda made you! Mr. Summer Fun.*

"It is my business! Ya'll serious?...Yeah, ya'll serious; he's buying cute, little engagement rings. Did you say yes?" She folded her arms. He pulled the ring out and snatched her hand, "Put it on. If you're going to marry him, put it on!"

"No." She tried to pull her finger back, not wanting him to notice that she'd slipped on the spoon ring last night while he slept.

"Take off my ring and wear this crap." His hand shook as yanked on her finger.

"Owww!" Raven tried to pull her hand back, but he pulled off the spoon ring, tossing it over his shoulder and pushed the engagement ring on, it fit snug and perfect. His jaw tensed.

"I hope you live happily ever after with that bastard!" Jon opened the bedroom door and stalked to entryway.

"No, wait!" She pulled on his shirt, and leaned back. Bare soles starting to burn from scrapping over the rug runner.

"You took the ring. You made your choice."

CHAPTER 47

Charlene took her daughter's hand as they sat in the back of a Lincoln. The driver pulled away from the curb at an airport in Alabama. Her empty chest expanded as she took a deep breath. The awful day had been filled with rushing and faltering. She'd almost missed–not boarded–her flight from L.A.

Why wasn't Roy Timmons dead or a revered or small town hero? At the least, he could've been a father with a family that loved him so much that she couldn't break their hearts, by breaking his.

"How are things going?" Charlene asked. *Please say something, get my mind off Roy.*

"That was a great party for Trinity. I think she's the first toddler that wasn't afraid of a clown."

Charlene smiled, even though Raven had skirted around her question. Trinity's first birthday party had been the only day she hadn't worried about Stork.

She chatted with Raven about funny Trinity moments as the toddler tried to pull on a pony's tail or climb into the cages where the zoo animals were stationed in the backyard. A few laughs later, and then the car was cloaked in an overpowering silence. Tense shouldered, she wanted to yell at the driver in a black cap and stuffy suit.

Finally, she scratched the scar. *I shouldn't have brought Raven along. She's clearly nervous.* Charlene reached for the speaker button as the car lurched to a stop. Too late to make this U-turn in life. Glancing out the window, she peered past morning haze as the driver handed papers to a gun-clad officer. The tight-lipped guard, in turn, scanned documents from Stork before waving them in. She turned to look out the back windows to see them pass through iron gates that stretched toward the heavens and the bars closed. They were locked inside the pits of hell.

Stork had given specific instructions for her private meeting– scheduled by the warden, due to Charlene's celebrity status–with Royland Timothy Alder, alias Roy Timmons. His words were a never-ending recorder, embedded in her memory, in her soul: "Royland Alder is incarcerated in maximum security, separated from the general population; indicted on fourteen counts of rape, kidnapping, murder in the first degree. Attempted murder—one of his victims was buried alive and luckily found—and that's only what's been pinned on him. He's a sociopath, diagnosed with antisocial personality disorder. Royland's outwardly charming, charismatic even. His attentiveness captivates you, before your brain registers his true colors. He's a member of the KKK, dubbed 'The Black Beauty Murderer' in the 90s by the media in the South for targeting young African-American females. Remember, he's as sly as a fox…"

Unsure which—Storks' monotone or the true Royland Alder—Charlene felt a chill travel up her spine as she watched a gentle shower begin to beat on the windows. As instructed, the driver parked and opened the back door. He stood to the side with an umbrella and Charlene got out first.

"Are you sure you want to come?" She asked, glancing inside at Raven. Her voice had a flair of leadership. She'd used the same take-charge stance while being Meagan and during her action flicks. Though, this was for the benefit of her daughter.

"Yes, Mom." Raven scooted out after her and the driver shut the door.

Cold stung, making Charlene's lambskin gloved fingers wriggle. She dipped them inside her cashmere jacket. Bones frozen.

Finally, her daughter seemed to spring to life. Raven took a mitten hand to pat her back. They walked through a cement structure with multiple iron fences. "You can do it, Mom."

A prison guard stood at a station just inside the entrance. His tone drummed so powerful that it knocked on Charlene's chest cavity. She didn't know whether to get down and give him "twenty push-ups" or nod. She dared not open her mouth or ask him a question. His voice ended with a much slower, yet still strong, "…do ya'll unda'stand?"

"Yes," Raven replied.

Charlene nodded her hundredth nod and with shaking legs, placed her purse on the rolling table and went through the body scanner. She watched his bugged eyes as he stared at the machine. Not making any sudden movements, she took her purse on the opposite. As instructed, Raven did the same routine, but the body scanner beeped as she passed through.

"Did ya just hear what I told you?" The guard gave her a look of disgust, his eyelid twitched as he pulled out a wand. Gold tooth showing as his teeth gritted. "Spread 'em wide!"

"I'm sorry?" Raven's legs parted. The wand roamed over her body, buzzing on her coat pocket.

"What's this?" The guard pulled out a nail clipper.

"Well, it's a nail clipper…"

"It's a lethal weapon! Stand aside." The guard turned to Charlene. "You need to continue walking, ma'am. You *cannot* stand here!"

"But, I…" *I can't see Royland all by myself!* The look on the guard's face as he pointed to a red-bold, sign that indeed indicated the area as a no-stopping-zone, made her rigid legs move. She scurried to the bus that would take her to the maximum security section.

The second set of Storks words slithered through her mind, "It is important that you be prompt. The warden will only close the visiting section for fifteen minutes for your private meeting with Alder. Whatever you have to say, make it quick."

Grilled by Stork, she knew exactly what to expect when stepping into a cement-walled, empty visiting room with tables and chairs bolted to the floor. One way windows to one side and the grey October sky to the opposite side peeked through barred windows. Then her breath caught…

Roy…Royland Alder sat in the middle of the room, in an orange jump suit. Blond, wavy hair with a silver streak neatly combed back. Face freshly shaven. He was handsome. It instantly dissolved her tension. She pictured this as the setting of a movie, with an attractive yet villainous costar. Royland's elbows were planted on the tables with hands clasped together, eyes closed, almost as if he were praying. The shackles that held his arms together met at a chain draping down on the table and underneath to his shackled feet.

She sank onto the hard bench on the opposite side.

Eyes the color of a field of Texas bluebonnets opened and he smiled so charismatically. *Charismatic!* Stork's words came back in a flash. She felt ashamed by being temporarily plunged back into her fifteen-year-old-self. Naïve.

"Hello, Charlene." His voice enveloped her, hugging softly. As hard as she tried, her eyes were glued to his. Her body went numb with fear when Royland reached his hands across the table. The chains clanked in his movement, causing her to jump.

One of the guards tapped his Billy Club. "Don't go there, Alder!"

His hands recoiled. She read the tattoo on his knuckles "K-I-L-L" and "C-O-O-N." There were skull heads on his thumbs.

"I miss you, Charlene. Do you miss me?" His baby-blues glazed over with lust.

Squaring her shoulders, she said, "Roy–uh, Royland, I'm here to understand why you–"

"All you niggers ever want to know is why. *Why this? Why that?* I thought you came to see *me!*" A dog with rabies, Royland shouted through gritted teeth. With his forearm, he wiped spittle from his chin and mouth. Speechless, she watched as he stood and grabbed his penis. "I thought you wanted more."

"Sit down, *Alder!*" The guards yelled.

"You want to know why?" Smirking at the guards, he sat. The dog was gone. The evil glare abandoned. As if a temporary exorcism had made the devil flee his body, his eyes, were once again, cloudless summer skies. Then he began, with a haughty flare. "Simply because I can. I had to show ya'll that you were nothing!"

"I am something," Charlene found her voice as her mind flashed back to all she'd endured in this lifetime. *I've been raped, left for dead, I've gone through emotional turmoil. This year has been ridiculous while trying to get my daughter back!* She stood; eyes narrow. "I'm a strong woman! You have to go around, drugging and raping girls–not even women, just teenagers–taking their innocence because you hate the color of their beautiful black skin!"

"Let's get this straight." He put his hand up, ready to philosophize. "I didn't drug girls or females. I drugged coons." He slapped his knees laughing. "You think I can't get a woman? I get conjugal visits all the time. I get—"

"You're sick, pathetic." She cut through his arrogance. "The pain you put me through didn't stop me. I continued on. You're nothing but the devil!"

He yanked the necklace around his neck from under his shirt and kissed the pendant, the very same Jesus cross that haunted her dreams for years. "Bull! You're going to hell. God don't want no darkies in heaven."

"You're evil!" She started backing away from this useless conversation. He had empty eyes, even emptier than her stepfather Otis's eyes when he threatened her mother's life the night before she ran away. Royland would enjoy arguing with her forever, if given the chance. *My time is worth more than this.* Rearing on her heels to leave, she paused when he spoke.

"Oh, yeah? Don't *nobody* want your old ass." His tormenting eyes stopped piercing through her soul as if arguing with her was of no importance. For a moment, Charlene's head tilted in confusion. He'd been trying relentlessly to defend his warped mindset. Now, lust returned, but his gaze stayed just past her.

"I want her!" Royland pointed with his hands close together. The chains around his wrist clinked off the tabletop. "She's a tad old. Heck, I'll make an exception. *Conjugal visit time!*"

Charlene whipped around and her eyes bugged out. *My God, what have I done?* She opened her mouth to speak, to say something, anything, but couldn't. She couldn't alter this dire situation.

Raven stood at the door, eyes wide with fright.

~~~

In the hotel shower, Charlene scrubbed her skin. Royland's stench was just beneath the surface. She rubbed more hotel soap on her towel and cleansed until her skin began to ache and tears stung her eyes.

Tears for herself, and, most importantly, for her daughter.

Ten minutes later, the room fogged with steam when she opened the bathroom door. Her skin was taut from cheap soap and harsh cleaning. Raven sat on the full-sized bed closest to the window, but the curtains were drawn. They hadn't talked since leaving the prison. Getting her daughter to communicate was the hardest achievement that she'd never been able to crack.

"Raven, I'm so sorry for bringing you." Charlene wanted to reach over, hug daughter and say just how much she loved her. She took two steps in her child's direction, but Raven's voice ruined her resolve.

"I offered." Monotonously, Raven shrugged, not even turning around.

They went to bed early and didn't even venture to the lobby for a continental breakfast. The next morning during the plane ride, Charlene asked about Jon.

"I'm dating Bill now." Raven said; her face an emotionless-slate.

"I just don't think you're happy with Bill," Charlene replied, hesitantly. She thought about the day she'd seen Jon at Bella's Jewelry. Teresa was right, he hadn't been flirting and Raven hadn't been happy since they were together. "You can't let other people dictate your relationship. Tell him about the way Pierre treated you at the party. Did you talk to him about Camille?"

"No," came her muffled reply. She leaned against the window as clouds zoomed by.

"Bill is good for you. He'll keep you grounded. But Jon, he's the best choice. You challenge each other..." Charlene stopped talking when her daughter wouldn't turn around. Every day speaking to her child had come easier, except for today.

CHAPTER 48

Mom is right. Raven let herself into the glass house. She showered and donned new Victoria Secret lingerie and Dior stilettos. Placing two glasses and a chilled bottle of wine on the dresser, she propped herself on an abundance of pillows.

Jon should be home any minute. It had been three weeks since he'd blown up about the rings. During the Royael-exchange, he would *not* speak to her. She closed her eyes thinking of what her mom said. *Jon's the best choice.* She'd been trying to make Bill fit into a puzzle in which he didn't belong. Raven hugged a pillow to her chest and tried not to smudge the makeup on her face.

She fell asleep.

The beep of the downstairs door alarm awoke her. With one glance at the clock, it read 4am. She slipped on the stilettos and walked to the banister to see Jon at the front door with a woman in an ultra-short miniskirt–slutty-club-attire. They slobbered and groped each other, and then the woman back stepped into the Koi pond. Raven's heart sunk. She wanted to slink back into the room, but the ditz hiccupped and looked up.

"You didn't tell me you were married." The lady wiped her red-smeared lips.

"I'm not." Jon's eyes went from a narrowed look of lust to aggravation as he noticed Raven.

"Well, it looks like she belongs here." The girl pointed with an attitude then turned and stormed out, slamming the heavy door as hard as she could.

"Why are you here?" His tone was even harsher than the guard at the body scanner.

"I…" Throat gone dry, she gulped and continued. "I wanted to start over."

"Are you crazy? I've given you *100%* of me." Words slurred from too many drinks, he ascended the stairs. "When you came to my office for the first time, you tried to blackmail me. Now, I learn you've been seeing Bill behind my back. You're probably sleeping with Stephen. Only Lord knows your plans with Tyriq, after I seen ya'll on the balcony in Florida. I'm so disappointed in you."

"Jon…" she began as he stopped at the landing.

"Naw, Raven. As far as I'm concerned, you are no better than my mom. She told me how you cornered her in the hotel bathroom. You threatened her seriously? You made her go bald." His hand went to his forehead, "Did you even think to bring up how you broke in my parents' and made her go bald! I coulda gotten over that, but to go threatening her. Seriously?"

Raven put her hand over her mouth, the man before her was brand-new and he *hated* her. A sliver of moon from the skylight made his facial features hard, zapping the morsel of courage she fed on. Throat constricted, and mouth dry, she began in a stutter, "Jon, I wasn't going to blackmail you."

"Look me in the eye, and tell me yes or no. Were you plotting anything?"

His hazel eyes were on fire. Her eyes cast down to the floor, and she opened her mouth to reply. As if her actions were all the answer he needed, he shrugged out of his suit jacket and tossed it across the hallway. Taunting, he spat the words, "Cat got your tongue?"

"Yes, but–"

"We're done."

"Jon," she began as the giant passed by her and into his bedroom. "It's not what you think. I'd never embarrass you or our child like that. It didn't involve Scandalous magazine or–"

He chortled. "I own Scandalous magazine!"

She sighed, and tried to touch his arm, but like a flea, he flicked her away. Resolve gone, she held on to the truth as it trembled in her heart. She murmured, "I was just going to leave you before y–"

"What's this?" In disinterest of her story, his laser gaze roamed around the room. He slapped the wine glasses onto the floor. Raven jumped as it shattered near her feet. She felt naked in the worst of ways as he glared at her lingerie.

"Let me show you something." Jon's shoulders sunk as if all that animosity had been stolen.

She watched him move toward the painting next to the bedroom door and open the contraption. He pulled out a royal purple box. Getting a whiff of his cologne, the lady's perfume, and an abundance of alcohol and cigarettes as Jon neared. Her eyes widened as he opened it to a marble-sized blue heart-shaped diamond with a diamond incrusted band.

"If you weren't scheming, this would be yours." He snapped the box closed in her face. He stepped closer to her, she moved back. Cat and mouse. "Get this through your head, I don't want you anymore. Don't come by, if you don't have my child. Do you understand?"

Rendered speechless, she nodded. To her dismay, she'd succeeded in part of her plan after all. She'd made him love her again and broken his heart. In her attempt to leave him before he left her, well... now, she was at the scary part. She'd desired to love him most of all. As Sharon said, our deepest desires are our worst fears... Too bad loving him to carry out her plan was the heart's game of Russian roulette. Karma had boomeranged. The lowest of vermin, she slinked around to grab her jacket and bags. In an inconsolable daze, she headed for the stairs.

'Guess we know how this ends.'

The voice was back.

CHAPTER 49

Pulling the cell phone away from her ear, Raven turned the volume down as Jon ranted about wanting to see Royael for Thanksgiving. *Too late.* She smirked and pressed the message delete button. She'd moved from the condo that he'd bought, almost three weeks ago while he was in Chicago overseeing the hotel construction. She couldn't help the grin on her face when applying lip gloss in the guest bedroom at her mom's home. Back to her original act of vengeance, the one she'd second guessed. The first plan had been scrapped when she found out just how much Royael would miss her dad while he left after her first bout of drunken psychoness. Finally, now, she'd conceded to an overdose of scandalous deeds. Like a light switch, her emotions for him had flipped to OFF. *If Jon thinks I'm as conniving as Elise, hell, I'm up for the challenge.*

A rap came at the door. Raven gave one last look of satisfaction then said, "Come in."

"Re-Re," Charlene's head was just in the door. "Damien's been calling up the stairs for you for the last five minutes. You have a visitor."

"Who?" Raven tugged at her turtle neck sweater.

"I don't know, but hurry up. We're going to miss the Black Friday sale. You know Momma made me eat all that food, so I overslept. You barely ate anything and shoulda woke me up. Besides, Damien won't dream of letting me blow a ton of dough like this every day."

"All right," Raven replied to her mother's giddiness and stuffed her feet into suede boots. She hurried down the stairs. A man stood at the door with a bouquet of roses. Bill? Unlikely. They'd broken it off before the plane could launch. She'd apologized and he'd even admitted some of the blame for always putting school first.

In a noisy jogging suit, he reached out and handed her the red bouquet and asked for her signature. When she did, he said, "You've been served."

Grumbling, she slammed the door as he winked. Upper lip curled, she opened the envelope.

"What's that, Raven?" Damien asked, walking down the hall. "You look worried."

"Jon wants *joint* custody." She handed him the court petition, not the least bit fazed, irritated beyond repair, but not *worried*. This was only the beginning of hurting Jon. Heck, he was the *new list*. There'd be no crossing his name off and starting in on Jonathan Dubois. She'd focus all of her attention on the man that hurt her the most. Her ex-best friend, ex-lover, ex-everything.

"I thought you two had that all arranged?" He scanned the documents. When Raven looked down at the floor in response, he added, "Royael's been cranky; when's the last time she saw him?"

"About a week ago…" *Three weeks to be exact–the beginning of forever, as far as I'm concerned. After some time she'll be okay. Hell, I didn't grow up with a dad, and a lot of others don't either.*

"Raven, you can't keep Jon from seeing his daughter," he chided.

Not interested in a fatherly scolding, Raven crossed her arms. "Why not? I should tell the judge about his family and how they tried to pay me to get rid of Royael. He can't just come back and decide he wants her. Let him try, the judge will know all about his grimy-ass family. If that's not enough, the whole world will, too!"

"Aw, Raven. You said that Elise did that, not Jon." Damien patted her shoulder.

"Uh-huh. Tell Mom, I'll be back." Raven grabbed her keys and hurried out of the house.

~~~

Descending in torrents, rain began to seep into her sweater as she stood outside of her car in Jon's driveway. She leaned down to give the steering wheel a good, long honk.

Hands stuffed in his leather jacket, he hurried through the front door, jogged over the fragmented stone bridge and she tossed the court papers at him. Sighing, he took hold of the soggy papers that were pressed against his chest. "Raven, I'm sorry for the way I acted–I was

Miss Scandalous

drunk. But, I still want to see my child. Can we go into the house and talk?"

"You think you can come into my life and take my child?" Her voice was eerily calm–too calm for the pounding of her heart and the shaking of her angry spirit. On fire, the blood in her body burned. The rain pummeling her skin, started to boil.

"I'm not trying to take Royael," Jon sighed. "Come inside. We can communicate like grownups, for the sake of our child. We're soaking wet."

"I'm the one who takes care of Royael." Her lips barely moved as she spoke, stilling the teeth-chattering coldness. She didn't even wipe the rain and tears from her face. "I've nurtured every cold; changed every stinky diaper. I breastfed her! You don't know the pain of birth! If you know what's good for you, you'll just leave us alone!"

"No, Raven, everything can't go your way. I love you. I just don't trust you anymore. We have to make this about Royael."

"Hell, no! You tried to take *my child*." Her hair was drenched and her clothes stuck to every inch of her body. "I guess you think Scandalous is the only magazine. Come at me with all you got. I dare you. Try to take *my* child! I'll have every dirty secret that you, your mom, that bastard Jonathan–I'll have the Dubois and Devereux names looking so dirty that it'll take–"

"C'mon, Raven. Let's go inside and–" He took hold of her arm. She winced. He let go. "What's wrong with your arm? I barely touched you."

"Don't pretend to care!" Taut lips bluer than her eyes, she looked at the man she'd love to hate.

Taking her all in with his eyes, he zeroed in on her ring finger. It was empty. "Did Bill hurt you? Well, you always knew how to pick 'em. First Chris, now Bill! You broke up with him and he–"

"Get over yourself!" She got back into her car and pressed the lock button.

Pulling at the doorknob, he tried to open it. He jumped back when the Challenger roared to life and she sped in reverse. The car almost

273

hydroplaned in the rain. "Raven, wait!"

Wiping tears from her face, she forced the stick into drive and mashed on the gas. *You won't be taking my child!* Focusing on that thought, her foot pressed harder. She rounded the first curve and zipped by massive pine trees. Body tensed with anger, she took to the next bend. The car swiveled as it rode over the third arc. Hydroplaning over the sleek road, it veered toward the opposite side and flipped sideways skirting toward the low railing… heading for the cliff. The drop off.

CHAPTER 50
THREE WEEKS EARLIER

Raven breathed in and out, mentally calculating how long she held the breath in and the length that it took to let it escape. It didn't cut through her anxiety as she sat on the bed, in her condo. She turned on the TV. Stork told her to turn to channel five at approximately 3:00 pm for the afternoon news. Every once in a while Stork paid the main anchorman to deliver a code, the answer of which would only be known by a select person. Seeing dollar signs, the newscaster always obliged. Today. This was the day. As the recipient of the code, only she knew the answer.

"…That's awful. What's the world coming, to?" The main anchorman shook his head; his perfectly rosy cheeks almost made this a joke. "Soon we're going to hear that there has been a sighting of a purple-spotted chicken."

She gasped for breath as the newscaster gave the sign and the co-caster laughed in High Definition. This was no laughing matter. Picking up the remote, she rewound the program and paused.

(During her private meeting with Stork, prior to visiting the prison, he'd outlined a set of instructions. "Remember everything, verbatim. There's no room for error. When you arrive at the guard station, you'll stay behind. The guard will find a nail clipper in your pocket and hold you aside. The money should be in your boot."

The domineering guard had gotten chummy-chummy after Charlene left, and she'd handed him a thick wad of cash—more money than she'd made in the last couple of years at the coffee shop.

She'd smiled at Royland upon entering the visitor room that day. He'd been enraged at Charlene. His anger meant nothing—for him. The switch to her heart was OFF. Then her mother turned around. Raven stood stark still, pretended to be in shock. She'd faked fear but was not afraid. Not one iota. She knew his fate…

The guard, that chummy guard, had gone to Royland's cell and left a rather large present. As soon as Royland was escorted back to his cozy-cemented chamber, he'd be beaten within an inch of his life by three of the roughest, anti-KKK prisoners that Alabama had to offer. After which, he'd do a stint at the informatory and *there, amongst healing wounds and unbeknownst to him, his DNA would be tested.)*

Feeling like she'd sink through the mattress and suffocate slowly, Raven hopped up. Every filament in her body was on fire, every sense hyped. She pressed the rewind button again. Let it play, and then mash the rewind button, repeating the process over and over again as the tip of her thumb lost all blood circulation. Self-torture.

"*...Sighting of spotted-purple chicken...*" The screen froze on the co-anchor's wide mouth, teeth, and cocked head.

"Royland Timothy Alder was my father..." Raven whispered into the empty room. Falling back on the bed, she could gouge out her eyes...his eyes. They were his blue eyes. She turned her arms over in front of her, looking at the lightness of her skin because of Royland Alder.

Instead of letting the hate break through, she went to Victoria Secret. She let her mom's words motivate her as she found the right lingerie to win back love.

Except, love didn't love her anymore.

~~~

"Only family and friends, sir," the lady with Dallas Cowboy scrubs instructed at the nurse's station. This was Jon's umpteenth time asking about Raven's status. Her tone had gone from empathy to apathy.

"I'm family. I'm her fiancé..." he spoke fast, hands on top of his head.

"Ms. Shaw is still in surgery. I, or her doctor, will inform you the moment we have an update."

Damp jeans stuck to his thighs as Jon sat. He glanced at the wall clock. Raven had been in surgery for hours. He felt like going to beat the hell out of Bill Mack but needed to know how she was first. He could only imagine what Bill had done to her arm and why she wasn't wearing the nerd's ring. Thinking about Charlene and having to tell her the news, he pulled his cell phone out for the first time. There were eleven missed calls and even more text messages from her, looking for Raven.

He called back and Damien answered. In an out-of-body experience, he spoke with Raven's stepdad. A while later, a doctor in green scrubs came to introduce himself as Charlene ran into the waiting room. The wetness had done a number on her hair, transforming her into the Medusa he remembered, fitting her demeanor.

"I'm Dr. Abdu." He addressed the jumble of nerves, shaking her hand. "...Raven's stabilized." The doctor looked back and forth at them and explained her condition.

"She's okay?" Charlene's hands were at her chest.

"Yes, ma'am, given the level of the car accident. She had lacerations to the head, and we had to clean a lot of glass. Her left ankle is in a cast. She's resting now." He led them into her room.

Raven's eyes were closed as she lay in a sanitized bed with bandages to her forehead. The beep of the heart rate monitor cut through the silence as they crowded around the thin bed. It had stopped raining outside, and the only window cast a dim light from a gloomy day.

"I do have a few things I need to discuss with you," Dr. Abdu said, turning to Jon.

"What do you mean to *him*? I'm surprised you've even allowed him in here. He's not family." Charlene huffed, pulling the ribbed coverlet to Raven's neck.

"You're the fiancé, right?" Dr. Abdu asked.

"He's not the fiancé!" Charlene cut in, turning away from her child.

"You're the baby's father, right?" Dr. Abdu looked down at the medical charts.

"Yes—" Jon began only to be cut off.

"He's her *baby's daddy*, but he's not in the picture," she assured, turning to shoo Jon away. "You can go now. I'm here, *family* is here!"

"Sir, are you or aren't you the baby's father?" Dr. Abdu's bushy eyebrows crinkled together as he watched Charlene shove Jon. He scanned the chart, saying, "Raven is about... five weeks pregnant."

Recalling the day he'd dropped off Royael and came back with Mookie, Jon nodded, taking a seat. Charlene glared at him. "You bastard. Can't strap it up?"

Ignoring her flair for the dramatics, he ignored the nutcase and asked, "Is-Is the baby okay?"

"Yes." Dr. Abdu name was called over the intercom. "This is urgent. I'll be back."

When he walked out of the door, Charlene walked over to Jon. She looked down at him with disgust. "I want you to leave! If you had any respect for Raven, you'd go, now!"

Head in his hands, Jon's voice was muffled, "No."

"It's clear that you don't care anything about my daughter, so you need to go." She started tugging at his bicep, but he didn't budge. "Raven told me all about Camille Laurent, *cheating bastard.*"

"I never cheated. She did. Bill proposed to her." *She broke my heart. He probably broke her arm. I'll break his legs.*

"You idiot, she didn't cheat." Charlene stopped tugging his arm and paced over the vinyl floor. "I'll admit she was trying to get over *you*—for reasons that I'm not sure, since you're a sneaky snake—but she never said yes. Granted, Bill is a much better man than you and your sick family. Your grandfather insulted Raven during that hotel opening. He said you'd play with her for a while! At least, he's honest. I took up for you, and told her you'd changed because she was so happy. Right now, I hope your nasty ass catches something with those sluts you've been sleeping with. Oh, and if my daughter gets an STD, I'm beating your ass, then I'm suing your ass!"

"Excuse me, Charlene." Jon lit up and looked down at the psycho. "I've loved Raven the whole time." His voice decreased as Dr. Abdu strolled into the room and handed him an ultrasound picture. Charlene tried to snatch it from him, but he sidestepped her.

Dr. Abdu scratched his shiny beard. "Now, we have a more pertinent matter to discuss. We're keeping Raven for observation."

"I thought she was just sleeping." Charlene sank into the chair, trying to calm her beating heart. His stance foreshadowed doom better than any costar she'd ever worked with. Jon took a seat next to her, in his own state of panic as she tossed a sequence of questions.

The doctor held up his hand to cease her inquiry. "We've noticed wounds of a self-inflicted nature along her forearm, in addition to old scars across her left wrist."

Jon massaged his temple. *So Bill hadn't hurt her?*

"Have any of you observed behavior typical to self mutilation. Wearing long sleeves in the summer? Periods of depression? Have you seen any unexplained scars? She had leather wristlets in her belongings—besides style—that is a prime indicator..." He went on to explain the warning signs.

"Oh, my God! The day...the day that Marcus Weber came to my house," Charlene sputtered, and then put her hand over her mouth stifling a sob. "Her hand was cut when she washed dishes. I never put knives in the sink, and I didn't remember the cut when we went downstairs, maybe... But I'm her mother, I should know these things."

"I haven't..." Jon scoured his brain for signs. He'd seen a scar on her calf, but it was old and she'd been the world's most adventurous tomboy as a kid. As for her wrists, she always wore bangles or the wristlets.

"What's going to happen now is, Dr. Stanton will perform a psych evaluation and we'll go from there." Dr. Abdu made for the door.

"This is my fault. I shouldn't have served her those papers." Jon stopped pacing back and forth to stand in front of Raven. He touched her cheek and hoped she was comfortable in her dreams. "I never apologized for leaving her..."

"No, this isn't your fault. It seems I've blamed you for everything," Charlene started. Jon opened his mouth to say something in his confusion, but he was at a loss for words. "I wasn't paying attention. And then we went to see Roy Tim—Royland..." Her voice broke and she told him the story.

~~~

Pain medicine plunged Raven into a dark, shameful sleep. After humiliating herself in front of Jon, she went home. In her room the windows were drawn. A blue glow from the paused TV was her only light. The co-anchor's face was still tilted in a hearty laugh and the studio lighting caught his chiseled cheekbones in a perfect shot. The main anchor, that Stork had paid to deliver the sign, had a carefree smile. With tear stained cheeks, she slid onto the floor, holding her beloved tin box. She had decided to never do this again. The euphoria commenced by accident while at her godmother's house at the age of fourteen, when she'd wanted to know more information about her mother. The accidental cut while slicing apples for a pie had sparked something inside of her. She'd been afraid of in the beginning. It was years later and in a state of chaos before she'd cut again. And now, as she leaned against the wall, feet planted before her, her hands grazed the box.

"*I won't ever let Jon hurt me, again,*" *she vowed. Slowly, her fingertips went from the top of the box to the latch and she opened it. Taking out its only contents, a razor, she contemplated if she wanted to make this next move. Yes, she felt the numbness that overtook her in her Godmother's kitchen the first time. She felt nothing, like she'd done so many times before while cutting. Breathing came easy as she watched red liquid pooling around her arm.*

It burned when the bright light flooded into Raven's eyes. She lay on a firm bed with her left ankle encased. Through shaded eyes she watched Jon and Charlene at the foot of the bed, their back to her. A man with a Middle Eastern accent spoke. When he mentioned pregnancy, she bit her lip so as not to scream. Yes, she'd stopped taking her pills. She'd only been keeping preoccupied with Bill when Jon weaseled his way back into her bed. Now, a foreign being grew within her.

Then she heard the doctor telling them about the cutting. *Maybe it's a good time to say the kitchen scene after Marcus was an accident?* But that would be a lie. She listened as her mom talked about Royland Alder. There was tenderness in Jon voice. She hated that. For her sake, they spilled their hearts out to each other. He told Charlene how he got a letter from Raven–Elise–that she wasn't going to keep the child. That was the reason he'd left. He thought Raven hadn't wanted to see him again. He mentioned a call he'd made about seven months later. Raven tried hard, but she didn't remember a call. Then again, she'd chucked her cell phone into the meadow by then. Heart laden with anger at the words he spoke. *Here he is trying to make himself sound good in front of my mom!* She blacked out again.

CHAPTER 51

There were five–as Annette would say "kiddies"–elders standing around her in a yellow kitchen. All taking notes as she taught them how to make a cream puff. Charlene felt the excitement her momma exuded while cooking. *Aw, Momma, I wished only for the best for us.*

"What we're going to do now is…" Annette's voice trailed off. Noticing her daughter, she took off her sunflower mittens.

It was too late for Charlene to relax her tensed shoulders or to even attempt to form a smile, with her lips set in a line, as Annette quickly delegated a woman with puffy pinkish-white hair to take over.

"Ladies and Gentlemen don't burn down *my* kitchen while I'm out," Annette added at the door.

My kitchen, Charlene shook her head. The class was held in the general kitchen where all the residences' meals were prepared, but leave it to her momma to stake claim on the place. They linked arms and walked outside to the garden in the center of the home. Without a word, they passed rose bushes and took a seat on the couch.

"How's Raven?" Annette's hand went to her chest.

"She's all right," Charlene started. She'd told Annette about the car accident yesterday but had to look away. "Actually Momma, she's not all right. Physically, she'll make it…"

"Tell me." Annette patted her arm, with strength in her older eyes.

"You know, Momma, I shouldn't have taken Raven when I went to see Roy–Royland…" Charlene stumbled over the words. "I should've gone alone. There was the fire, and then her getting back with Jon–and Lord, those kids are so in love but don't know how to act. They've hurt each other so much… Raven's been burdened by more hurt than most people know in a lifetime. I've abandoned her. Momma, she's been cu–cutting herself."

"Not my grandbaby." Her eyes shaded when Charlene told her the warning signs. Slowly, she nodded. "When Jon left her pregnant, she stayed in her room most of the time and didn't eat. It's a wonder that Royael was a healthy infant. But scars...after Otis died, she wore long sleeves and pants but, then again, it was spring. Not too hot to send up a red flag."

"She has a fear of... abandonment." Charlene's shoulders slumped, *and it's all my fault.*

"I thought I raised her right. To just be cutting herself," Annette's voice trembled with anger. Her lips pursed and she shook her head. She wiped away tears with a shaky hand. "My grandbaby. I just can't believe it."

"Momma, it's all might fault," Charlene said as Annette kept mumbling her grandchild's name. "I left her. Now, we just run around forgiving each other, just saying sorry and the other person saying, "okay" because it's the godly thing to do. Have we really gotten over what we've all done to each other? Has she really gotten over the fact that I neglected her? God, can't I just turn back time? Leaving her is my biggest regret." Charlene plucked at one of the pink roses and twirled it in her hand.

They sat quietly for a while, each lost in their own thoughts of shoulda, coulda, woulda. Charlene plucked at the rose reflecting on the many things she hadn't gotten right in this lifetime. Raven was the most profound one.

"We all need to be straight with each other, Momma. We all have to be open and real." She began, letting the petal-less rose fall to the cement near her leather booties. I'm going to tell her about Otis."

"Naw, you was right. There's no need telling her now. Not with all she been through."

"I know not now, but later–sometime after she's had counseling. I don't want to tell her just because I wouldn't have been a donor match. I really just want her to know everything. We're Shaw women." Charlene wrapped an arm around her momma. "We have to be clear with each other and tell each other everything. We have to support each other."

A deep sigh of doubt escaped Annette's lips. "I agree. We do need to support each other, but this clearing the air, that's going to require some divine intervention. We gonna have to pray for it—and I mean pray *a lot* before we even get to this clearing-the-air-business."

Turning to her daughter, she added, "And then we got to get Raven to fess up, too."

Charlene looked into her momma's eyes. Uncertainty coated the lining of her stomach. The way Annette said it, Charlene became sure Raven had secrets nobody knew.

CHAPTER 52

All black. A black hoodie, black jeans, and black shoes. Raven determined the person, five yards away and heading her direction in the corridor, had no face. She craned her neck as she walked with the nurse to Dr. Stanton's office. The nurse had offered to use a wheelchair, but no she needed the practice and opted to meander with a cane. Her five-two height wouldn't allow her the ability to fully see the individual giving off ominous vibes. Patients and visitors traveled both ways, further obstructing her view. Gripping the cane tighter, she inched toward the wall, and could see a black-gloved hand skim the wood railing as her nurse chattered.

"…We just finished reconstruction of the children's ward. It was a hassle. We would've had to walk around the entire hospital."

Raven mumbled a reply as the nurse continued. Eyes narrowed, she looked harder, but a boy moved in front of this person—man or woman—she couldn't tell. The little boy, with his little afro, was guided hurriedly by his mom, and in his opposite hand a "Get Well" balloon tottered in front of the individual's face.

"Do you know this hospital is almost a mile long? When they finished construction, the children were so happy. That made the chaos worth it."

"I didn't know," Raven murmured as they continued. She blinked, but her heart felt unsettled. This was nothing like those *realistic* images of Elise in a trench coat and cap. This was profound, undeniably *real*. The black-wearing figure zeroed in on her as they continued to near each other; now, less than a yard away. She glimpsed the tip of a nose, peeking just outside the hoodie.

"This way," the nurse waved, bending the corner. "By the way, you're doing well on that ankle."

The hoodie person stopped as the corridor led to a T and leaned against the wall. A shadow of a face tracked Raven's gaze as she slowly turned away. When she looked at the ceiling mirror that hospital staff used to quickly cart bedridden or disabled patients around the corner, the person in black vanished. *Maybe I need to take my pills again...*

~~~

Raven tapped her fingernails on the armrest of the chair, listening to Stanton's low-key voice. She continuously reminded herself to *pretend to pay attention* and forget about that hallucination a mere hour ago. The motto helped aligned her back muscles and provide eye contact. After being asked a tense battery of questions about suicide, she wanted to chill. She'd passed the psych evaluation, wouldn't be held–*indefinitely*–for attempted suicide, but something in his tone implied that she wasn't free.

"We need to reevaluate our relationship. What was occurring is: You'd see me or call when your tolerance level for anxiety would reach its max." Stanton pushed his glasses up the bridge of his nose. "Raven, it's imperative that you realize I'm only a guide. Consider me as a roadmap; there when you need a nudge in the right direction; not when you're trekking through the desert. But you wanted to be on a sky resort, so to speak. Only, you must gage which road to take. One day you're going to be the master of your own destiny. For now, you need a certain level of guidance."

Raven squirmed in her seat. She stared at the bandage around her arm, wanting to pull it off and see the wound. *Dang, I hadn't meant to cut so much. And I ain't suicidal!*

"It's time to say goodbye to 'the voice.'"

Tuning back in, she cleared her throat. *Come again?* Eck. She forced herself not to frown at Stanton's recommendation. *The voice tells me when I'm being misused. I just got it back!*

"It's a defense mechanism that keeps you from experiencing life. It hinders you from fully trusting or learning when not to trust." He stapled his fingers in front of his mouth, and then he smiled. "I understand your hesitance, Raven. You've invented 'the voice' out of a need to cope as you've grown. It came from your desire not to fight, except you've focused all of your survival tactics into *one* entity."

~~~

Jon sneezed from all the flowers Raven had gotten; from Stephen and Melody, Manna Church, Sharon Riley, Cassidy and the coffee shop, and more. He stood and stretched, staring at rumpled covers on the hospital bed. Though Raven wouldn't speak to him, he'd spent the night. He couldn't see himself leaving her, even if she gifted him with fleeting looks of hatred.

His cell phone buzzed another call from Grandfather. Sighing, he wondered when her counseling would be finished, though he needed to answer this call. He walked through the artsy lined hallways that displayed Christmas pictures from the children's ward. He passed through the electric sliding door to the picnic area and answered just in time.

"Why haven't you been at work?" Pierre inquired. No hello.

"Raven's still in the hospital." He took a seat, rubbing his eyes as they adjusted to the sun.

"When we spoke yesterday, I thought you said Raven was only scraped up?"

"Yes, Grandfather, but she's still here and this is where I'll be until she gets out." He picked at chipped paint on the table. "Most of the office is gearing toward the holiday season—"

"Jon, inefficiency is an attribute that—"

"I'm not slacking off. Are you going to ask how she's doing?" Noticing a trio of nurses gobble on hoagie sandwiches, his stomach growled in response.

Pierre groaned. "Why must you associate with that woman? She's tarnishing our image."

"Are you serious?" Jon asked through gritted teeth. "I know you don't like Raven, but I plan to marry her one day." *If I can get her to forgive me for everything I've put her through…*

"That's absurd!" He gasped. "Listen, my son, she's unstable. In the hospital for self-mutilation! If I can gather this type of information, consider what our enemies will do?"

While young, just the mention of "son" from his grandfather made him feel loved. He'd rarely hear Jonathan say as much. "I love Raven. I do *not* care about an image. I've hurt her enough. She needs to know that from now on, I'll always be there. If there's one thing you've taught me as a business man, it's to be persistent with what I want." *Raven's the only one I've ever wanted.*

"I understand," Pierre's tone softened. "Take care of her. She's enduring a difficult season. I'll send Laurent to oversee the Chicago hotel. When you're ready, come back."

"Yes, Grandfather." He clicked off the phone and leaned his elbows on the table. Rubbing the back of his neck, he had a flashback to when he was fourteen years old and his mother had sent him to France. He mulled over one day in particular. He'd been walking to his grandparent's bedroom to show Grandfather, something that slipped his mind even now.

The door swung open and Pierre hastened out. His hard features softened as he noticed Jon. "Hello, my son. I must go out-of-town. When I return, I'll take you to the Devereux headquarters, and we can talk business."

Jon's chubby cheeks jiggled a nod as Pierre left. He hadn't been interested in talking family business, just bonding. As he turned to walk away, an antique vase of flowers soared out of the double doors so close to his nose that he felt the swish. Estella stormed through, tears streamed down her face. Model façade contoured in a mask of murder.

"Pierre—" Her waved fist lowered as she stopped short in front of him. "Jon, I'm sorry…"

He was confused. She spoke English. After all the reprimanding he'd received because he couldn't speak French, he was speechless.

"I've failed teaching you French and you haven't lost much weight." Her voice trembled and she sniffled.

Jon touched her purple cheek, still in shock that she could speak his language.

"Silly me; forgot to put on makeup." She winced then gave a weak smile. "Please speak French when Pierre comes home."

He nodded, but all his mind could register was that she spoke English.

"How about I teach you to make pancakes? It's the only thing I can cook. A girl, who wanted to be a model, followed me around constantly that was during my prime. Well, I taught her to walk, she taught me to cook pancakes. Now her

runway strut rivals mine," she paused and laughed a feminine laugh. "Anyhow, I'll let you have one pancake to celebrate your birthday and then we have to exercise and you..."

"I have to speak French," he finished off the memory.

That day was captured in the photo that Raven had given him. In his bewilderment about Nana speaking English and not looking at him like a fat slob, he'd forgotten all about the fun they had. *What if it wasn't anger or annoyance that she looked at me with while we ate? What if Grandfather forced her to make me speak French–forced her to make me lose weight?* He mumbled, "All for the sake of an image."

He remembered all the times Pierre mentioned image; even chastising Estella before they'd gone to the opera one night. *She's a model. Why would he be lecturing her about her looks?* Stiff legged, he went inside. Dr. Abdu stood at the door to Raven's room, talking with Charlene and included him in the conversation.

The psych team has determined that Raven will continue to see Stanton during multi-weekly sessions. She'll either have to be transferred to a facility or can one of you provide Raven with round-the-clock supervision, until the therapist states otherwise."

"She lives with me," Charlene replied hastily.

"If you are willing to provide all the attention that she requires, that is the ultimate option for recovery." He handed Charlene forms to sign.

CHAPTER 53

Session three. Raven sat in Dr. Stanton's office for her biweekly dose of therapy. The windows were wide open to a swirl of gray clouds, and she missed the flowers that would bloom come springtime.

"I was overwhelmed. Speak with Mom, forgive Jon, talk to my father... all of it was just too much." She straightened in the posh tan seat. It helped take the venom out of her voice while referring to her father. At the time Stanton had, unknowingly, wanted her to speak with Jonathan. *If you only knew.*

"How is your relationship with Jon? We haven't discussed him, yet, or your father for that matter." Stanton bit on the rubbery tip of his glasses.

You won't ever be hearing about Royland. Nobody will! "Jon comes around every day." Raven wanted to smile, but she knew she shouldn't. It would take time for the love she felt for him to dwindle. "I don't want you to help me work things out with him. I don't want him in my life."

Stanton's silver, bushy eyebrow rose. "Have you told him so?"

"Of course, I tell him to go home. *All the time.*" She let her head fall back as she sighed. Composing herself, she continued, "I'm meaner to him now than when we were kids and I'd boss him around. *Every day* he comes back! Asks me about the baby, how I'm feeling, yada, yada."

"Seems like he carries some of the blame on his shoulders?"

Raven scoffed. *It's all Jon's fault.* She envisioned the day she'd gone to his house to reason with him that they should start over. That day, her body navigated in overdrive and he, her childhood friend, was the only person she could tell about Alder—every dirty piece of information.

"Raven?"

Can you read my mind? "Yes?" Raven found herself restructuring her posture, yet again, and kept her face blank as possible.

"We were talking about Jon and his feelings about your cutting."

"Yes, maybe he feels to blame. That would be the only logical reason he would stay around." *Why doesn't he just mess with long-legs-and-exotic-looks Camille?*

"Are you in pain?"

None. "Not much." She grimaced for effect and tapped her bandaged ankle, resting on her opposite thigh. While exercising, she welcomed pain. Growing up in Bellwood, she wouldn't complain about anything. While cutting, *that was good pain.* Endorphins. This was not pain.

"How do you feel about the baby?"

~~~

Leg propped over a silk pillow on the den coffee table, Raven grumbled under her breath as Jon towered inside the doorframe. Who'd let him in? Charlene went to pick up Royael from school and she'd fought for this crumble of solidarity, with Damien upstairs asleep after a redeye flight from L.A.

"Hello, Raven. Did you take the prenatal vitamin today?"

She cackled at the raunchy-comedy movie and reached over for a glass of Sprite when he re-asked his question. She narrow eyed his jeans and vintage Armani shirt. Not his usual sexy/stuffy work attire. Not at all. The *lucky* shirt strained over bulging biceps. "Why aren't you at work?"

Hazel eyes squinted as he asked, "Is that water or soda?"

In response, Raven turned the volume up and laughed at an actor falling down the stairs. The spoof barely boarded on funny, but she improvised. His cologne lingered and slowed her breathing as he reached around her and picked up the drink, tasting it. When he walked to the door with her soda, she exclaimed, "Good riddance!"

Two fake forced laughs later and he returned, holding a glass of water, which he again—rudely, in her opinion—reached past her and placed on the side table. Double rude, he went to open the blinds to a sunshiny day, casting a glare on the HDTV. He sat next to her. "Did you take the pill?"

"You confiscated my drink."

Voice edgy, he replied, "Take it with the fresh glass of water I just

Miss Scandalous

brought."

"I took the damn thing!" She kept her eyes on the TV.

"How are you?... Is everything okay?... Are you in pain?... How's the baby?"

Still attempting to watch the movie, she felt his eyes roaming over her in concern and mouthed 'OMG' to the usual verbal-questionnaire. He should've been a private nurse. He'd probably be the highest paid. Beautiful tan skin, wavy sandy-brown hair, muscles for days. *Oh, the things he could do with them lips! –Stop it, Raven! Don't turn dum-dum for him again. Keep watching the television.* And she did, laughing at the end of another half-baked joke. Then the TV went black. He had the remote in his hand, and she felt him testing her. Minutes passed as he tapped it in the palm of his hand.

"I'm getting rid of it." She stared at a slight glow on the screen from being on all day. Though she didn't look at Jon, she could feel the pain of the moment. If captured on film, blue would be the essence. *Yes. I vow never to be hurt by Jon again and getting rid of this baby will hurt him.*

He didn't say anything for a while. She didn't expect it. He wasn't the type to argue or complain–except for that night he'd obliterated her heart. His voice cloaked her in shame as he consented, "I'm with you, whatever choice you make."

He tried to take her hand, but she crossed her arms. Turning to look into honey eyes that she'd never–not in a zillion years–forget, monotone, she asked, "Can you go now?"

"I think Royael's here. I won't bother you any more today, my Raven." Jon stood. "I love you."

Abdomen churning, she chose not to acknowledge how he towered in the doorframe again. Picking up the remote, she pressed the power button. With the movie on commercial, she flipped channels and waited for the door to close. Less than a minute later, he kneeled between her legs.

"I promise that I'll never leave you, Raven. I'm staying. You're stuck with me, no matter how long it takes." Heart bleeding, he searched her face for an expression. She looked through him.

~~~

In a daze of anger, sadness, pain, Jon stood in the living room as Royael showed him an ornament she'd made at school, a painted gingerbread man. He took a seat on the white and black paisley chair, nodding his head as she rattled on about her list for Santa. All the while his thoughts were in the den with Raven. *How can I get through to her? She's so cold?* He hated himself for not fighting harder while Raven was pregnant with Royael. Easy Bake Oven went through one ear and out the other as he stared at the large, empty stone fireplace. The stew simmering in the kitchen should've made him feel cozy—at home.

Now, I'm back at square one again. His family had been snatched away from him. His mom had ruined what he'd had with Raven as a child. Jonathan called after seeing Raven's totaled car on the front page of a gossip magazine—one that rivaled the Devereux's Scandalous publications and needless to say, it included a controversial headline. During their detached conversation, Jonathan mentioned how Elise finally confessed to him that Jon wasn't his son. Jonathan always had his doubts. *That's why Dad and I were never close.* Their call ended cordially, but Jon wasn't sure where that would lead for their relationship. A few months ago, he'd gotten his love back.

This time I ruined my happiness.

"Daddy, are you listening!" The snappy, chipmunk voice made him look down and nod.

All this wouldn't have happened if I'd have stayed in Bellwood with Raven.

"Pick me up!" Royael raised her arms.

Jon hoisted her on his shoulders and she placed the ornament on a frosted tree that dominated soaring ceilings. Hugging his daughter, he said, "I'm going home, now."

"I want to spend the night with you! We gotta go shopping, Daddy. We have to make sure Santa—"

"Not today, Royael. I'm sure Saint Nick knows exactly what you want." He winked, smiling through the pain. "I promise that after Christmas, we'll have all the time in the world."

CHAPTER 54

The wonderful smell of pine tree and a crackling fire, mixed in with the honey glazed ham wafting through the house. There was total chaos as Royael and Trinity, who kept toppling over, tried to keep up with Oscar's older grandchildren. A childcare center worth of kids bolted up and down the stairs, adding a beat to Nat King Cole's Christmas Song.

"Momma, come *out* this kitchen," Charlene chided as Annette sat in the breakfast nook. A flurry of servers placed food in silver chafing dishes and the double wall ovens were all occupied. When Annette didn't reply, she added, "I told you the chef has prepared food for Denzel Washington and–" Charlene abruptly stopped talking, noticing a notepad in her hand.

Annette gave her an you-better-not-say-nothing look.

Grinning, she leaned toward the hallway–for everybody to hear– and shouted, "Annette's getting *cooking tips*!"

"Char!" Annette got up from the table. She zipped past a server and out of the kitchen. Giggling, she ran to her Uncle Oscar in the living room where he, Damien, and the rest of the men watched a football game.

"Help me, Unc! Momma is tryna kill me," she pleaded.

He patted her shoulder, but his eyes never left the TV. "Tell Nettie it's a holiday."

A few of her male cousins grunted for her to get the doorbell and they shooed her out.

Annette winked and backed toward the kitchen with a sly grin, saying, "I'll get ya later, chile."

Running her fingers through her pressed hair, Charlene fixed disarray pieces and tugged at the itchy sweater Annette knitted. She strolled down the scone-walled entryway and opened the glossy, black door. "Merry Christmas, Jon, glad you made it."

"Merry Christmas, come in," Charlene heard Damien say as he

wrapped his arms around her and kissed the back of her neck. "You're going to have these kids thinking there isn't a Santa Claus with that bag full of gifts."

"I had to bring something." Jon dropped the bag at the door and peeled off his damp camel coat as Damien closed the door to the rain.

"We been waiting for you." Annette slipped the notebook in her jean pocket and gave Jon a hug. "Let's go eat, before there's a mob of angry black folk."

They headed into the formal dining room. A picturesque Christmas it was. The table stretched the length of the area, with a white lace cloth and a shiny red runner. Tall glass cylinders were filled with gold and silver ornaments, adorning the center. Poinsettias gathered around tapered candles on either side.

Jon looked past all the faces that he'd been introduced to. He knew Oscar from camping trips at Rover Valley. He tried to remember the rest of them as Annette made introductions, but had only one thing on his mind. "Where's Raven?"

"We ain't waiting on Scrooge," Oscar replied, taking a seat.

"She's been acting crunchy all day," said a teen girl that he already forgot the name of.

Royael folded herself around his leg, making it hard to walk, as he passed the kitchen. She let go when he knocked on the den door. No answer. He opened it to a dark room. Even on an overcast Christmas day, he'd prefer to open the blinds. He squinted, making out Raven asleep on the pullout couch. He pulled the door shut.

"Mommy said the baby makes her sleepy." Royael twirled a long pigtail as they walked.

"What else does she say about the baby?" Just outside the double doors of the formal dining room, Jon squatted down to her level.

"Nothing," Royael shrugged and ran inside as people began to repeat that it was *time to eat*.

~~~

"Momma, I know you're not in this kitchen tryna clean?" Charlene's hand went to her hip as she stood in the archway.

"Girl, naw." Annette turned around and shut the refrigerator door with her hip. Pulling out a one-shot bottle of brandy from her bra, she poured it into a glass of eggnog. "Sorry about that, baby, but I can't drink eggnog straight. Let's go outside on the deck and talk. I need some fresh air–love the smell of rain–but, I gotta keep warm."

"Okay." Charlene took a second glass, without the alcohol. They walked to the back door. Before they could take one step onto the deck, they noticed Raven and Jon.

"Aw, shucks. Let's go 'round to the front," Annette said.

They sat on the swing, silently looking at God's creation of towering trees and the vibrant, rolling grass at the empty golf course. Finally they were on the level where they could be comfortable with each other without thinking about how their words or lack of words might rub the other in the wrong way.

Sometime later, Annette broke the silence. "How's Re-Re doing with the therapist?"

"We went together this past week. It was a really constructive session. I'm just worried about her hormones. I'm surprised she's in the back talking with Jon, right now."

"Have you been praying for her?"

"Yes, every day." Charlene shook her fists. "She's just so angry."

Annette huffed. "Let's pray for her."

Charlene looked at her mom; beautiful eyes of wisdom looked back. She rubbed at the scratchy sweater, knowing she'd never wear it in front of the paparazzi or as Meagan. With her momma, she got to be herself, but this "praying together" was new. Of course, they'd prayed in the company of each other during dinner or even at Manna Church with a congregation of people. They hadn't prayed for her deepest desire. Raven's happiness.

Hesitance threatened to strangle her as she considered Annette's strict way of raising her, making her feel like a sinner as a child. The words that she'd said when finding her fifteen year old daughter in her bedroom with eighteen year old Jonathan came to her mind in a flash. Biting her lip, Charlene took Annette's hands in hers and they prayed.

CHAPTER 55

An auburn sun peaked through cypress trees. The beautiful sight would've been lovely to capture on film. Raven imagined photographing the rains pitter patter on the crystal-blue pool as she closed the French doors. The smell of food made her want to vomit. While everyone stuffed their faces, gluttony on Christmas, she'd snuck out. Sinking into the thick-white cushions, she lifted her feet off the deck, favoring her left ankle. Sighing in comfort, she snuggled under a burgundy cashmere blanket.

"Merry Christmas, Raven."

She closed her eyes as Jon stepped outside. *Please think I'm sleep.* The sound of his boots on the wood planks, and the movement of the cushion next to her, indicated that he didn't take the hint. She watched sprinkles of rain patter on the pool again, and like a good Christian, mumbled, "Merry Christmas."

She sighed when he placed a flat, rectangular gift on her lap. Snail paced, she slipped her index finger between wrapping paper with shimmery Christmas trees and a whole roll of scotch-tape. He'd packaged it himself. A jewelry box. She thought of a smart retort about him buying jewelry, and then determined the less communication they had, the better. Opening it, she saw a white-gold heart locket. Using her thumb, she unclasped the elaborate-pattern locket to two small pictures.

Breathtaking. She studied a girl with black hair in frazzled pigtails that came down past her shoulders. A cocky smile. Eyebrows thick, *twelve-year-old thick. I remember that day. I was so happy.* On the opposite side was a picture of a fat boy with chipmunk cheeks and kind eyes. The sunlight set fire to his afro, making it almost blonde. He'd be handsome one day, but he didn't know it–didn't have swag yet. *Jon was so happy.*

The facial shots came from a photo that would forever be imbedded in her memory. They were at the river in Rover Valley,

North Carolina. Uncle Oscar had taken the picture as she and Jon held up a big fish while Grandpa Otis bragged his head off. Throat heavy and batting back tears, she saw an image of pride in her grandpa's eyes. *Jon and I were so close.* Every earthly object Raven had, she'd gladly give away to go back to that time.

Start.

Over.

Raven felt the side of her mouth twitch. A grin fought against her. She wanted to smile, but she wouldn't. The locket snapped shut, and she placed it back in the box, submerging the two happy children back in the dark. That's where they should be. Nobody should have to remember those good times–*you can't remember the good ones, without the bad ones.* She wrapped it back in the paper. With frosty-blue eyes, she handed him the gift. "I didn't get you anything."

He unraveled the shiny paper, once more, and pulled out the locket. "I had this picture when I first realized I liked girls. This girl was the only one I wanted, *ever.*" He looked up at her as he pointed to her side of the locket and she rolled her eyes. "I took the picture with me when I went to France to start high school. It got me through years while I was away. It was there when I came back, and like a fool ran away to college."

"Is that so?"

He had a wry smile, adding, "I did some real stupid stuff to the girl. Guess you don't know how important someone is until they're gone."

"Guess so," she shrugged.

"I left her and my child. I'll be trying to make up for that for the rest of my life."

"No need."

Raven tried to get up, but he placed his hand on her knee and kept talking. "The picture got me through the pain I caused this beautiful girl. I didn't know how I would ever see her again or apologize for the stuff I'd done."

Through gritted teeth, she replied, "Maybe she doesn't care anymore."

"Yes, she does."

Annette's voice was in her ears. The usual words of wisdom: "Just forgive…" "God is love…" *But, I can't. I've given him all of me. Every last piece of my soul has been taken by him!*

"Damn it, Raven, I didn't cheat on you with Camille, and Charlene told me about the jail visit."

Raven wrapped the blanket around her tighter as if the mere act were shielding herself from his words. *Mom told you what* she *knows about Royland Alder. She didn't tell you–*

"I will always love you. There wasn't a day that went by that I didn't think about you while in France. I believed you wrote the letter to me, Raven. It wasn't my fault. I swear, when I got your letter, I was coming to see you. I was going to force you to keep the baby, but my grandfather…" He looked for any sign that she cared, but she didn't show it.

Doesn't matter. If you cared, you would have come to me and wanted to keep our child! Then I could have told you I hadn't written it. I searched for you so long.

"If you *can't* forgive me," he said, with an uncanny ability to read her thoughts.

She finally looked him in the eye. "*Then what?*"

"We don't ever have to see each other again. Is that what you want? I can have my assistant pick up Royael and drop her off, if your mom is not in town." His last words came out as a mere whisper. "All right, Raven, you can get rid of the baby."

One day you'll leave again and I have to prepare myself for that.

"I said I'll never stop loving you, Raven. I'll always be there, but only if you want me."

But how can live without him?

'*Look at his pain. It'll strengthen you. Make his heart break for what breaks yours.*'

"I'm leaving." Slowly, Jon strolled toward the sliding door. "I won't come back…"

"Don't." Face as frigid as the air, she turned to look at the peaceful pool. A tear slipped down her cheek, landing on her collarbone. *God,*

I'm suffering, too.

"I won't come back." That front that he'd put on, crumpled down around him.

The meadow, it was a cold night while you waited, pregnant and alone. The vow. You wanted to tell him about Alder, to tell him everything!"

Raven shook her head.

He walked out.

Her mind flashed back to the day that he'd compared her to Elise. That day, her body had been submerged in quicksand. Suffocating. Slowly dying. One entity in the universe could save her.

Jon.

She'd gone to him in her weakness, needed comforting about Royland Alder. A sob escaped, Raven opened her eyes.

"What if he still can save me?" She whispered.

'Living in the world of "what if" can be dangerous.'

Her thumb caressed the swirly shaped heart that dangled in her lap. *Can "what if" be safer than not knowing...* She gripped the necklace in her hand, arose slowly, favoring her right ankle. She limped back into the house.

"Where's Jon?" The sense of aloneness stormed through her spirit. Her chest heaved. The pit of her empty stomach felt heavy. Her family grubbed on dessert. Some, she knew, were on their second or third slice. Damien wasn't even using a dessert plate. He had slices of different pies and cakes on a dinner plate.

"Just walked out," he said, spearing his fork into a slice of pound cake.

"Daddy left me here, again! He said after Christmas, I'd go with him! I didn't even get all my gifts, because he gave some to the other kids!" Royael pouted, swinging a designer doll by the hair. Mookie, that tired bear, was nestled in her other arm—comfy and cozy, her baby.

Fingernails digging into her palms, Raven walked as fast as she could. Heart beating, throat clamped shut. She hurried out the front door. Sprinkles came down around her. Tiny bumps prickled her shoulders and arms. She'd left the blanket on the wicker couch in the back. Coldness trickle through her camisole and Capri sweatpants. She looked past Uncle Oscar's car and other family member's cars scattering the sidewalk. Across the street, about a block down, Jon opened the door to the Chevelle. *He brought the classic.*

"Jon," she called.

He turned around.

"What if I see you as the fat, little boy I once knew in Bellwood?" She bit her lip as the voice screamed about abandonment. "What if I just want my friend back?"

Chest heaving, her eyes were wide with concern. But every step he took closer to her, she could breathe again. Inhale and exhale freely. She breathed Jon in as he swooped her into a bear hug.

~~~

They sat in the Chevelle. He told her everything that happened since he'd gone to college. She'd consoled him as he realized how much of a role Pierre played in keeping them apart.

"When I moved to Paris, Grandfather had a loft readied for me, bought me a new Porsche and everything changed. I felt so guilty for leaving you, that it took so long for me to call…"

They told each other everything—well, she'd been as open as can be about the visit with Royland. The comfort in Jon's eyes read that he understood her need for more time. He pulled her hand into his. The subject switched gears, and every conversation began with "remember that time…," and ended with them laughing until their sides ached.

"You can't tell me that I didn't have yo' back," Raven joked.

"Yeah," he started sarcastically. "You had my back after an array of best-friend-peer-pressure-activities. Let's not forget my concussion in the meadow. Oh, and after making me jump off that boulder—as I tried to imitate your triple flip—at the gorge and almost killed myself; how about this one? Picture us about ten, *you had my back* when you forced me to eat the batter of Miss Wimble's sock-it-to-me-cake, though I'd already been promised a slice of fudge cake."

"Dang, you know the batter taste *better* prebaked. I didn't want to get caught eattin' by myself."

"We did get caught. All you said was 'Jon made me do it'...Yup, you had my back–"

"Hey, hey, at least I stuck around and we both got our asses beat together. It didn't hurt much. Miss Wimble was already a thousand years old by then." She leaned back on the headrest, beaming from ear to ear, remembering a few more "ass beatings" that she'd signed them up for. "All right, so, I was a crappy friend."

"Naw, you were the best friend anybody could ever have." He looked in her eyes and said, "You made me live."

When he licked his lips, her gaze took in his perfectly shaped mouth as every inch of her body went hot. They'd put the Chevelle to good use as seniors. Maybe they'd even conceived Royael in the front seat with her on top of him or possibly the backseat with him on top of her. Slowly, she stopped gawking and tore her gaze away from well-defined arms. Letting the beating of her heart diminish, she started another round of "remember when we...," plunging the heat of the moment back into the friend-zone. She'd dreaded this tactic in the past, while dating Chris and seeing Jon on the side. Right now, she needed the friend-zone more than the desert needed rain as the voice ranted tales of neglect and Jon–*the Legacy*–moving on to the next best thing.

As dusk claimed the sky, they sat in the car and made promises, *best friend* promises. Hand in hand, they ambled back into the house. Everyone was sitting in the living room, on the sectional couches or rugs, bellies protruding, watching a movie.

"Raven, you haven't opened your gifts." Remote in hand, Damien paused the TV.

Charlene placed a wingback chair in the middle of the room. Raven took a seat and Uncle Oscar handed her scattered presents that were under the tree.

"I'm surprised there isn't coal in that." A cousin joked as she pulled out a sweater from a candy-cane, gift bag marked "Granny." It matched Charlene's with a lopsided Christmas tree.

"Gosh." Raven toyed with the locket around her neck as she continued to open presents. She even got Royael's handprint wrapped in newspaper. They'd threatened to kick her out–for the sake of a paused movie– when she'd stopped to put on a pair of leather Chanel boots with spikes that Charlene had bought, to which, she giggled, saying, "Ya'll know I got a boot fetish."

"All right, Re-Re. This is the last one. *Somebody really loves you,*" Oscar assured with a whistle as he handed her an impeccable blue box with a gauzy-silver ribbon.

Raven rubbed her hands together, as the box sat in her lap then pulled at the tie. It floated to the plush carpet. Biting her lip in excitement, she pulled the top off the gift box. "It looks unnecessarily expensive. Ya'll know I don't like flashy things."

She looked at Jon. He must have gone to one of those designer stores to have it wrapped. He shrugged. *Oh, is Mom trying to make up for missed holidays?* Raven imagined Charlene floating through B'Jori or another high-priced boutique, picking up a pair of jeans that were off the "*frivolocity* scale."

Moving the opal-colored tissue paper, her lovely smile of contentment twitched. She had to make it plastic and keep the frown– that battled against her–upside down. *Who gave me this? It's not funny!* The hard beam on her face made her cheeks ache as she stilled herself from scouring through the tissue paper to see if a card or some other form of identification was on the gift.

"What's in the box, Scrooge–uh, Re-Re?" questioned one of her cousins.

Raven held onto that cheek-shattering grin.

"You've been trippin' all day… Grumps, what's in the box?"

The crackle of the stone fireplace made her skin burn. The heat got closer and closer. The Christmas music sent an eerie prickle down her spine as she mentally faded out of the present. Only seeing blue eyes and wavy blond hair, she looked through her family.

Roy… Royland. Alder.

Controlling her breathing, she thought of *her* father. Air swished quietly passed an overzealous smile. Cramming all recollections of Alder to the darkest, most *scandalous* parts of her mind, she allowed her sparkling, *happy* eyes stopped on her mom. Mustering enthusiasm and appreciation, she said, "Thanks Mom."

Charlene's mouth slowly opened, but Raven gave her a look of adoration. "It's a secret gift from my mom, since we've missed so many Christmases."

Charlene's eyes furrowed, but she didn't challenge her child's lie.

Eyes moving away from her mother's lips as they finally formed and voiced a "you're welcome," Raven looked down at the box on her lap. She inwardly hoped nobody noticed the slight shake of her fingers—spirit trembling with fright—as she placed the lid back on the gift.

Author's Note

Thank you for reading this book. Feel free to sign up at http://www.nicoledunlap.com for updates, connections with book clubs, and I'll be sure to keep you posted about valuable discounts and offers. I love to hear from readers and welcome reviews.

If you have enjoyed *Miss Scandalous*, the second installment of the Shaw Family Saga, and didn't get a chance to read the first, I'd recommend taking a look at *Miss Nobody* to see how the saga began. You can sample the beginning or watch the book trailer (for both books) on my website. Stick around for the third book, *Miss Perfect*. It will pick up with the family drama and leave your jaw dropped in suspense and guessing at the intense mystery. The Shaw women's heart wrenching battle to keep the faith all begins Summer/Fall 2013.

Until then, be blessed!
Nicole Dunlap

Made in the USA
Charleston, SC
21 May 2013